Key Thinkers in Industrial and Organizational Psychology

Key Thinkers in Industrial and Organizational Psychology explores the lives, ideas, contributions, and impact of key figures who have shaped and developed industrial and organizational (I-O) psychology.

Through a chronological lens, the book traces the history and context behind the groundbreaking work of a diverse group of individuals who have influenced the field. Among those featured are pioneers such as Walter Dill Scott, Charles S. Myers, Lillian Evelyn Moller Gilbreth, Francizka Baumgarten-Tramer, Chen Li, and Bernard M. Bass. The book offers the reader a comprehensive understanding of the evolving ideas and discoveries that have shaped I-O research and practice over time.

This book is an invaluable resource for all scientists and practitioners of I-O psychology and historians of psychology, as well as anyone interested in how psychology has transformed workplaces and influenced organizational practices.

Laura Koppes Bryan is the inaugural T.G. Lewis Faculty Scholar in Organizational Behavior and former Interim Dean of the University of Kentucky Lewis Honors College, USA. She is a U.S. Fulbright Scholar and a fellow of the American Psychological Association (APA), the Association for Psychological Science, and the Society for Industrial-Organizational Psychology (SIOP). Her work on the history of I-O psychology has been published in the *Journal of Applied Psychology* and as book chapters, and she edited both editions of *Historical Perspectives in Industrial and Organizational Psychology* (2007; 2021).

Andrew J. Vinchur is Charles A. Dana Professor Emeritus of Psychology and former Psychology Department Head at Lafayette College, USA. During the first half of his professional career, he published research on topics such as employee selection, meta-analysis, job analysis, and psychometrics; however, for approximately the last 20 years his primary research focus has been the history of I-O psychology, especially the early history of the field. He is the author of *The Early Years of Industrial and Organizational Psychology* (2018).

Key Thinkers in Psychology and Neuroscience

Key Thinkers in Psychology and Neuroscience is a collection of books focusing on the lives, work, and thought of the most influential figures in a given field. The books examine how these disciplines have been shaped and developed throughout history to the present day, and the impact of theory, research and practice from some of the most significant minds in psychology and neuroscience. These are insightful and indispensable companions for students in psychology.

Key Thinkers in Industrial and Organizational Psychology
Edited by Laura Koppes Bryan and Andrew J. Vinchur

Key Thinkers in Individual Differences
Alex Forsythe

Key Thinkers in Neuroscience
Andrew P. Wickens

Key Thinkers in Industrial and Organizational Psychology

Edited by Laura Koppes Bryan
and Andrew J. Vinchur

Routledge
Taylor & Francis Group
NEW YORK AND LONDON

Designed cover image: Getty Images @Trifonov_Evgeniy

First published 2025
by Routledge
605 Third Avenue, New York, NY 10158

and by Routledge
4 Park Square, Milton Park, Abingdon, Oxon, OX14 4RN

Routledge is an imprint of the Taylor & Francis Group, an informa business

ISBN: 9781032516455 (hbk)
ISBN: 9781032506340 (pbk)
ISBN: 9781003403258 (ebk)

DOI: 10.4324/9781003403258

Typeset in Sabon
by Newgen Publishing UK

Access the Support Material: www.routledge.com/9781032516455

Contents

Contributors

William K. Balzer
Bowling Green State University
Bowling Green, Ohio

Laura Koppes Bryan
University of Kentucky
Lexington, Kentucky

Geoffrey C. Bunn
Manchester Metropolitan University
Manchester, United Kingdom

Katrina A. Burch
Western Kentucky University
Bowling Green, Kentucky

Nathan T. Carter
Michigan State University
East Lansing, Michigan

Wayne F. Cascio
University of Colorado Denver
Denver, Colorado

Jeffrey M. Cucina
U.S. Customs and Border Protection
Washington, DC

David Devonis
Elms College
Chicopee, Massachusetts

Jennifer Feitosa
Claremont McKenna College
Claremont, California

Sharon Glazer
Rutgers University – New Brunswick
Piscataway, New Jersey

Mark Griffin
Curtin University
Perth, Australia

Rebecca Grossman
Hofstra University
Hempstead, New York

Rosemary Hays-Thomas
University of West Florida *Emerita*
Pensacola, Florida

Scott Highhouse
Bowling Green State University
Bowling Green, Ohio

Leaetta Hough
The Dunnette Group, Ltd
St. Paul, Minnesota

Yeh Hsueh
University of Memphis
Memphis, Tennessee

Jerard F. Kehoe
Fellow, Society for Industrial and Organizational Psychology
Olympia, Washington

Janet L. Kottke
California State University, San Bernardino
San Bernardino, California

James T. Lamiell
Georgetown University
Washington, DC

Samuel T. McAbee
Bowling Green State University
Bowling Green, Ohio

Stephanie C. Payne
Texas A&M University
College Station, Texas

Kathie L. Pelletier
California State University, San Bernardino Emerita
San Bernardino, California

Jesús F. Salgado
University of Santiago de Compostela
Santiago de Compostela, A Coruña, Spain

Jeffrey S. Schippmann
Schippmann Consulting
Calgary, Alberta, Canada

Elizabeth L. Shoenfelt
Western Kentucky University *Emerita*
Strategic Performance Solutions
Bowling Green, Kentucky

Jessica J. Sim
Elmhurst University
Elmhurst, Illinois

M. Dale Smalley
Retired
Amelia, Virginia

Jeffrey M. Stanton
Syracuse University
Syracuse, New York

Thomas A. Stetz
Hawaii Pacific University
Honolulu, Hawaii

Miki Takasuna
Tokyo International University
Toshima, Tokyo, Japan

Andrew J. Vinchur
Lafayette College
Easton, Pennsylvania

Jonna Williams
University of Baltimore
Baltimore, Maryland

Mengting (Rachel) Xia
Curtin University
Perth, Australia

Fan Yang
Texas A&M University
College Station, Texas

Stephen J. Zaccaro
George Mason University
Fairfax, Virginia

Steven Zhou
George Mason University
Fairfax, Virginia

Michael J. Zickar
Bowling Green State University
Bowling Green, Ohio

About the Editors

Laura Koppes Bryan is the inaugural T.G. Lewis Faculty Scholar in Organizational Behavior and former Interim Dean of the University of Kentucky Lewis Honors College. She is also the Founder and CEO of LLBryan Consulting in which her consulting and coaching practices are based on positive organizational psychological science. She is a U.S. Fulbright Scholar and a fellow of the American Psychological Association (APA), the Association for Psychological Science, and the Society for Industrial-Organizational Psychology (SIOP). She authored *Shaping Work-Life Culture in Higher Education: A Guide for Academic Leaders*, co-authored *EEO Law and Personnel Practices*, and co-edited *Using I-O Psychology for the Greater Good: Helping Those Who Help Others*. Her work on the history of industrial and organizational psychology has been published in the *Journal of Applied Psychology* and as book chapters, and she edited both editions of *Historical Perspectives in Industrial-Organizational Psychology* (2017; 2021; Routledge). Bryan is past-president of the College and University Work–Life–Family Association, past elected officer of the SIOP executive board, former SIOP historian, and is currently an elected member of the APA Board of Educational Affairs.

Andrew J. Vinchur is Charles A. Dana Professor Emeritus of Psychology and former Psychology Department Head at Lafayette College. During the first half of his professional career, he published research on topics such as employee selection, meta-analysis, job analysis and psychometrics; however, for approximately the last 20 years his primary research focus has been the history of I-O psychology, especially the early history of the field. He is the author of *The Early Years of Industrial and Organizational Psychology* (Cambridge University Press) and is a former historian for SIOP.

Preface

The Editor of Routledge/Taylor & Francis Group approached Laura to write this text for their series of key thinkers. Laura knew that given the number of key thinkers, this effort would require more than one person, thus, she was willing if she could create an edited text with a coeditor who has historical knowledge of industrial-organizational (I-O) psychology. She invited Andy Vinchur to join her on this endeavor, and we are pleased to jointly provide this text.

I-O psychology, the scientific study of behavior in organizations, particularly work organizations, has a long and rich history. It has been well over a century since the first industrial psychologists applied a new scientific psychology to increasing productivity and efficiency in organizations and improving the satisfaction and well-being of organizational members. As the field expanded in both size and scope, many individuals contributed to its growing knowledge base. This volume highlights a sample of those contributors. It is, at heart, a history of ideas. Ideas that were original, ideas that were influential, ideas that were thought-provoking, ideas that been supported empirically, and ideas that have moved the field forward. Every chapter provides a biographical sketch of one or more contributors, a synopsis of the contribution of these individuals to I-O, and a summary of why these individuals and their ideas were important. Each of the 43 key thinkers (48 if you include the brief sketches in the concluding chapter) had a major influence on the science and practice of I-O psychology.

How were these key thinkers chosen? Inclusion presented a classic selection problem: too many worthy applicants for too few positions. To manage the problem, we made a few initial decisions. I-O psychology developed across many countries; we wanted the book to reflect this by including individuals from across the globe. We were willing to sacrifice some depth for breadth, keeping chapters relatively short to include more key thinkers. We focused on psychologists, while remaining open to non-psychologists who were influential. While we tried to include key thinkers from the beginning of the discipline until the present, we limited inclusion to those individuals who had completed their careers. We developed an initial list of potential key thinkers, which we shared with colleagues knowledgeable in the history of I-O psychology, asking them to review the list and include additions and deletions. We then invited these colleagues to prepare contributions as well as suggest other potential authors. Additionally, we reviewed the literature for potential authors who would be interested in preparing contributions.

The result was a representative sample, not the population, of key thinkers in I-O psychology. The process was unavoidably subjective, and while we are confident that the 48 key thinkers included in this volume are a deserving group, there are certainly many others who could have easily merited inclusion. We could have easily filled a second volume with those individuals.

A similar structure is apparent throughout this text with chapters providing biographical information and the key thinker's contribution to I-O psychology. There is some variation in headings, breadth, and depth of content because we wanted to give authors flexibility with their approach. The key thinkers are presented in chronological order based on the individual's birth year and years of accomplishments. A benefit of this approach is that the reader can gain an understanding of I-O history if the chapters are read in the order as presented. Although the chapters are unique to each key thinker, it is true that none of these key thinkers operated in a vacuum and that the times and context around them were important. They also had mentors, collaborators, and students who helped them in ways large and small.

This book is for current and aspiring scientists and practitioners of I-O psychology and other disciplines, such as the history of psychology, human resource management, organizational behavior, and organizational psychology. The reader will learn that many key thinkers faced and overcame tremendous challenges, and that there was no one pathway to become a scholar of applied psychology in business and industry. Their stories are an inspiration, and you may gain insights or find yourself asking more questions after reading them. If this is true, then the authors have been successful.

Chapter 1

Frederick Winslow Taylor (1856–1915)

Elizabeth L. Shoenfelt

Frederick Winslow Taylor's 1911 book *The Principles of Scientific Management* was elected the most influential management book of the 20th century by the American Fellows of the Academy of Management and was further described as the most influential management book ever (Bedeian & Wren, 2001). Who was this individual and what is so influential about his work? This brief biography will provide some insight into this question and will likely prompt a desire for further reading about Frederick Winslow Taylor. This narrative tells the story of Taylor's life and of his work's legacy that is still impactful.

Biographical Overview

Early Years

Frederick Winslow Taylor was born March 20, 1856, in German Town (Philadelphia), PA, the second of three children born to Franklin Taylor, an English Quaker and a Princeton-educated attorney who built his wealth on mortgages, and Emily Annette Taylor (nee Winslow), whose ancestor was one of the original Mayflower Pilgrims, well-grounded in Puritanism, and for many years the Governor of Pennsylvania. Taylor's mother was among the earliest suffragists and, in 1842, was a delegate with Lucretia Mott to The International Anti-Slavery Convention in London. His familial upbringing likely resulted in the role of technique and ethics in Taylor's *Principles of Scientific Management*. Taylor was compelled by social consciousness evident in two forces: one to investigate and invent and the other to ensure these inventions served society. Even as a boy, although Taylor was very generous

DOI: 10.4324/9781003403258-1

to his opponents, he was intent on strict observance of rules of a game and keen on determining the one best way to, for example, brake a bob-sled, vault a fence, or stroke a croquet mallet. He used a quasi-experimental method to develop a harness to ensure he slept in a specific position that he ascertained would prevent his chronic night terrors (Copley, 1923).

Following rigorous homeschooling under the tutelage of his mother and with the intention of becoming an attorney, Taylor attended Phillips Exeter Academy and then passed the Harvard entrance exam with honors. He declined admission because his avid studying by candlelight at night had so fatigued his eyes that he temporarily had to give up reading. Instead, he became an apprentice machinist at the Enterprise Hydraulics Works in Philadelphia (owned by a family friend) and, noting the prevailing bad industrial conditions, devoted much time and thought to possible remedies (Copley, 1923). In 1878, he completed his four-year apprenticeship and became a machine shop laborer at the Midvale Steel Works, where he was quickly promoted to time clerk, journeyman machinist, machine shop foreman, research director, and, finally, chief engineer while simultaneously serving as machine shop foreman. His quick ascension through the ranks has been attributed to both his talent and his father's close relationship with Edward Clark, part owner of the Steel Works. While at Midvale, in 1883, Taylor completed a bachelor's degree in mechanical engineering from Stevens Institute of Technology via correspondence study.

Taylor was an accomplished athlete. In 1881, with Clarence Clark (Edward's son and later Taylor's brother-in-law), he won in straight sets the inaugural United States (US) National Tennis Doubles Championship (later to become the US Open). In the 1900 Summer Olympics, Taylor finished fourth in golf, just out of the medals. On May 3, 1884, Taylor married Louise M. Spooner of Philadelphia. The couple had no children of their own, but in 1901, after the untimely death of their friends William and Anna Potter, the Taylors adopted their three children, Kempton, Robert, and Elizabeth.

Career Notes

Taylor's employment included general manager and consulting engineer to management at Manufacturing Investment Company of Philadelphia from 1890 to 1893, when he opened his independent consulting firm specializing in systematizing management and manufacturing. In 1895, Taylor published his first paper, "A Piece Rate System," in the *Transactions of the American Society of Mechanical Engineering* (*ASME*). From 1898 to 1901, Taylor joined Bethlehem Steel to solve expensive machine shop capacity problems. He and Maunsell White III conducted comprehensive empirical tests there to develop high-speed steel cutting tools that revolutionized metal-cutting techniques.

Scientific Management and Growing Notoriety

In 1901 at the age of 45, Taylor retired from Bethlehem Steel after discord with other managers. Until his death 14 years later, he promoted scientific management and his machining methods through lectures, writing, and consulting. Taylor provided highly detailed consultations with hundreds who visited him at his home and who were taken by Taylor to neighboring plants to observe his methods in actual operation (Copley, 1923). Indeed, in the final paragraph of Taylor's (1911/1998) book, he welcomes all who are interested to visit his home in Philadelphia where he would be pleased to show them how scientific management is practiced in nearby organizations, indicating that "he regards visits of this sort as a privilege, rather than as an intrusion" (p. 76).

In 1906 (published 1907), the same year he was elected president of *ASME*, he presented his highly regarded paper, "The Art of Cutting Metal" (Taylor, 1907), which reported more than 30,000 experiments conducted at Midvale Steel Company in the 1880s. In these studies, he scientifically varied the speed, feed, and shapes of cutting tools to determine the one best way to do any metal-cutting task. Taylor invented procedures still in use including cooling metal-cutting operations with a stream of water; he developed the charts or slide rules for feed, speed, and depth of cut. *ASME* published many of his influential papers including "Notes on Belting" (Taylor, 1894), "A Piece-Rate System" (Taylor, 1895), and "Shop Management" (Taylor, 1903).

Taylor gained international fame in 1910 when he testified in the Eastern Rate case. The Eastern Rail Road Company (ERRC) application to the Interstate Commerce Commission to increase freight rates was characterized by opposing attorneys as inevitably increasing prices of consumer goods. The attorney representing Eastern shippers, future US Supreme Court Justice Louis Brandeis, coined the term "scientific management" in his argument that, rather than increasing rates, railroads could reduce expenses by adopting the efficient methods of scientific management. Taylor, in an amicus capacity, explained the cost efficiency of scientific management. Taylor's testimony was bolstered by well-known business leader, Harrington Emerson, a proponent of scientific management who testified that, in his estimate, it could save ERRC a million dollars a day. Scientific management was then promulgated worldwide as an elixir for industrial inefficiency (Wren, 2011).

One year later, 1911, Taylor presented his paper "The Principles of Scientific Management" to *ASME*; he published his book of the same title the same year. Taylor stated the purpose of his paper was to convince through illustration of successful applications that "whenever these principles are correctly applied, results must follow which are truly astounding." (p. iv). Indeed, his book recounts in detail the most well known of his interventions. Within two years of the book's publication, it had been translated into French, German, Dutch, Swedish, Russian, Lettish, Italian, Spanish, and Japanese, and shortly after Taylor's death, into Chinese (Copley, 1923).

In 1912, Taylor testified before the Special Investigative Committee of the House of Representatives examining his and other shop management systems. Taylor explicated how scientific management could address the issues brought before Congress by organized labor. This committee work preceded the 1913 establishment of the Department of Labor to promote the welfare of workers and improved work conditions (Copley, 1923).

The Taylor Society was formed in 1912; it joined the Society of Industrial Engineers and became the Society for Advancement of Management. Taylor received an honorary doctorate from the University of Pennsylvania in 1906; he eventually joined the faculty at the Dartmouth College Tuck School of Business. On March 21, 1915, after catching pneumonia, Taylor died in Philadelphia one day after his 59th birthday.

Scientific Management

Any biography of Taylor would be incomplete without including the four key principles of scientific management. The interested reader can consult any of numerous sources including most modern management books. Taylor (1911/1998) cited these as the four key principles:

1. Development of a true science for each task.
2. Scientific selection and subsequent training of first-class men and the elimination of men who are unwilling or unable to adopt the best methods.
3. Bringing the first-class worker and the science of the task together through constant cooperation, helpfulness, encouragement, and watchfulness of management; and paying each man a large daily wage for working quickly and obeying management.
4. Almost equal division of work and responsibility between workers and management. Intimate friendly cooperation between the management and the men, with management working almost side by side with the worker.

Taylor indicated that

> the most important objective of both the workmen and the management should be the training and development of each individual in the establishment so that he can do (at the fastest pace with maximum efficiency) the highest class of work for which his natural abilities fit him.
>
> (p. 3)

Taylor's Influence in Industrial-Organizational Psychology

Taylor proved prescient as many of the principles and practices he put forth in his renowned volume blossomed into full-blown theories that are foundational in modern industrial-organizational (I-O) psychology. For example, Taylor originated and pioneered the recognition of "the human side of enterprise" in the mid-1880s (years before McGregor), identifying the important role of management in equitable treatment of workers. In addition to direct influence of Taylor and scientific management to the essential I-O practices of selection, placement, and training, their influence in I-O psychology is evident throughout Taylor's book as it references:[1]

- Superiority of data-based scientific decision making over judgment (p. 46)
- Job analysis and job design (foundational in scientific management; pp. 9, 26, 51, 61)
- Physical ability testing (p. 29)
- Mandatory rest breaks at scientifically determined intervals (p. 47)
- Quality control (p. 45)
- Return on investment/utility analysis (p. 35)
- Accurate performance measurement (p. 46)
- Well-planned tasks with specific, challenging objectives for the day's work (goal setting) (pp. 33, 34, 37, 47)
- Motivational and cueing functions of feedback (pp. 33, 41, 48)
- Norm of systematic soldiering (years before the Hawthorne Studies) (pp. 3, 7)
- Theory X beliefs of management (pp. 1, 6)
- Addressing the fallacy that technology will displace workers (p. 4)
- Motivating effects of pay for performance versus demotivating effects of uniform pay for a day's work (pp. 6, 36, 48)
- Overcoming resistance to change (p. 60)

Criticisms of Taylor and Scientific Management

Taylor and scientific management were not without criticism, both in his day and in more modern times, albeit for different reasons.

Contemporaneous Criticism

Early 20th-century criticism centered on the perceived exploitation and dehumanization of the worker. Jobs were simplified into the one best way to perform a task, were repetitive, and were closely supervised. Link (1919) indicated these perceptions, conflated by management with industrial psychology, created a hurdle for acceptance of the work of industrial psychologists. Viteles (1932) criticized scientific management, yet acknowledged scientific management laid the foundation for industrial psychology. Muscio (1920) distinguished between Taylor's scientific management and others who professed to but did not follow scientific management and who were deserving recipients of many of the criticisms leveled at Taylor. Muscio argued there was little factual support at the time for the criticisms of Taylor and scientific management.

Taylor (1911/1998) himself indicated management resisted the required large capital outlay for the scientific studies, the planning and management oversight, the extensive training of workers, and change itself. Workers disliked that they were required to repeat the same task and to operate strictly according to their foreman's instructions. Yet, most of the workers in the steel mills were illiterate immigrants who benefited from the system that frequently doubled their wages for the same hours of work and increased their standard of living.

Contemporary Criticism

More recently, Taylor has been criticized for dehumanizing and demeaning workers, reducing them to machines that repeat the same oversimplified task under micromanagers, creating monotony and alienation in the workforce, and that requiring the one best way precludes innovation and can reduce feelings of autonomy, ownership, satisfaction, and responsibility. Taylor's work was innovative and revolutionized steel manufacturing. His one best way, grounded in science, greatly increased efficiency and profitability. Even so, Taylor (1911/1998) indicated that, once workers were proficient in the one best way, they should be encouraged to suggest improvements to methods and tools.

Critics who claim that Taylor's focus on wages doesn't appropriately address worker motivation fail to acknowledge Taylor's use of goal setting and feedback, now recognized as key motivational techniques and that money is a primary motivator for most workers (Locke, 1982). Taylor has been criticized as anti-union when, in fact, Taylor expressed that if scientific management is properly implemented, worker welfare is prioritized and unions are not needed. Taylor implemented better wages, shorter work hours, and rest breaks – issues commonly at the forefront of labor–management conflict.

Taylor did use what now we would consider condescending language. For example, that there are different classes of men, those with "insufficient mental capacity" must be guided by management, and that a man suitable for handling pig iron must be so stupid that his mental capability resembles an ox. Indeed, this is condescending language but should be considered in light of the culture of the time. Today, I-O psychologists hire or reject applicants and classify workers based on cognitive ability but use more respectful language.

Contemporary criticisms reflect modern prioritization of worker well-being and disacknowledge the prevailing industrial culture and zeitgeist of Taylor's time; that is, the turn of the 20th century in the midst of industrialization when economic survival was the paramount motivation for most unskilled workers, many of whom were minimally literate. These contemporary criticisms are akin to criticizing Edison for failing to devise the LED light bulb. When carefully examined in light of what Taylor actually wrote, spoke, and practiced, there is little factual support for most of these criticisms; many of Taylor's insights remain relevant today (Locke, 1982). Bedeian and Wren (2001) summed it up nicely when they recognized Taylor's book as the most influential management book of the 20th century, "Although Taylor remains the favorite bogeyman of the popular press, the fundamental principle of Taylor's philosophy — the rule of knowledge as opposed to tradition and personal opinion — is as valid today as it was in his time" (p. 222).

Conclusion

Taylor arguably is one of the most influential management theorists of the 20th century. His principles of scientific management (1911/1998), still influential, had global impact when first published. Taylor's rigorous use of the scientific method identified innovations that revolutionized the steel industry. Perhaps Taylor's greatest contribution was his prescient insights into work performance, anticipating many of the principles and practices foundational to I-O psychology. Although Taylor and his methods were criticized both contemporaneously and contemporarily, his influence on I-O psychology cannot be denied.

Note

1 Page numbers referenced here are from Taylor (1911/1998).

References

Bedeian, A. G. & Wren, D. A. (2001). Most influential management books of the 20th century. *Organizational Dynamics, 29 (3)*, 221–225. https://doi.org/10.1016/S0090-2616(01)00022-5

Copley, F. B. (1923). *Frederick Winslow Taylor father of scientific management.* Harper and Brothers Publishers. https://archive.org/details/frederickwtaylor01copl

Link, H. C. (1919). *Employment psychology: The application of scientific methods to the selection, training, and grading of employees.* Macmillan.

Locke, E. A. (1982). The ideas of Frederick W. Taylor: An evaluation. *Academy of Management Review, 7*, 14–24. https://doi.org/10.2307/257244

Muscio, B. (1920). *Lectures on industrial psychology* (2nd Ed.). Routledge.

Taylor, F. W. (1894). Notes on belting. Transcript. *American Society of Mechanical Engineers, 15*, 204–238.

Taylor, F. W. (1895). A piece-rate system, being a step toward partial solution of the labor problem. Transcript. *American Society of Mechanical Engineers, 16*, 856–883.

Taylor, F. W. (1903). Shop management. Transcript. *American Society of Mechanical Engineers, 24*, 1337–1456. Republished as Taylor, F. W. (1911). *Shop management.* Harper and Brothers.

Taylor, F. W. (1907). The art of cutting metal. *American Society of Mechanical Engineers.* https://doi.org/10.1038/scientificamerican01121907-25942supp

Taylor, F. W. (1911/1998). *The principles of scientific management.* Harper and Brothers. Reprint of unabridged volume, Dover Publications.

Viteles, M. S. (1932). *Industrial psychology.* Norton.

Wren, D. A. (2011). The centennial of Frederick W. Taylor's *The Principles of Scientific Management*: A retrospective commentary, *Journal of Business and Management, 17(1)*, 8–22.

Chapter 2

James McKeen Cattell (1860–1944)

Andrew J. Vinchur

James McKeen Cattell was not an applied psychologist. Unlike contemporaries such as Walter Dill Scott, Hugo Münsterberg, and Walter Van Dyke Bingham, he did not conduct research or practice in any substantive area of industrial-organizational (I-O) psychology. The first American to receive a doctorate from Wilhelm Wundt's foundational psychology program at the University of Leipzig, Cattell was a pioneering experimental psychologist in his early career who spent the bulk of his later career in editorial and administrative positions. Yet his contributions to psychology and the subfield of I-O psychology were substantial. Napoli (1981) states that Cattell's 1890 article on mental testing was the beginning of applied psychology, and Landy (1997) includes Cattell with Scott, Münsterberg, and Bingham as "the four leading figures in the formation of I/O psychology" (p. 468). Cattell had a substantial influence on the early development of psychology in general, and he played a key role in shaping the public's perception of the new science. This chapter will concentrate on Cattell's specific contributions to I-O psychology while occasionally touching on his more general achievements.

Biographical Overview

The Life

Cattell was born in Easton, PA, in 1860. His father William became the president of Lafayette College in 1863; his mother, Elizabeth McKeen, was the daughter of a wealthy foundry owner and College benefactor (Sokal, 2006). While attending Lafayette,

DOI: 10.4324/9781003403258-2

Cattell was influenced by pioneering philologist Francis Andrew March's lectures on Francis Bacon and the inductive Baconian method (Bjork, 1983). Following his graduation in 1880, Cattell briefly studied philosophy in Europe before returning to America to spend a year at Johns Hopkins University with G. Stanley Hall. Then he returned to Europe to receive his doctorate in 1886, the first American to do so in Wilhelm Wundt's psychology program at the University of Leipzig. It was at Leipzig that Cattell first demonstrated an interest in human performance variability (Woodworth, 1944). After graduation, Cattell lectured briefly at Bryn Mawr and the University of Pennsylvania. Unable to find a suitable position at an American university, Cattell left for Great Britain and Cambridge University to study neurology. While in England, Cattell found a mentor in Charles Darwin's polymath cousin Francis Galton, who was interested in anthropometric measurement. Galton encouraged Cattell to apply quantitative measurement to the individual characteristics he studied in Wundt's laboratory (Sokal, 1987). In 1888, Cattell was able to procure a position as a lecturer of psychophysics at the University of Pennsylvania (U. Penn Catalog, 1888–1889). In 1889, his title was changed to Professor of Psychology (U. Penn Catalog, 1889–1890); he was one of the first to hold that title in the United States.[1] In 1891, Cattell moved to the psychology program at Columbia University. In 1894, Cattell and Mark Baldwin cofounded the journal the *Psychological Review*.

Cattell's progressive politics and argumentative nature kept him in conflict with the administration at Columbia University, particularly with Columbia president Nicholas Murray Butler. Cattell's pacifist opposition to America's involvement in World War I gave Murray the excuse he needed to fire Cattell in 1917 (Sokal, 2009; Summerscales 1970). This effectively ended his academic career. Cattell spent much of his post-academic career in an editorial role. He was involved as a publisher and/or editor of the journals *Science, Popular Science Monthly, School and Society,* and *The American Naturalist.* Cattell edited *American Men of Science* and played a key leadership role in the American Association for the Advancement of Science (AAAS) (Coon & Sprenger, 1998). Through his publishing, editing, and leadership efforts, Cattell played a large role in how psychology was perceived in America. In 1921, he founded The Psychological Corporation, a holding company for psychologists with the goal of advancing psychology through research and practice (Cattell, 1923).

Cattell experienced both a great deal of success and failure throughout his long career as a psychologist. While "he possessed a courage which led him to fight for his principles against the greatest odds" (Kunkel, 1944, p. 5), he could be stubborn and argumentative, and his colleagues at times found him alienating (Sokal, 2006). Active in psychology until the end of his life, Cattell died in Lancaster, PA, in 1944.

The Work

While Cattell never practiced as an industrial psychologist, his work, both experimental and administrative, had an important influence on the field. The functionalist approach to psychology, emphasizing the usefulness of psychological processes, that he championed while heading the psychology program at Columbia University was amenable to applied psychology.[2] Cattell's focus on quantification and measurement provided a foundation for early industrial psychology. He believed that unless psychology was firmly based on accurate measurement and empirical research, it would never obtain parity with the physical sciences (Cattell, 1890/1947).[3]

Cattell was a key figure in the development of psychological testing. He focused on anthropometric testing, primarily physiological but also including measurement of some simple psychological characteristics (Sokal, 2006). While his anthropometric measures were not successful in predicting criteria of academic success (Wissler, 1901), his overall approach of carefully measuring of individual difference characteristics provides the foundation for psychology applied to employee selection. In 1898, Cattell developed a rank-ordering method, his order-of-merit method, for ranking stimuli on effectiveness. This methodology proved valuable to psychologists working in advertising (Kuna, 1979).

In 1921, Cattell founded the Psychological Corporation, a holding company for psychologists whose purpose was to advance psychology through practice and research (Cattell, 1923).[4] The firm had 20 prominent psychologists as directors, including pioneering industrial psychologists Walter Dill Scott, Walter Van Dyke Bingham, and Harry Hollingworth. Cattell's goals for the Psychological Corporation were very ambitious. In addition to promoting research and providing psychological services, Cattell wanted the organization to improve the finances, visibility, and social standing of psychologists. Unfortunately, in its early years, the Psychological Corporation floundered under Cattell's leadership. It was not until a 1926 reorganization under the industrial psychologists Bingham, Scott, Elsie O. Bregman, and Paul Achilles that the organization achieved a measure of financial success (Achilles, 1957).

Cattell devoted much time and effort to improving the visibility and standing of psychology. He was a strong advocate for psychology as a profession, and he argued for its usefulness beyond the laboratory. Through his editorial and publishing duties, his work in organizing and promoting the American Psychological Association (APA), and his own writing, Cattell did much to popularize psychology to the public and to increase its standing in the scientific community. He was recognized for his contributions. Cattell was elected APA president in 1895. He was the first psychologist elected to the National Academy of Sciences in 1901, preceding William James. Cattell was president of the AAAS in 1924, and president of the International Congress of Psychology in 1929. His obituary (*New York Times*, January 21, 1944) referred to him as the dean of American science, noted his international reputation as a psychologist, and that, along with James, he was a pioneer of American psychology.

The Legacy

Cattell's place in the history of psychology is secure. He is widely viewed, with others such as William James, Hugo Münsterberg, G. Stanley Hall, and Edward Titchener, as one of the founders of American psychology.[5] Cattell's career in psychology can be divided into three major stages, each beneficial for I-O psychology. In graduate school and in his early academic career, he conducted empirical research on individual differences, measurement, and quantification that were foundational to the development of I-O psychology. In Cattell's second stage as a leading educator at Columbia University, he administered a program that produced a number of influential industrial psychologists. His final stage was as a journal editor, publisher, and promoter of psychology. Cattell's founding of the Psychological Corporation provided an outlet for industrial psychologists to practice and a model for future consulting activities. Other efforts in promoting psychology, including applied psychology, through his editorial and publishing ventures did much to increase psychology's visibility and acceptance by the public. As Sokal (2006) observed, Cattell was a promotor of "an applicable psychology" that "provided their science and discipline with the institutional infrastructure that enabled it to grow and prosper as it did in the 20th century" (p. 19).

Notes

1 While Cattell is sometimes cited as the first one to hold the title of professor of psychology in the United States, Joseph Jastrow was appointed professor of experimental and comparative psychology at the University of Wisconsin in 1888. Jastrow's title was shortened to professor of psychology in 1903 (Cadwallader, 1987).
2 Many prominent early industrial psychologists received their graduate degrees at Columbia under Cattell, including Elsie Oschrin Bregman, Harry Hollingworth, and Edward K. Strong, Jr., all who have chapters in this volume. A partial list of other early Columbia graduates who contributed to the field include Paul Achilles, James B. Miner, Sadie Shellow, and Herbert Toops (Vinchur, 2018).
3 In that 1890 article Cattell was one of the first, perhaps the first, to use the term *mental test.*
4 The Psychological Corporation was not the first successful industrial psychology consulting firm, that honor goes to Walter Dill Scott's short-lived Scott Company, founded in 1919. There was an earlier unsuccessful attempt, the Economic Psychology Association, founded in New York in 1915 as a cooperative venture between psychology and business (Hollingworth, 2013 [written in 1940]). The Division of Applied Psychology, also founded in 1915 at the Carnegie Institute of Psychology in Pittsburgh, was an academic program that provided industrial psychology consulting.
5 Cattell (1903) had a small group of prominent psychologists use his order-of-merit method to peer-rank American psychologists on eminence. He did not publish the identified results until 1933. Cattell ranked second, after William James. Positions three through 10 were held respectively by Hugo Münsterberg, G. Stanley Hall, James

Baldwin, Edward Titchener, Josiah Royce, George Trumball Ladd, John Dewey, and Joseph Jastrow (Over, 1982).

References

Achilles, P. (1957, November 30). [Letter to Leonard W. Ferguson] Carnegie-Mellon University (Ferguson Collection, Box 2), Pittsburgh, PA.

Bjork, D. W. (1983). *The compromised scientist: William James in the development of American psychology*. Columbia University Press.

Cadwallader, T. C. (1987). Origins and accomplishments of Joseph Jastrow's 1888-founded chair of comparative psychology at the University of Wisconsin. *Journal of Comparative Psychology, 101,* 231–236. https://doi.org/10.1037/0735-7036.101.3.231

Cattell, J. M. (1890/1947). Mental tests and measurements. *Mind, 15,* 373–381. Reprinted in *James McKeen Cattell: Man of science, Vol. 1: Psychological research* (pp. 132–141). Science Press.

Cattell, J. M. (1903). Statistics of American psychologists. *American Journal of Psychology, 14,* 310–328. https://doi.org/10.2307/1412321

Cattell, J. M. (1923). The psychological corporation. *Annals of the Academy of Political and Social Science, 110,* 165–171. https://doi.org/10.1177/000271622311000117

Coon, D. J., & Sprenger, H. A. (1998). Psychologists in service to science: The American Psychological Association and the American Association for the Advancement of Science. *American Psychologist, 53(12),* 1253–1269. https://doi.org/10.1037/0003066X.53.12.1253

Hollingworth, H. L. (2013). *From Coca-Cola to chewing gum: The applied psychology of Harry Hollingworth,* Volume II (L. T. Benjamin, Jr. & L. R. Barton [eds.]). University of Akron Press.

Kuna, D. P. (1979). Early advertising applications of the Gale-Cattell order-of-merit method. *Journal of the History of the Behavioral Sciences, 15,* 38–46. https://doi.org/10.1002/1520-6696(197901)15:1%3C38::aid-jhbs2300150105%3E3.0.co;2-b

Kunkel, B. W. (March 26, 1944). Memorial to James McKeen Cattell. Graduation exercises, Lafayette College. Lafayette College Archives, Easton, PA.

Landy, F. J. (1997). Early influences on the development of industrial and organizational psychology. *Journal of Applied Psychology, 82,* 467–477. https://doi.org/10.1037/0021-9010.82.4.467

Napoli, D. S. (1981). *Architects of adjustment: The history of the psychological profession in the United States*. Kennibat Press.

New York Times (1944, January 1). Dr. Cattell dead; scientist, editor: Noted psychologist a former professor at Columbia – Headed publishing firm. 17.

Over, R. (1982). The durability of scientific reputation. *Journal of the History of the Behavioral Sciences, 18,* 53–61. https://doi.org/10.1002/1520-6696(198201)18:1%3C53::aid-jhbs2300180106%3E3.0.co;2-t

Sokal, M. M. (1987). James McKeen Cattell and mental anthropometry: Nineteenth century science and reform and the origins of psychological testing. In M. M. Sokal (ed.), *Psychological testing and American society 1890-1930* (pp. 21–45). Rutgers University Press.

Sokal, M. M. (2006). James McKeen Cattell: Achievement and alienation. In D. A. Dewsbury, L. T. Benjamin, Jr., & M. Wertheimer (eds.), *Portraits of pioneers in psychology, vol. VI* (pp. 19–35). Erlbaum.

Sokal, M. M. (2009). James McKeen Cattell, Nicholas Murray Butler, and academic freedom at Columbia University, 1902-1923. *History of Psychology, 12,* 87–122. https://doi.org/10.1037/a0016143

Summerscales, W. (1970). *Affirmation and dissent: Columbia's response to the crisis in World War I.* Teachers College Press.

University of Pennsylvania Catalogue and Announcements (1888–1889). Retrieved from: https://colenda.library.upenn.edu/catalog/81431-p3xd0rj6p

University of Pennsylvania Catalogue and Announcements (1889–1990). Retrieved from: https://colenda.library.upenn.edu/catalog/81431-p3sn01r3d

Vinchur, A. J. (2018). *The early years of industrial and organizational psychology.* Cambridge University Press. https://doi.org/10.1017/9781107588608

Wissler, C. (1901). The correlation of mental and physical tests. *Psychological Review, 3,* 1–63. https://doi.org/10.1037/h0066617

Woodworth, R. S. (1944). James McKeen Cattell 1860-1944. *Psychological Review, 51,* 201–209. https://doi.org/10.1037/h0063297

Chapter 3

Hugo Münsterberg (1863–1916)

Nathan T. Carter

> The time seems ripe for bringing the psychological work into full contact with the practical efforts of civilization.
>
> (H. Münsterberg, 1914, p. vii)

Münsterberg had a strong influence on the development of multiple fields including forensic psychology, film studies, psychotherapy, and of course industrial-organizational (I-O) psychology. His research on employee selection and his advocating for a focus on worker well-being was ahead of its time. His work received mixed reviews from subsequent psychologists citing his subjective approach, however, it is difficult to disentangle this later criticism from national politics, which caused strained relations between himself and American colleagues as he defended Germany as World War I (WWI) began. Regardless, Münsterberg's legacy includes mentoring future leaders in psychology, advocating for women in the field, and his efforts to bridge American–German cultural understanding. His impact on applied psychology and his role in shaping I-O psychology were undeniably significant.

Biographical Overview

Early Life and Education

Hugo Münsterberg was born in 1863, in the city of Danzig. At the time, Danzig was part of a Prussian province of the same name and is currently known as Gdańsk (the Polish form of Danzig), Poland. His father Moritz was a well-to-do lumber

DOI: 10.4324/9781003403258-3

merchant who bought up forests in Russia, selling the exploits to England. His mother, Anna, was Moritz's second wife, who gave birth to Hugo and his brother Oscar, and raised Hugo's half-brothers, Otto and Emil. Both Moritz and Anna were fervent advocates of intellectual and artistic life. Moritz's travels for business opened the household not only to his own recounting of his adventures but also to a literature beyond the confines of their hometown. Anna was a talented painter and sketch artist. His mother's interest in art had a particular impact on Hugo, and although he did not practice visual arts himself, he became an avid consumer of varied forms of art and literature. At age 7, Hugo began writing poetry, an area in which he achieved some distinction, writing lyric, epic, and dramatic poetry throughout his life (M. Münsterberg, 1922). His mother's passing when he was only 12 years old is noted to have transformed Hugo from a "carefree child to a serious little boy" (p. 12).

Hugo's education began with kindergarten, then a private school, and then the Germanic "Gymnasium," which he entered at 9 years old. The Gymnasium is a sort of cross between collegiate structure and standardized state-controlled schooling, with a timeline corresponding to grade school and high school, but extending into what in contemporary American education is the sophomore year of college. At that point, final examinations termed the "Abiturium" are administered, and those who pass – as did Hugo – are admitted to study at any German University. Hugo's activities in Gymnasium were multifaceted. He published with a friend a college-type periodical entitled *Loose Leaves*, developed a lexicon and etymology of German words, studied Arabic to the point of being capable of reading the original Quran, played cello in an amateur orchestra, and maintained a group of friends whom entertained themselves by reenacting plays in a casual way, and read their own works of literature and poetry to one another (M. Münsterberg, 1922).

At the age of 19, Hugo entered the University of Leipzig, concentrating on obtaining a medical degree. While there, he took a lecture from Wilhelm Wundt, who is generally credited as founding the first experimental psychological laboratory. Wundt's lectures inspired Münsterberg to pursue becoming a psychologist. One co-worker in Wundt's lab was the American student

James McKeen Cattell, who would make his own large contributions to psychology. Upon completion of the medical degree, Münsterberg began pursuing completion of a dissertation to obtain a PhD under Wundt. However, the topics Münsterberg chose were not popular with Wundt; in particular, Hugo had become fascinated by individual differences, which Wundt was not ready to tackle as a strict structuralist aiming to find universal laws of human behavior (Keller, 1979). Additionally, Münsterberg's dissertation contradicted many of Wundt's most basic beliefs, claiming that each physiological action possessed a correspondent psychological action, and that the sense of willed behavior was the result of physiological sensation (Spillmann & Spillmann, 1993). Despite Wundt's reservations, Münsterberg completed the PhD in 1885, moving first to Heidelberg University and then to Freiburg University two years later (Hale, 1980; Landy, 1992). Just before settling at Freiburg, he would also marry Selma Oppler in the small town of Vosges, Weissenberg. He would have two children with her: Margaret, who would go on to write a biography of her late father, and Ella, whose paintings of her father can be found in the Harvard Art Museum collections.

At Freiburg, Hugo would hold the position of a "privatdocent." In this position, a scholar received no salary or compensation other than fees they charged to students to attend their lectures. During this time, the scholar waited to be appointed to a professorship at another university (M. Münsterberg, 1922). While at Freiburg, Hugo began to publish – in fact, one of those publications would be a thesis idea that Wundt had rejected years earlier – and set up several rooms in his personal home as laboratory space (Landy, 1992).

Around 1890, William James – at the time a very prominent American psychologist – began to correspond with Münsterberg after having met him in Paris, and even sent a student to work with him at Freiburg. James would champion Hugo, and even send him words of encouragement after a sharp critique from an elder colleague, going as far to say "... I will back you to beat the whole army of your critics before you are forty years old" (M. Münsterberg, 1922, p. 32). In February of 1892, James first floated the idea to Münsterberg of coming to Harvard to take over the psychological laboratory there, to which Hugo was interested; by March, Hugo received a telegram from James reading in German "Alles gelungen" ("Everything settled") (M. Münsterberg, 1922, p. 35).

The Harvard Years

When Hugo arrived at Harvard, he did not yet speak English but learned quickly during his three-year term. He quickly became a favorite lecturer among students and mentored graduate students on their dissertations (Spillmann & Spillmann, 1993). His work was still largely focused on the psychophysical, and during this time he published a piece that lead to the discovery of what is now often referred to as the "Münsterberg Illusion" (Münsterberg, 1894; other names for the illusion include the Café Wall and Kindergarten Illusion) in which parallel lines with staggered blocks appear to have opposing slopes despite their parallelism.

After his three-year term (1895–1897), Hugo and his wife returned to Freiburg. However, Harvard beckoned him again. He hesitated to commit and asked the President of Harvard to allow him to return first without his family, for them to follow after he had made up his mind. The President was clear in correspondence that this would not fly and that the university would not accept anything less than he and his family "burning [their] ships" upon their return. Thus, in September 1897, the Münsterberg family would return for good, establishing their roots in Cambridge (M. Münsterberg, 1922).

It was during this period that Münsterberg's originality truly began to flourish. In 1898, he was elected as the seventh president of the American Psychological Association. His address dealt with the interrelation between the disciplines of history, the arts, natural science, and physical sciences, and is a compelling and insightful read (see H. Münsterberg, 1899). He also began to write in English. Münsterberg's early experimental work was all written in German (W. James and other colleagues could read German and so were able to read these works), greatly strengthening his fame, writing for popular press publications such as the *Atlantic* and the *New York Times*. In fact, Landy (1992) notes that he published in the latter on average once a month with a "pro-psychology opinions" (p. 794).

From the late 1900s to his death, Münsterberg would publish significant works and conduct other activities that would influence various – as of yet mostly undefined – subfields of psychology and other disciplines. His book *On the Witness Stand* (1908) is considered one of the first works in forensic psychology, and among the first to consider jury research, and the fallibility of confessions and eyewitness accounts. *The Photoplay: A Psychological Study* (1916) is often credited with having founded the field of Film Studies, drawing parallels between certain cinematic techniques (e.g., closeups, flashbacks) with correspondent mental processes (e.g., focused attention, memory). He made contributions to clinical psychology in his work *Psychotherapy* (1909). Despite early statements strongly against the application of scientific psychology to the classroom (see Benjamin, 2006), Münsterberg made contributions to educational psychology, including *Psychology and the Teacher* (1910).

Most pertinent to the current chapter is his *Psychology and Industrial Efficiency* (1913a), which is often considered the first major work in I-O psychology. In this work he built upon the scientific management idea of Frederick Taylor, suggesting vocational guidance and the selection of workers as a psychological problem, presenting his famous "trolley car" studies, which tests to select out accident-prone trolley operators via simulations to determine candidates' ability to, for example, avoid pedestrians and make fast decisions. Further, Münsterberg's (1913a) work suggested that in addition to the mechanics of work, the mental structure of the worker must also be understood, and one could argue that he foresaw the evolution of work in job satisfaction and well-being in that he sought to promote better "inner harmony" in workers (cf. Wozniak, 1999). Thomas (2021) noted Münsterberg was to be included on the editor list of the newly founded *Journal of Applied Psychology* prior to his death, and Stern (1917) wrote a memorial article in its first issue. Moreover, Münsterberg introduced the concepts of job analysis, job design, the scientific study of training methods, and was an early advocate of psychological testing for selection (Landy, 1992; Münsterberg, 1913a; Spector, 2008).

Death and Legacy

On December 16, 1916, Hugo Münsterberg suffered a fatal cerebral hemorrhage while delivering a lecture at Radcliffe College. After his passing, the next generation of applied psychologists would conduct an autopsy on his work that was less than favorable. Münsterberg's work was often highly subjective and lacking in statistical analysis and/or details, and this was not to the liking of Morris Viteles or Edward Titchener, the latter of which would claim that Hugo "degraded" psychology while at Harvard. It is difficult to disentangle much of the anti-Münsterberg sentiment from politics. Despite the lack of warmth he found from his American friends and colleagues – including William James – in the last years of his life, he founded the Amerika-Insitut at Berlin – part of his legacy of attempting to "explain" Americans to Germans and vice versa during the highly contentious time of WWI – and often published works intended to promote American–German intercultural understanding and exchange (e.g., Münsterberg, 1901; 1904). Upon his death, Harvard would print only a brief note in commemoration in the *Harvard Gazette* (see Spillmann & Spillmann, 1993).

In addition to his direct influence on academic psychology and other disciplines, his work as a mentor also had major impacts. Münsterberg was among the first at Harvard to encourage women to work in his lab, despite his expression of chauvinistic opinions – both hostile and benevolent – in works like *American Patriotism* (1913b). Mary Calkins – the first female president of both the American Psychological Association and American Philosophical Association – recounted stories of Münsterberg forcing a head waiter at Harvard to allow a luncheon to proceed despite her attendance, which was not allowed by Harvard (Calkins, 1930; cf. Prieto, 2012). Furthermore, after presenting her dissertation Münsterberg lobbied hard for Calkins to be awarded the PhD from Harvard; the school conceded to allow her to accept one from Radcliffe – the "women's college" of Harvard – but she declined the degree in the end. Dr. Calkins went on to found one of the earliest psychological laboratories in the United States at Wellesley College. Notably, Gertrude Stein was another female student who worked in Münsterberg's lab. He told her in a letter in 1897:

> ... if in later years, you look into printed discussions I have in mind to publish about American students, I hope you will then pardon me if you recognize some features of my ideal student picture as your own. I hope to hear about your skill often and expect the best from you.
>
> (Martin, 2019, p. 43)

In addition, Münsterberg is the academic grandfather of seven Society for Industrial and Organizational Psychology presidents via their advisors Harold Burtt, Gordon Allport, and Sidney Pressey (Landy, 1992).[1]

Conclusion

Hugo Münsterberg was a complex individual, full of contradictions and controversial opinions, as noted by historians (Benjamin, 2006; Landy, 1992). His impact on the field of applied psychology writ large and specifically on I-O psychology is undeniable. He conducted perhaps the earliest work on selection and foresaw the coming of well-being and job satisfaction research. He proselytized applied psychology in a way few have, directly corresponding with presidents of the United States including Theodore Roosevelt, William Taft, and Woodrow Wilson. He mentored many of the next generation of thinkers that would see applied psychology through the formation of I-O psychology and was an unlikely champion of female students at a time when Harvard did not recognize their contributions. Whether one considers his actions wrong, right, or somewhere in between, Münsterberg clearly sought to leverage the power of psychological theory, principles, and methods for the betterment of society, a spirit that should forever inspire and energize both the scientist and the practitioner.

Note

1 These presidents were Carroll Shartle (1949–1950), Edwin Henry (1956–1957), Douglas Bray (1971–1972), Edwin Fleishman

(1973–1974), Donald Grant (1974–1975), Paul Thayer (1976–1977), and Paul Sparks (1978–1979).

References

Benjamin, L.T., Jr. (2006). Hugo Münsterberg's attack on the application of scientific psychology. *Journal of Applied Psychology*, *91*, 414–425. https://doi.org/10.1037/0021-9010.91.2.414

Calkins, M.W. (1930). Autobiography of Mary Whiton Calkins. In C. Murchison (Ed.), *History of psychology in autobiography*, Vol. 1, pp. 31–61. Clark University Press. https://doi.org/10.1037/11401-002

Hale, M. (1980). *Human science and the social order: Hugo Münsterberg and the origins of applied psychology*. Temple University Press. https://doi.org/10.1126/science.208.4445.714

Keller, P. (1979). *States of belonging: German-American intellectuals and the First World War*. Harvard University Press. https://doi.org/10.1086/ahr/85.3.729-a

Landy, F.J. (1992). Hugo Münsterberg: Victim or visionary? *Journal of Applied Psychology*, *77*, 787–802. https://doi.org/10.1037//0021-9010.77.6.787

Martin, L. (2019). The making of men and women: Gertrude Stein, Hugo Münsterberg, and the discourse of work. *Modernism*, *26*, 43–65. https://doi.org/10.1353/mod.2019.0002

Münsterberg, H. (1894). *Pseudoptics*. Milton Bradley.

Münsterberg, H. (1899). History and psychology. *Psychological Review*, *6*, 1–31.

Münsterberg, H. (1901). *American traits from the point of view of a German*. Houghton-Mifflin.

Münsterberg, H. (1904). *Die Amerikaner.* E.S. Mittler & Sohn.

Münsterberg, H. (1908). *On the witness stand: Essays on psychology and crime*. McClure. https://doi.org/10.1037/10854-000

Münsterberg, H. (1909). *Psychotherapy*. Moffat, Yard. https://doi.org/10.1126/science.30.761.150

Münsterberg, H. (1910). *Psychology and the teacher.* D. Appleton. https://doi.org/10.1037/11339-000

Münsterberg, H. (1913a). *Psychology and industrial efficiency*. Houghton-Mifflin.

Münsterberg, H. (1913b). *American patriotism and other social studies*. Moffat, Yard. https://doi.org/10.1126/science.38.967.56

Münsterberg, H. (1916). *The photoplay: A psychological study*. D. Appleton.

Münsterberg, M. (1922). *Hugo Münsterberg: His life and work*. D. Appleton.

Prieto, L.C. (2012). Women issues to Wonder Woman: Contributions made by the students of Hugo Münsterberg. *Journal of Management History*, *18*, 166–177. https://doi.org/10.1108/17511341211206834

Spector, P. E. (2008). *Industrial/organizational psychology: Research and practice* (5th ed). Wiley.

Spillmann, J., & Spillmann, L. (1993). The rise and fall of Hugo Münsterberg. *Journal of the History of the Behavioral Sciences*, *29*, 322–338. https://doi.org/10.1002/1520-6696(199310)29:4<322::aid-jhbs2300290403>3.0.co;2-1

Stern, W. (1917). Hugo Münsterberg: In memoriam. *Journal of Applied Psychology*, *1*, 186–188.

Thomas, R.K. (2021). “Pure” versus “applied” psychology: An historical conflict between Edward B. Titchener (Pure) and Ludwig R. Geissler (Applied). *The Psychological Record*, *72*, 131–143. https://doi.org/10.1037/h0074508

Wozniak, R.H. (1999). *Classics in psychology, 1855-1914: Historical essays*. Thoemmes Press.

Chapter 4

Jòzefa Joteyko (1866–1928)

Jesús F. Salgado

Marie Curie (1867–1934) is a scientist known worldwide for her discoveries in physics and chemistry. Twice winner of the Nobel Prize, she was Polish and moved to Paris to study at university. In the same year that Marie Curie arrived in Paris, another young Polish student also came to Paris to study for her doctorate in medicine. Today, she is fairly unknown, but due to her research in fields such as physiology, experimental psychology, industrial psychology, education, and for being one of the European creators of a science of work, she deserves to be rescued from oblivion. I refer to Jòzefa Franciszka Joteyko, whom we might call *the Madame Curie* of work psychology, based on the national parallelism – both were Polish and studied in France – and the influence in their respective disciplines. In addition, both conducted research during the same period and received awards in the same year from the French Academy of Sciences (1898). It is sad that Joteyko and her contributions to industrial, work, and organizational (IWO) psychology are virtually unknown today outside of her native Poland.

Biographical Overview

The eminent Polish physiologist and psychologist Jòzefa Franciszka Joteyko (spelled Ioteyko in many of her French publications) was born in the village of Pochuiky (which now is a part of Ukraine) on January 29, 1866, and died in Warzaw on April 24, 1928. Her family was descended from Lithuanian nobility and were members of the Polish intellectual elite. When Joteyko was 7 years old, the family moved to Warsaw, where she received private instruction

DOI: 10.4324/9781003403258-4

at home. She passed the high school examinations, and the family moved to Geneva to allow her to continue her undergraduate studies in the physical and biological sciences at the University of Geneva, where she graduated with a bachelor's in science in 1889. Subsequently, she enrolled at the Faculty of Medicine of the Free University of Brussels where she obtained a degree in medicine. Next, she completed her doctoral dissertation at the University of La Sorbonne-Paris in 1896 under Charles Richet, winner of the Nobel Prize in Medicine in 1913. The title of her dissertation was *La fatigue et La Respiration Élémentaire du Muscle* (Fatigue and Elemental Muscle Respiration). She practiced medicine in Paris for a couple of years and then returned to Brussels where she remained until she moved in 1915 to London and later to Paris (1916–1918) because of World War I (WWI). In 1919, after Poland became an independent republic, she returned to her country. Despite her extraordinary research merits, the University of Warsaw denied her a professorship position, but she found a position as a lecturer at the National Pedagogical Institute and the National Institute for the Deaf. During her life she had three main research partners: Michalina Stefanowska (Poland, 1855–1942), Barbara "Varia" Kipiani (Georgia, 1879–1965), and Marja Grzegorzewska (Poland, 1887–1967). In her last years, she suffered a painful liver illness. In 1927, Joteyko's health conditions became worse, and Grzegorzewska took care of her until her death in April 1928 at the age of 62. In Krakow, a street is dedicated to her.

From 1898, she lectured on experimental psychology at the Kasimir Laboratory of the Solvay Institute of the Nouvelle University of Brussels. In the first eight years, more than 400 students from the University of Brussels received psychology training on this course. At the Solvey Institute, she was successively hired as assistant researcher (1902), physiologist (1903), and *chef de travaux* of psychology (1903). In Brussels, she edited the *Revue de Psychologie* (additional information about Joteyko's life can be found in Konieczna, 2019; Pekacka-Falkowska & Pekacka-Eglis, 2019).

Awards, Honors, and Recognitions

She received numerous awards, the first one being the Mention Honorable de la Faculté de Medicine de Paris for her doctoral thesis in 1896. In 1900, she also obtained the Prix Desmeth de la Societe Royale des Sciencies Medicales et Naturales de Bruxelles, and the Prix Montyon de Physiologie Expérimentale of Académie des Sciences de Paris. In 1901, she was awarded the Prix Dieudonné de Médecine de la Societe Royale des Sciences Medicales et Naturales de Bruxelles, shared with M. Stefanowska. In 1903, she received the Prix Lallemand of the Académie des Sciences de Paris; in 1909, she received two Prizes from the Academy of Sciences of Paris for her book on the psychophysiology of pain and muscular function, respectively; and in 1916, the Academy of Sciences of Paris awarded her a prize of 4000 francs.

When WWI interrupted her research activities because the Belgian universities were closed, she moved to Paris in 1916, where after the vote of a professorial committee, she received the *Michonis endowment chair* for teaching experimental psychology in the Collège of France, the most prestigious French academic institution, established in 1530. She was the first woman in history who gave lectures at the Collège de France. In 1917 and 1918, she also lectured at the University of Sorbonne and the University of Lyon.

Main Contributions to IWO Psychology

Along with Alfred Binet (1857–1911), Emil Kraepelin (1856–1926), Ètienne-Jules Marey (1830–1904), Angelo Mosso (1846–1910), and Charle Richet (1850–1935), Joteyko is one of the great European figures in the early research of psychology applied to the study of physical and intellectual fatigue. She introduced new concepts in science such as the *fatigue quotient*, the *law of pain*, and the *law of minimum available* (LMA). In the XIII International Congress of Hygiene and Demographics, held in Brussels in 1903, Joteyko was the first researcher to declare the necessity of measuring the aptitudes guiding young workers in choosing a profession by means of laboratories intended for the scientific study of work.

A short chronological summary of some of Joteyko's main books and scientific contributions is as follows. In 1905, she published a book that was highly praised at the time *Entrainement et Fatigue au Point de Vue Militaire* (*Training and Fatigue from the Military Point of View*) (Joteyko, 1905) in which, based on her experiments, she concluded that military training (service) would be more effective if it had a duration of between 6 and 12 months, and that a longer training period as performed by the armies of the time (between two and three years) was useless and even harmful from the military point of view.

In her book of 1909, *La Psycho-physiologie de la Douleur* (*Psycho-physiology of Pain*), a result of her research with Stefanowska, she established the *Loi de la douleur* (*Law of pain*), as a complement to Weber's psychophysical law (Joteyko, 1909). According to Weber, excitation grows faster than sensation. Joteyko's studies indicated to her that pain behaves inversely to Weber's law: sensation grows faster than arousal. She also examined individual differences in pain according to the sex, age, race, and profession of the individual.

In this book, in addition to examining the causes of professional fatigue, she insists on the importance of determining fatigue curves by mathematical methods. According to her studies with Victor Henry, fatigue curves conformed to a third-degree parabolic equation. $N = H - at3 + bt2 - ct$, where N is effort in each instant, H is maximum initial effort, t is time, and a, b, and c are the parameters of the equation. The calculation of the parameters makes it possible to say whether an action is central or peripheral and to situate the modifications produced. This study could be fruitful for the evaluation of the degree of fatigue of workers. At the 6th International Congress of Psychology, she indicated the rules to be followed in the study of professional fatigue and insisted on the importance of mathematics and the discovery of the general equation of fatigue curves. Great intellectual fatigue, such as that which an adult may experience due to a great effort of attention, would be accompanied by a decrease in sensitivity to pain. In this book, she also studied what today we call post-traumatic stress and its effects on people's lives and work (see also Joteyko, 1908, 1921).

Joteyko was also one of the first researchers to propose a new Science of Work in a book published in 1917, a name that was later adopted by many other authors such as Otto Lipmann and Walter Moede in Germany, Jean-Maurice Lahy in France, and Morris Viteles (1934) in the United States. For her, the science of work referred to the psycho-physiological (experimental) study of worker behavior and characteristics in industry (Joteyko, 1917, 1919). The main topics would be (a) job learning and job adaptation, (b) the study of professional fatigue, (c) the study and prevention of accidents at work, (d) personnel selection and vocational orientation, and (e) the study of individual aptitudes. In this book, she also made a critique of Taylorism, a critique that she shared with Jean-Maurice Lahy, and like Lahy she believed that general intelligence was becoming increasingly important for workers' productivity.

In her book *La Fatigue* published in Paris in 1920, she summarized over 20 years of research findings (Joteyko, 1920). She argued that intellectual *surmenage* (intellectual exhaustion) was a form of mental fatigue that irritates the nervous system, causing decreased appetite, sleep suppression, hypotension with slowing of the heartbeat (bradycardia), and increased blood pressure. Joteyko defined intellectual fatigue as an abuse of attention, which would produce an attenuation of various psychic processes. Fatigue of attention manifests itself as a delay in the execution of work or a defective execution of work. Therefore, time and errors would serve as a basis for measuring the intensity of intellectual fatigue. Joteyko made a distinction between the effects of fatigue and monotony, the latter resulting from the uniformity of work. In her opinion, the intensity of work does not change with monotony. She also argued that fatigue should not be confused with distraction, which is a lack of attention. According to Joteyko, intellectual fatigue would depend both on the type of work and on the characteristics of the individual.

Joteyko (1920) introduced the LMA. According to the LMA even when fatigue is taken to the extreme, there always seems to be a residue of energy in reserve and this occurs in muscular fatigue as well as in intellectual fatigue. She considered it out of the question that a human being might be fatigued to the point where all memory effort is impossible. The LMA would be a defense mechanism created to protect a weakening organism. A normal person totally devoid of memory and attention was inconceivable.

Based on her studies on intellectual fatigue, Joteyko's (1920) recommendation for producing good intellectual work was to reduce fatigue and take advantage of the benefit of acquired training. She also pointed out that intellectual work would be subjected to the same laws of fatigue as physical work, requiring rest and sleep. According to Joteyko, fatigue, like pain, would be a defensive response of the organism that would play a prophylactic role allowing for a more economical energy consumption by the organism. Fatigue would be a feeling that regulates energy consumption.

In *Fatigue,* Joteyko (1920) formulated three major proposals: (1) If daily work follows an arithmetical progression, the wage should follow a geometrical progression. The coefficients of growth would be established experimentally in each occupation taking into account the methods of work; (2) For equal work, equal wages; so, women should receive the same salary as men if they do the same job. The amount of work to be produced will be established in each industry; and (3) The number of hours of each trade must be limited to achieve optimum production.

The last three years of her life (1926–1928) were devoted to editing the *Polish Psychological Archives* in collaboration with Marja Gregorievna. There, Joteyko published her last articles that were devoted to some of the psychological topics that had interested her for the previous 20 years: active education and methods for children's education, vocational and personnel selection orientation, Gestalt psychology, and the perception of sensations and the creation of mental images in the blind. When she died, she had produced over 250 research pieces presented in international conferences and published as articles and books. She was a feminist convinced of the equality not only of rights but also of abilities between men and women. The Nobel Prize laureate Charles Richet once wrote that Joteyko was the most intelligent and industrious student he had ever had.

Conclusion

Joteyko was one of the most eminent European IWO psychologists (and the most eminent Polish one) of the early 20th century. Like Emilio Mira and J-M Lahy, she deserves to be rescued from oblivion for her many scientific contributions in numerous applied psychological domains. Her scientific production includes over 250 books, articles, and conference presentations. She was the founder and first editor of the *Journal of Psychology* (Paris) and the *Polish Psychological Archives* (Warsaw). Few psychologists of her time received so many awards and recognitions. She was the first woman to lecture in psychology at the Collège of France, the most prestigious French academic institution.

References

Joteyko, J. (1905). *Entrainement et Fatigue au point de vue militaire* [*Training and fatigue from the military point of view*]. Misch & Thron.

Joteyko, J. (1908). *Etudes sur la fatigue professionnelle* [*Studies on professional fatigue*]. Misch & Thron.

Joteyko, J. (1909). *Psycho-physiologie de la douleur* [*Psychophysiology of pain*]. Alcan.

Joteyko, J. (1917). *Le science du travail and son organization* [*The science of work and its organization*]. Alcan.

Joteyko, J. (1919). *The science of labor and its organization*. Routledge.

Joteyko, J. [(1920), *La fatigue* [*The fatigue*]. Ernest Flammarion Editeur.

Joteyko, J. (1921). *La productivité et la durée du travail* [*Productivity and duration of work*]. Institute Solvay.

Konieczna., S. (2019). Professor Jòzefa Joteyko: The distinguished Polish scientist at the turn of the 19th and 20th century. *Nauka, 1,* 149–158. https://doi.org/nauka.2019.126185

Pekacka-Falkowska, K. & Pekacka-Eglis, A.M. (2019). Jòzefa Franciszka Joteyko (1866-1928). *Journal of Neurology, 267,* 2774–2775. https://doi.org/10.1007/s00415019-09512-9

Viteles, M. (1934). *The science of work*. Norton.

Chapter 5

Mary Parker Follett (1868–1933)

M. Dale Smalley and Jeffrey S. Schippmann

Mary Parker Follett (1868–1933) is likely the most significant contributor to the study of leadership, organizational theory, and management principles, who is completely unfamiliar to most students of industrial-organizational (I-O) psychology. If we learn that Warren Bennis stated, "just about everything written today about leadership and organizations comes from Mary Parker Follett's writings and lectures;" or, if we find Peter Drucker proclaimed her to be "the prophet of management," then we should try to discover if these claims are justified. Curiosity alone should beg the question, "Mary who?" (see Graham, 1995).

To address this question, we offer a synopsis of Mary Parker Follett's seminal and oftentimes unrecognized contributions. That said, our goal is larger than setting the record straight about her influence on I-O psychology. Just as important, we wish to bring to light her ideas because they are relevant not only to the concerns of our practice and research but to the "social order" at large.

Biographical Overview

Mary Follett was born in 1868 in Quincy, MA near Boston (Graham, 1995). Her mother came from a prominent family in the league of descendants of John Adams. Her father's prospects were much less auspicious and were worsened by a drinking problem that plagued him throughout his adult life (Tonn, 2003). Also, his devotion to responsibilities as a husband and father was suspect, as he abandoned his family twice after hardships before dying at age 43; Mary was 16, her brother was 7. Her mother was described as "incompetent, demanding,

DOI: 10.4324/9781003403258-5

and 'alien to Mary's interests' " (Tonn, 2003, p.16) and began deteriorating in 1885 to a state described as a "nervous invalid" (Graham, 1995, p. 13). The backdrop for this difficult upbringing included remnants of the Victorian Era, which discouraged and often prohibited women from engaging in public life, including education, vocation, and suffrage. Mary was thus pressured throughout her life to devote herself fully to caring for her mother and brother. Her accomplishments demonstrate that she did much more.

Within this brewing storm "Minnie" entered school at age 4 to receive instruction on subjects normally reserved for boys, and at 11, she was among select students in their teens to be admitted to the prestigious Thayer Academy, where she was introduced to rigorous critical thinking. Accounts from older classmates and teachers say she was an amiable prodigy (Tonn, 2003). After graduating from the Academy in 1884 and soon after her father's death, Mary began completing rigorous correspondence courses for the next three years in the evenings as a respite from her familial duties and to assuage her need for learning.

In the Fall of 1888, she was accepted by the Society for the Collegiate Instruction of Women, known as "the Harvard Annex" (later Radcliffe College) where she was *allowed* to attend classes taught by willing Harvard professors. A pivotal interlude in her studies occurred in 1890–1891, when she attended Newnan College at the University of Cambridge (Metcalf & Urwick, 1941/2013). The cumulative effect of her experiences there fortified her desire to seize a place in public life upon her return to the Annex evinced by the expansion of a paper she presented to the Newnan Historical Society into her first book, *The Speaker of the House of Representatives* (Follett, 1896). Tellingly, the book was written while Follett taught history at a private school in addition to her own college studies.

This auspicious book was regarded by many, including Theodore Roosevelt, as a perceptive exploration of the gap between the executive and legislative branches of government and ways to bridge it, but it received disapproval because of the audacity of inferences made by a young, female author. She graduated summa cum laude from Radcliffe two years later (Shapiro, 2011).

Impact

Throughout her education and career, Follett had the privilege to interact with an array of eminent advocates, public officials, educators, scholars, and businesspeople, as well as hard-pressed people from all walks of life. Notably too, during her last 29 years of work, her most outward reaching and creative period, she struggled with pain and suffering due to an undiagnosed kidney tumor that necessitated hospitalization or bed rest for weeks and months at a time. *The New State*, her second book, was published in 1918 and achieved wide acclaim, especially among philosophers, despite defying norms that constrained women from challenging social and political conventions and principles. As her tumor worsened and metastasized, her physical strength and stamina were increasingly compromised. Yet she managed to complete and publish her acclaimed magnum opus *Creative Experience* in 1924, and she continued to travel and lecture in several cities in the United States and abroad until just before her death in 1933.

In evaluating her work, it is useful to know she drew upon hands-on experience at the turn of the 19th century as a reformer striving to mitigate pressing immigration and poverty-related problems in Boston neighborhoods. She was instrumental in establishing social centers that expanded the use of school buildings by providing education, vocational training, recreation, childcare, and employment resources (placement services) to foster connections with community groups and businesses. That escalating work exposed her to the practical realities of societal institutions, as well as to business leaders and government officials at city, state, and national levels. President Theodore Roosevelt consulted with Follett on how to organize and manage social and civic organizations across the country. Aside from her writings, her many lectures and speeches to students, academics, business leaders, and government officials were consistently well received, and individuals she met found her to have a "stimulating presence" that belied the forcefulness of her views (Metcalf & Urwick, 1941/2013, p. 20). So much so that a presentation on Constructive Conflict at a Bureau for Personnel Administration Conference in 1925 initiated her welcomed involvement in the affairs of business management (Metcalf & Urwick, 1941/2013).

Excepting books by Tonn (2003), Graham (1995), and Metcalf and Urwick (1941/2013), the relatively sparse literature that does cite her contributions tends to single out only a few of her ideas (e.g., coordination, power-with, constructive conflict) with a relatively narrow acknowledgment of relevance to contemporary practices such as conflict management, kaizen, or network organizations. Yet, her work in real-world public service, and publications and lectures (see Metcalf & Urwick, 1941/2013) represented a synthesis of some of the most cogent thinking of "giants" regarding the human condition in the broad sense. That consilience, moreover, anticipated varied contemporary views that are gaining prominence today.

By asserting "creative experience" or variously "interpenetrating," "integrating," and "unifying" in thought, feeling, and action with one's fellows she deliberately sought to reify "the fundamental law of existence ... of the utmost importance for the continuance of civilization" (Follett, 1918, p. 36). In the full context of her writings and lectures, she represented ideas ranging from Confucious and Aristotle to Adam Smith, Charles Darwin, Émile Durkheim, Max Weber, William James, and Josiah Royce, to name a few. A shared theme among these thinkers that Follett *consistently* explicated, culminating in Creative Experience, was that people do not fully "realize" their "true natures" until they honor their roles as participants ("citizens") in an endeavor with interdependent members of a social collective. In "groups," not "crowds," people are afforded opportunities to express latent potentials, particularly the virtue of empathy ("ren" for Confucious), and thereby "evoke" their "true self," "each from the other" ("reciprocal freeing"). To the extent they and their fellows "integrate" their uniquely diverse talents, their group may accomplish something more significant ("creative") than those same individuals may achieve working independently (to Euclid, something greater than the sum). She contended that as empathy emerges from participants for one another within a group due to their "interplay" ("interweaving," "self-organizing"), it can be extended via "relations" with other groups leading to awareness of the necessity of generalizing internal coherence to external coherence as well. With that, the stage may be set for groups to "self-manage" ongoing "harmonization" with other systems in their environments while influencing them in turn. Thus, "co-adapting" ("co-creating," "reciprocal relating") as the progressing "situation" demands becomes a necessary ongoing process of continuous change (i.e., improvement), the essence of evolution. In Follett's "advanced thinking," leaders and managers bear the responsibility to provide the means and support to enable individuals to fulfill their natural bent – to bond, actualize, and act in collectives – in service of themselves and their environments – the "total situation"(see, for example, Follett, 1924). Above all, she believed business organizations by way of their positions in larger social structures have the most potent capacities to "creatively" contribute to the advance of societies, and she repeatedly called upon the social sciences to discover ways to support this aim. Indeed, that work began during her lifetime with the likes of the Hawthorne studies of Mayo, Roethlisberger, and Whitehead, followed by Chester Barnard's (1938) concepts of efficiency, authority, coordination, and the informal organization, Herzberg et al.'s (1959) two-factor theory, McGregor's (1960) theory Y, on to Ouchi's (1981) theory Z and to adaptive leadership (Nohria, 2022), and "humanocracy" organizations (Hamel & Zanini, 2020).

The construct validity of her ideas continues to be supported by applied research, practice, and an assortment of theories and principles from a variety of disciplines such as general systems theory (Drack et al., 2017) and its many variations (cf. Parsons, 1970), particularly the concepts of complex adaptive and living systems, spontaneous order, and emergence. The feedback loops that boost the orderly manifestations of systems are indicative of Follett's "reciprocal relations" ("circular responding"). Even the application of the laws of thermodynamics and the concept of entropy to open, closed, and isolated systems are connected to her ideas regarding "energy release," "relations," and "gaps" in organizations and societies. The thrust of research on collective intelligence supports her unfaltering contention on the prowess of groups comprised of "diverse individuals" with "integrated interests" engaged in the "group process" (Katzenbach & Smith, 1993; Riedl et al., 2021). Her search for methods by which "the full integrity of the individual shall be one with social progress" (Follett, 1924/2013, p. xiv) speaks to the fruitful theories of social identity and self-categorization (see Tajfel & Turner, 1979; Turner et al., 1987). And, to cite one more example, her far-reaching views on "experiencing" an ever-changing "total situation" – "progressive integratings' [sic] as the process of all organic life" and the necessary "conditions for the productive relating of human beings" (Follett, 1924/2013, p. 225) now see relevance in the rising field of evolutionary developmental psychology (see Machluf et al., 2014). Follett's profound *primitive notion* was that individual differences regardless of origin represent opportunities for emergent ("creative") manifestations when commingled in a group, which, in turn, provide opportunities for solutions to demands of ever-changing situations, just as variations in phenotypes within species (industries) afford survival options in evolution (economies). "We must face life as it is and understand that differences are its most essential feature" (Follett, 1924/2013, p. 232).

Prescience

Looking ahead, we believe the troubling trends in related topics such as alienation, loneliness, and disengagement can be addressed with approaches underpinned by Follettian concepts. Relatedly, existential problems such as the fragmentation of societies, growing distrust in social institutions, declining social rectitude, the rising threat of climate change and artificial intelligence, and diminishing planetary resources in the face of increasing population size, to name a few, likely cannot be solved solely by "experts" or by any consolidated authority, as Follett often warned. This is currently illustrated by the struggles of traditional centralized organizations in business, government, and religion in their dynamic environments to solve these problems.

The open question is whether means (technologies, practices) will continue to be developed, which have the promise of facilitating the kind of vibrant group processes Follett considered necessary. The profession of I-O psychology is positioned at the intersection of business and science to further the creative advances required. At issue is the ultimate purpose of any association or discipline – to further parochial financial, political, or professional interests or to *integrate* economic necessities with an authentic "way of being" of humankind (Rogers, 1995). Mary P. Follett's contention that individuals must flourish so that civilizations may thrive has the makings of an elegant notion with profoundly prescient implications. Indeed, she was ahead of her time, and perhaps, her concepts may become most critically important when civilization *must,* for sake of sustainability, rise to meet the "law of situation." We can only wonder what Mary P. Follett would say, if she were with us now.

References

Barnard, C.I. (1938). *The functions of the executive.* Harvard University Press.

Drack, M., Apfalter, W., & Pouvreau, D. (2017). On the making of a system theory of life: Paul A. Weiss and Ludwig von Bertalanffy's conceptual connection. *The Quarterly Review of Biology. 82*(4): 349–373. doi:10.1086/522810

Follett, M.P. (1896). *The speaker of the house representatives.* Reprinted by Cornell University Press. www.archive.org/details/cu31924104018605

Follett, M.P. (1918). *The new state: Group organization: The solution of popular government.* Longmons, Green and Co.

Follett, M.P. (1924/2013). *Creative experience.* Reprinted by Martino Publishing.

Graham, P. (Ed.) (1995). *Mary Parker Follett: Prophet of management: A celebration of writings from the 1920s.* Harvard Business School Press.

Hamel, G. & Zanini, M. (2020). *Humanocracy: Creating organizations as amazing as the people inside them.* Harvard Business Review Press. ISBN: 978-1-63369-602-0

Herzberg, F., Mausner, B., & Snyderman, B.B. (1959). *The motivation to work.* Wiley.

Katzenbach, J.R. & Smith, D.K. (1993). *The wisdom of teams: Creating the high-performance organization.* HarperCollins.

Machluf, K., Liddle, J.R., & Bjorklund, D.F. (2014). An introduction to evolutionary developmental psychology. *Evolutionary Psychology, 12*(2), 264–272. https://doi.org/10.1177/147470491401200201

McGregor, D. (1960). *The human side of enterprise.* McGraw-Hill.

Metcalf, H.C. & Urwick, L. (Eds.) (1941/2013). *Dynamic administration: The collected papers of Mary Parker Follett*. Martino Publishing, Mansfield CT.

Nohria, N. (2022, July–August). As the world shifts, so should leaders. *Harvard Business Review*. *100*(4), 59–61.

Ouchi, W.G. (1981). *Theory Z: How American business can meet the Japanese challenge*. Addison-Wesley.

Parsons, T. (1970). *The social system*. Routledge & Kegan Paul. ISBN 0-7100-1931-9.

Riedl, C., Kim, Y.J., Gupta, P., Malone, T.W. & Woolley, A.W. (2021). Quantifying collective intelligence in human groups. *Proceedings of the National Academy of Sciences of the United States of America*, *118* (21). https://doi.org/10.1073/pnas.2005737118

Rogers, C. (1995). *A way of being*. HarperOne. ISBN: 9780395755303 ISBN-10: 0395755301.

Shapiro, M. (2011). *About Mary Parker Follett*. http://mpfollett.ning.com/notes/About_Mary_Parker_Follett

Tajfel, H. & Turner, J.C. (1979). An integrative theory of intergroup conflict. In W.G. Austin & S. Worchel (Eds.), *The psychology of intergroup relations* (pp. 33–48). Brooks/Cole.

Tonn, J.C. (2003). *Mary P. Follett: Creating democracy, transforming management*. Yale University Press.

Turner, J.C., Hogg, M.A., Oakes, P.J., Reicher, S.D. & Wetherell, M.S. (1987). *Rediscovering the social group: A self-categorization theory*. Blackwell.

Chapter 6

Walter Dill Scott (1869–1955)

Samuel T. McAbee

Walter Dill Scott was a pioneer in the field of applied psychology. He contributed to psychological research and practice of advertising and personnel selection, where he authored several of the first texts applying psychology to these areas and played a significant role in introducing psychological assessment to personnel selection in the military. He founded the first private personnel consulting company and was elected president of the American Psychological Association (APA) in 1919.

Biographical Overview

Walter Dill Scott was born May 1, 1869, in Cooksville, IL (Jacobson, 1951; Lynch, 1968). Scott attended Northwestern University in Evanston, IL. After graduating from Northwestern, Scott entered McCormick Theological Seminary in Chicago (Jacobson, 1951) where he completed his degree in theology. Around this time, Scott became aware of the psychological research emerging from Wilhelm Wundt's laboratory in Leipzig, which invigorated his interest in the field. Scott completed his dissertation under Wundt at Leipzig in 1900, titled, *Die Psychologie der Triebe Historisch-Kritisch Betrachtet* (*The Psychology of Impulses Historically and Critically Considered*), a non-empirical treatment of the psychology of impulses (Jacobson, 1951). After returning to America, Scott briefly worked with Edward B. Titchener at Cornell University to learn how to organize and maintain a psychological laboratory, before taking a faculty position at Northwestern from 1900 to 1916 (Ferguson, 1962; Jacobson, 1951). Although Scott contributed to a number of

DOI: 10.4324/9781003403258-6

areas relevant to applied psychology, his central role in the development of a psychology of advertising and personnel selection has had the most long-lasting impact on applied psychological practice (Lynch, 1968).

Contributions to I-O Psychology

The Psychology of Advertising and Suggestion

Scott's foray into the world of advertising represents a transition from his philosophical leanings toward a more applied psychology. His approach to advertising would include the formal methodological rigor he had learned during his time with Wundt but would also incorporate impressionistic principles (Kuna, 1976)—largely derived from his dissertation work on the psychology of impulses. Central to his theories of effective advertising was the concept of suggestion and the need to consider the aesthetic-emotional responses of the consumer. To Scott, advertising was not merely a means of communicating information, but rather, a form of persuading consumers to specific ends, where "the advertiser sought to influence the mind of the potential customer" resulting in "some particular action which would be carried out unhesitatingly, and unthinkingly" (Kuna, 1976, p. 350).

In 1902, Thomas L. Balmer, an advertising manager for Butterick magazines, contacted Scott about presenting a lecture on the role of psychology in advertising practices (Jacobson, 1951; Lynch, 1968). Although not initially attracted by the opportunity, Scott saw promise in the project as work in the field of advertising would allow him to test his theories about attention, suggestion, and persuasion in a practical context (Ferguson, 1962; Landy, 1997). Balmer convinced Scott to deliver a presentation on the subject (titled, "The Psychology of Involuntary Attention as Applied to Advertising"), at which many local advertising leaders were present (Lynch, 1968, p. 151). One of the advertising executives in attendance was John L. Mahin of *Mahin's Magazine*, who offered to publish Scott's research in a series of articles (Jacobson, 1951; Landy, 1997; Lynch, 1968). This research was later published in *The Theory and Practice of*

Advertising (Scott, 1903), the first book on the subject of psychology in advertising (Jacobson, 1951), and later in such books as *The Psychology of Advertising* (Scott, 1908) and *Increasing Human Efficiency in Business* (Scott, 1911).

Scott's sojourn into the psychology of advertising led to other areas where he believed psychological principles could have a functional value. In 1907, he published *The Psychology of Public Speaking* (Scott, 1907), another area of applied psychology which he was the first to address. Practical recommendations from the work included a variety of techniques available to public speakers, such as increasing group cohesion by seating audience members in close proximity and the use of audience co-action (e.g., sitting and rising in unison; Jacobson, 1951).

Personnel Selection

By 1910, Scott had begun to consider a wide array of psychological issues applicable to the business setting (Landy, 1997). One particular area of research that had long-lasting impact on the field of industrial-organizational (I-O) psychology was the application of psychology to the practice of personnel selection (Jacobson, 1951). Scott's writings on this topic "were inspired by the idea that man was [a] neglected factor in business," and that "little progress had been made in the ability to select and supervise men" (Lynch, 1968, p. 153).

In 1915, representatives of the American Tobacco Company approached Scott to assist them with their ongoing difficulties in hiring qualified salesmen (Jacobson, 1951). Scott developed a method for identifying psychological variables associated with success. He first interviewed current salesmen to ascertain which qualities they exhibited that contributed to success. From this, Scott and his colleagues derived a set of qualities that appeared to distinguish between successful and unsuccessful salesmen, and subsequently trained company interviewers how to assess potential employees for such qualities. Scott promoted the idea that mental (intelligence) tests, particularly those that emphasized abilities required to perform job functions, might be used to supplement interviews (Lynch, 1968).

The publication of Scott's research on the application of psychological principles to business and related areas between 1903 and 1917 "entitled him to be called the first business psychologist" (Jacobson, 1951, p. 75). In 1915, a likeminded psychologist named Walter V. Bingham became aware of Scott's research on selecting salesmen (Jacobson, 1951). Bingham, together with Edward A. Woods, approached Scott, offering him the position of director at their newly established Bureau of Salesmanship Research at Carnegie Institute of Technology (now Carnegie Mellon University; Ferguson, 1963a; Landy, 1997). Scott accepted the position, and in 1916 took a yearlong sabbatical from Northwestern to head the institute. In that same year, he was appointed as the first official professor of applied psychology to be authorized by an institution of higher education.

The work of Scott, Bingham, and their colleagues marked the transition of psychology from a purely academic endeavor to a formal profession (Jacobson, 1951). By applying the quantitative methods of individual difference psychologists in the creation of rating scales for psychological constructs, Scott was among the first to develop specific criteria for use in selecting employees for business purposes. This landmark practice has had tremendous and long-lasting implications for the field of I-O psychology. Scott and colleagues created several tools to assist in the selection of employees, including the *Interviewer's Scale and Rating Sheet.* Applicants were rated on four dimensions (appearance and manner, convincingness, industry, and character) to determine which applicants were the most qualified to be salesmen, using a variety of informational sources (e.g., applicant's personal history, interviewer judgments; Ferguson, 1963a; Jacobson, 1951; Lynch, 1968). These selection tools and a number of mental ability tests developed by the Bureau during this time were published in *Aids in Selecting Salesmen* (Scott, 1916). Many of these measures resemble modern methods of personnel selection, and the tests developed by the Bureau can be regarded "as the tests that most clearly introduced the idea of testing to an influential segment of American business" (Ferguson, 1963a, p. 61).

World War I and the Application of Psychology to the Military

World War I (WWI) marks a pivotal transition in the development of applied psychology. Scott saw an opportunity to apply the findings from his research on salesmen to assist the military in improving effectiveness (Jacobson, 1951). Scott and Bingham contacted the president of the APA, Robert M. Yerkes, to discuss the potential of the APA participation in military personnel selection; however, they were disappointed when the members of the APA appeared to be more interested in working with the military for the purposes of furthering psychological research, rather than applying its practices to improve military functioning and to further the American cause in the war (Ferguson, 1963b; Jacobson, 1951; Lynch, 1968).

Determined to move forward, Scott and Bingham contacted military personnel with the help of Edward L. Thorndike and Frederick P. Keppel, assistant to Secretary of War Newton D. Baker (Jacobson, 1951; Lynch, 1968). Although their proposal to develop a rating scale for selecting military officers was initially received with apprehension, Scott gradually persuaded high-level military officials that the use of selection tools (e.g., interviews, mental tests) would inevitably be useful for military applications. On August 5, 1917, Secretary of War Baker commissioned the Committee on Classification of Personnel in the Army (Jacobson, 1951; Lynch, 1968). Scott was appointed the director of the Committee, and Bingham served as executive secretary. As director of this group, Scott collected rating scales incorporating the most recent research in personnel assessment, which eventually formed the core material for what became known as the Army Alpha. In particular, Scott advocated for his "man-to-man" rating scale, in which officers were asked to evaluate soldiers' potential for promotion on a number of dimensions such as appearance, military experience, and judgement (Ferguson, 1963b) in comparison to known exemplars in officer positions. Indeed, Scott considered his rating scale as a more effective way of evaluating intelligence in large groups than the mental tests advocated for by Yerkes and others. Although development of the Army Alpha was housed under the Surgeon General with Yerkes, many of the measures included in the Army Alpha were adaptations of the selection devices Scott had developed with the Bureau of Salesmanship Research (Lynch, 1968). By the end of the war, Scott and his team of over 7,000 employed military personnel experts had evaluated the qualifications of over 3,000,000 soldiers in the army (Lynch, 1968), the first widespread use of rating scales (Strong, 1955). In recognition of his service to the military, Scott was awarded the Distinguished Service Medal in 1919 and was commissioned as a reserve colonel in the Adjutant General's department (Jacobson, 1951).

After the War: The Scott Company and President of Northwestern

After the end of WWI in 1919, Scott briefly returned to his work at the Bureau of Salesmanship Research (Lynch, 1968). In that same year, he was elected and served as the president of the APA (Landy, 1997; Lynch, 1968). Soon after his return to the Bureau, Scott was approached by several of his former colleagues, who "persuaded him to form a private company that would consult with business" (Landy, 1997, p. 474). He agreed and the first psychological consulting company was formed: the Scott Company (Lynch, 1968; Meyer, 2007). The Scott Company consisted of a staff of 8–10 psychologists whom Scott had worked with as part of the Committee on Classification of Personnel and several of his former colleagues from the Bureau (Jacobson, 1951; Meyer, 2007). Between 1919 and 1923, the Scott Company consulted with more than 40 major industrial clients on issues covering "the entire field of personnel management and as characterized by systematic research and the development of specific solutions" to meet business needs (Lynch, 1968, p. 166). Much of the practical experience Scott gained as a part of the Scott Company was reflected in his seminal book *Personnel Management* (Scott & Clothier, 1923).

Although the Scott Company was successful for its first few years, in 1920 Northwestern University offered Scott the position of president of the university; "and at the peak of his power and popularity, [Scott] left psychology for administration" (Landy, 1997, p. 474). With Scott's departure, no clear leader came forward from the remaining psychologists at the Scott Company, and the company disbanded several years later (Meyer, 2007). Scott served as president of Northwestern from his appointment in 1920 until his retirement in 1939 (Jacobson, 1951). After accepting the presidency at Northwestern, Scott's focus shifted away from applied psychological research, although he continued to revise and update his book *Personnel Management* through its fifth and final edition in Scott et al. (1954) (Lynch, 1968). Walter Dill Scott died on September 24, 1955—he was 86 years old (Strong, 1955).

Conclusion

As one of the earliest psychologists to apply psychological principles and theory to the problems of business, Walter Dill Scott had a tremendous impact on the field of I-O psychology. Scott was among the first to address the topics of a psychology of advertising and personnel selection. His efforts working with business and later in the military established systematic methodologies for identifying characteristics that distinguished between effective and ineffective personnel, and how decisions informed by such distinctions could contribute to organizational effectiveness. Scott also drew attention to the essential role of the employee in work, and the need to understand and explore the cognitive-emotional constructs that influence employee performance (Lynch, 1968). He was the first person to receive the title of professor of applied psychology and cofounded the first psychological consulting firm to apply psychology to business. There can be no doubt that Scott's academic and professional body of work helped pave the way for the field of I-O Psychology as it stands today.

References

Ferguson, L. W. (1962). Walter Dill Scott: First industrial psychologist. *Heritage of Industrial Psychology, 1*, 1–10.

Ferguson, L. W. (1963a). Bureau of salesmanship research: Walter Dill Scott, director. *Heritage of Industrial Psychology, 5*, 53–66.

Ferguson, L. W. (1963b). Psychology and the army: Introduction of the rating scale. *Heritage of Industrial Psychology, 9*, 125–139.

Jacobson, J. Z. (1951). *Scott of Northwestern.* Louis Mariano.

Kuna, D. P. (1976). The concept of suggestion in the early history of advertising psychology. *Journal of the History of the Behavioral Sciences, 12*, 347–353. https://doi.org/10.1002/1520-6696(197610)12:4<347::AID-JHBS2300120406>3.0.CO;2-M

Landy, F. J. (1997). Early influences on the development of industrial and organizational psychology. *Journal of Applied Psychology*, *82*, 467–477. https://doi.org/10.1037/0021-9010.82.4.467

Lynch, E. C. (1968). Walter Dill Scott: Pioneer industrial psychologist. *The Business History Review*, *42*, 149–170. https://doi.org/10.2307/3112213

Meyer, H. H. (2007). Influences of formal and informal organizations of the development of I-O psychology. In L. L. Koppes (Ed.), *Historical perspectives in industrial and organizational psychology* (pp. 139–168). Lawrence Erlbaum Associates.

Scott, W. D. (1903). *The theory and practice of advertising*. Small, Maynard & Company.

Scott, W. D. (1907). *The psychology of public speaking*. Pearson Bros.

Scott, W. D. (1908). *The psychology of advertising in theory and practice*. Small, Maynard & Company.

Scott, W. D. (1911). *Increasing human efficiency in business*. Macmillan.

Scott, W. D. (1916). *Aids in selecting salesmen*. Carnegie Institute of Technology.

Scott, W. D., & Clothier, R. C. (1923). *Personnel management: Principles, practices, and point of view*. Shaw.

Scott, W. D., Clothier, R. C., & Spriegel, W. R. (1954). *Personnel management: Principles, practices, and point of view* (5th ed.). McGraw-Hill.

Strong, E. K., Jr. (1955). Walter Dill Scott: 1869–1955. *The American Journal of Psychology*, *68*, 682–683.

Chapter 7

William Stern (1871–1938)

James T. Lamiell

On October 5, 1916, the German philosopher and psychologist William Stern (1871–1938) set about composing a relatively lengthy letter to his long-time friend, the Freiburg philosopher Jonas Cohn (1869–1947). Taking note of the burgeoning of practical efforts at the time to address 'issues in occupational psychology *(berufspsychologischen Fragestellungen)*,' Stern stated:

> For my part, I will try to ensure that in studies of occupational aptitude a social ethics rather than Taylorism prevails. What [we need] is not so much an industrial psychology but a psychology of capabilities.
>
> (Letter reprinted in Lück and Löwisch, 1994, p. 103)

This passage offers a small but instructive window onto Stern's thinking about 'occupational psychology' and on initiatives in applied psychology more generally. His concern for social ethics issued directly from his philosophical commitment to the system of thought he called 'critical personalism.' The conceptual cornerstone of that framework is the distinction between *persons* and *things*, and over the entirety of his scholarly career, Stern was at pains to make clear the full implications of that distinction for all of psychology, both basic and applied psychology. This is the context within which the historical significance of Stern's work for industrial-organizational (I-O) psychology is best seen.

Biographical Overview

Stern was born Louis William on April 29, 1871, in Berlin, to Jewish parents of modest means. Sigismund and Rosa Stern's only

DOI: 10.4324/9781003403258-7

child, he would come to identify himself simply as 'William.'[1] Following the completion of his *Gymnasium* schooling in 1888, Stern enrolled in philosophy studies at the University of Berlin (today the Humboldt University), completing his doctoral work in the sub-specialty of psychology there in 1893. In 1897, he secured a position as a lecturer at the University of Breslau, in the city that since World War II has been known as Wroclaw, Poland.

It was soon after Stern's marriage in 1899 to Clara Joseephy (1877–1945) of Berlin that Stern published a small book calling for the establishment of a 'differential psychology' (Stern, 1900). That new sub-discipline would be devoted to the systematic study of characteristic between-person *differences* in the manifestation of the basic human psychological functions of interest to the general experimental psychologists working in the intellectual patrimony of Wilhelm Wundt (1832–1920) and Hermann Ebbinghaus (1850–1909), who was Stern's senior colleague at Breslau, and others. A decade later, Stern would publish a much more expansive volume devoted to the same topic (Stern, 1911).[2] Hugo Münsterberg (1863–1916) would later note that the widespread embrace of differential psychology was fundamental to the establishment of applied psychology generally, and of I-O psychology in particular (see Münsterberg, 1913).

In 1906, Stern co-founded with Otto Lipmann (1880–1933) the Institute for Applied Psychology with headquarters in Berlin under Lipmann's direction. The two also founded and co-edited the German language *Journal of Applied Psychology (Zeitschrift für angewandte Psychologie)*, administered out of the Berlin institute. Historically, the existence of the institute would help to lend scientific credence to the very idea of practically applying psychological concepts and investigative methods beyond the confines of laboratories designed for controlled experimental studies in basic psychology. The journal would serve as a vehicle for publicizing the work of applied psychologists within the larger scientific community. Both of these developments would redound to the benefit of efforts in I-O psychology (as well as in other domains of applied psychology such as health/medicine and education).

In 1916, Stern relocated from Breslau to Hamburg, where he would help transform an existing entity known as the 'Colonial Institute' into the full-fledged university that was officially established there three years later. Under Stern's direction, that university's Psychology Institute would host many initiatives in applied psychology in subsequent years (Stern, 1933).

Soon after Hitler's accession to power in Germany in 1933, Stern's Jewish heritage resulted in his expulsion from the University of Hamburg. Under the threat of Nazism, William and Clara Stern fled Hamburg for the Netherlands in 1934, and then to the United States (US). There, William held a faculty position at Duke University until his death in Durham, North Carolina, on March 27, 1938.

Contributions to I-O Psychology

Most of Stern's efforts in applied psychology were in the pedagogical/educational domain. However, the differential psychology he launched with his 1900 and 1911 books (refer above) quickly became, and has remained to this day, the disciplinary home for virtually all forms of the psychological testing and performance appraisal procedures on which I-O psychologists have long relied so extensively. It was in this connection that Stern authored two conference presentations *cum* journal articles reflecting his hope, expressed in the above-cited letter to Cohn, that 'occupational psychology' *(Berufspsychologie)* be dominated not by Taylorism but rather by what he called a concern for a 'psychology of capabilities.' The first of those works was presented at the Fourth International Conference for Psychotechnics, held in Paris in 1927.[3]

Stern began that presentation by emphasizing the importance of recognizing the close complementarity between theoretical and applied interests in psychology. He then emphasized to his audience that from the philosophical standpoint of critical personalism, it is necessary both to *understand* and to *treat* persons as entities that are *unified wholes* having *depth*. The most important implication of unified wholeness for an I-O psychology that would become heavily invested in personality testing (cf. Vinchur, 2018) was to respect the fact that

> the human being is not a mosaic and therefore cannot be described as a mosaic. All attempts to portray a human in

terms of an ordered sequence of test results are fundamentally false.

(Lamiell, 2021, p. 134)

Stern (1929) implored I-O psychologists to keep ever in mind that the question of which individuals are best suited for a given occupation is entirely different from the question of which occupation is best for a given individual. Properly addressing the latter question, Stern emphasized, mandates consideration of the entire structure of an individual's personality. Hence, Stern argued, the tests used in occupational counseling must be designed much more in the fashion of personality tests than is the case in competition-based testing for selection. In the former case, he stated, "it is personal meaning that is decisive" (Lamiell, 2021, p. 145).

The personalistic grounding of Stern's concerns about the prevailing practices of occupational psychologists is starkly apparent here. Four years following the 1927 Paris Conference, Stern reiterated those concerns at the Seventh International Conference for Psychotechnics, held in Moscow in 1931.[4] There, Stern was especially critical of a view he found being often adopted by occupational psychologists, a view he called 'the harmony argument.' According to that argument, the occupational counseling that job applicants would receive when ability test results are viewed with the interests of the organization prioritized (interests Stern termed 'transpersonal') will by default also optimize the personal interests of individual clients. Stern challenged this view on a number of grounds, all of which appealed in some way to his personalistic convictions regarding not only the wholeness and depth of persons but also their inherent value as persons rather than things and the importance of their work in their overall psychological life.

In distinctly personalistic language, Stern reminded his audience in Moscow that

> the psycho-technician does not work on machines or on wares (in short, on 'things') but instead on human beings, and human beings are and remain, under all conditions, centers of their own meaning and values. They remain 'persons' even

when they are studied and treated from the standpoint of a transpersonal goal.

(See Lamiell, 2021, Chapter 8, p. 152, parentheses in original)

Conclusion

In an essay published in 1930, Stern expressed his concern over the proliferation of the 'testing culture' in the US, and his hope that this culture, which to him presented the clear 'danger of mechanization' in applied psychology, would "soon be a thing of the past" (Stern, 1930, p. 51). Ironically, the 'differential' psychology Stern had done so much to launch earlier in the century had by 1930 become the home for the very testing culture he was deploring—a culture that would reflect and perpetuate the triumph of trans-personalistic thought (refer above) over the critically personalistic ethos he hoped would be adopted broadly both within psychology and within societies more generally. Of course, the testing culture did not soon—and has not yet—become a thing of the past (cf. Hanson, 1993). Were it otherwise, William Stern's distinctly personalistic views would perhaps have been more historically prominent in I-O psychology (and in other applied domains) than they ever to date have been.

Notes

1 Contrary to what is suggested in some other extant sources, Stern's given name was *not* 'Ludwig Wilhelm.'

2 Stern stated explicitly in the 1911 book that it was to be regarded not as a revised edition of the 1900 book but rather as a new contribution to the literature. Unfortunately, that stipulation has subsequently been ignored by many influential differential psychologists (see Lamiell, 2019).

3 The paper was published in 1929 (Stern, 1929). My English translation of that text is available as Chapter 7 in Lamiell (2021), and my quotations of the work below are cited in accordance with that chapter.

4 A version of the text of that presentation was published two years later (Stern, 1933). My English translation of that text is available as Chapter 8 in Lamiell (2021). Here again, my quotation below from that work is cited in accordance with that chapter.

References

Hanson, F. A. (1993). *Testing testing: Social consequences of the examined life*. University of California Press.

Lamiell, J. T. (2019). *Psychology's misuse of statistics and persistent dismissal of its critics*. Palgrave-Macmillan.

Lamiell, J. T. (2021). *Uncovering critical personalism: Readings from William Stern's contributions to scientific psychology*. Palgrave-Macmillan.

Lück, H. E., & Löwisch, D.-J. (Hrgs). (1994). *Der Briefwechsel zwischen William Stern und Jonas Cohn: Dokumente einer Freundschaft zwischen zwei Wissenschaftlern* [*Letters between William Stern and Jonas Cohn: Documents of a friendship between two scientists*]. Peter Lang Verlag.

Münsterberg, H. (1913). *Psychology and industrial efficiency*. Houghton-Mifflin.

Stern, W. (1900). *Über psychologie der individuellen Differenzen (Ideen zu einer "differentiellen Psychologie")* [*On the psychology of individual differences: Toward a "differential psychology*]. Barth.

Stern, W. (1911). *Die Differentielle Psychologie in ihren methodischen Grundlagen* [*Methodological foundations of differential psychology*]. Barth.

Stern, W. (1929). Persönlichkeitsforschung und Testmethode [Personality research and the methods of testing]. *Jahrbuch der Charakterologie, 6*, 63–72.

Stern, W. (1930). Eindrücke von der amerikanischen Psychologie. Bericht über eine Kongreßreise [Impressions of American psychology: Report after travel to a conference]. *Zeitschrift für pädagogische Psychologie, experimentelle Pädagogik und Jugendkundliche Forschung, 31*, 43–51 and 65–72.

Stern, W. (1933). Aus den letzten Arbeiten des Psychologischen Institutes der Hamburgischen Universität [Report on the most recent works of the Psychology Institute of the University of Hamburg]. *Zeitschrift für angewandge Psychologie, 45*, 397–418.

Vinchur, A. J. (2018). *The early years of industrial and organizational psychology*. Cambridge University Press. doi: 10.1017/9781107588608

Chapter 8

Jean-Maurice Lahy (1872–1943)

Jesús F. Salgado

Jean-Maurice Lahy was indisputably one of the founders of European industrial, work, and organizational (IWO) psychology and one of its worldwide pioneers. His research preceded that of Hugo Münsterberg and the breadth of his scientific contributions and influence on the discipline in Europe was much greater, yet he is not as well known as Münsterberg, particularly among English-speaking researchers. His substantial scientific contributions are extraordinary for a person who had no university education and who had to combine unpaid scientific research with other jobs in order to make a living.

Biographical Overview

Jean-Maurice Lahy (who always signed as J.-M. Lahy) was born on August 7, 1872, in La Réole (Gironde, France) and died on August 22, 1943, in Sain-Léger-le-Guéretois (Creuse, France), from a heart attack while he was hiding from the Gestapo (Turbiaux, 1983; 2007). He had been a freemason since 1901, was a radical-socialist (later a communist between 1920–1923 and 1940–1943), and also a member of the French resistance. His father was Octave Lahy, a cabinet maker, and his mother Marie Julia Guithon, a seamstress. Lahy married Marie-Blanche Trouillet in 1901 and they divorced in 1919. In 1921, he married Marie-Charlotte Heloïse Hollebecque (1881–1957).

Lahy was a brilliant autodidact who, despite having no university studies, was extremely cultured (his library and archive, captured first by the Nazis and later by the Soviets, contained about 16,000 books). Throughout his life he had more than 180

DOI: 10.4324/9781003403258-8

scientific publications including books, articles, reports, and contributions to congresses. He was also very active in newspapers, publishing at least 150 articles.

According to Henri Jaskarzec, a former member of the Agni Lodge and fellow Freemason of Lahy, Lahy never subordinated Freemasonry to the interests of researchers, nor did he ever pervert research for the benefit of Freemasonry. His goal was human progress through the scientific study of exchanges between men, ideas, forces, and things. Lahy was a man of action, a rigorous experimenter, driven by an ethical ambition. Although much admired and with no known enemies, he could be hard to bear due to his very controlling and authoritarian nature and firm convictions.

He held various positions and received honors from international societies. For example, between 1921 and 1943, he was secretary general of the International Association of Psychotechnics; in 1925 he was appointed as a member of the French National Commission for Vocational Guidance; in 1926, he was appointed as a member of the editorial board of the journal *Industrial Psychology* edited by Donald A. Laird, Colgate University; in 1928, he was appointed as a member of the Board of Directors of the Institute National d'Orientation Professionnelle (INOP); in 1929, he co-founded the *Revue de la Science du Travail* (*Journal of Work Science*); in 1933, he founded the journal *Le Travail Humain* (*Human Work*). He also created several companies such as "*l'Établissement d'application psychotechnique*" [Company for the Application of Psychotecnics] to commercialize his scientific developments and at the same time contribute to social progress.

He started his scientific research in 1901 at the age of 29 as a "*student*" in the laboratory of experimental psychology of the École Politechnique des Hautes Études (EPHE) directed by Édouard Toulouse. In this laboratory, Lahy was successively appointed attaché in 1905, trainer in 1907, chef de travaux in 1908, and deputy director in 1925. At that time, none of these research activities were remunerated, so Lahy had to combine his research work with other jobs in order to earn a living. Thus, it is known that between 1892 and 1901, he was employed in the Post and Telegraph Service as a clerical staffer; between 1905 and 1908, he worked as undersecretary in the Ministries of the Interior, War and Commerce, Industry and Labor. Between 1908 and 1928, he was tax collector in the Oise and later in the Seine and Marne; in 1921, he taught a course at the Institute de Psychologie de l'Université de Paris in the section of applied psychology.

Lahy's main scientific influences were the sociologist Emile Durkheim, the ethnologist Marcel Mauss, the physiologists Auguste Chauveau and Jules Marey, the psychologist Théodule Ribot, and, above all, the psychiatrist and psychologist Édouard Toulouse.

Main Contributions to IWO Psychology

Lahy made contributions in many domains of science, including physiology, sociology, ethnology, morality, history, professional and vocational guidance, and, of course, psychology. In the particular case of psychology, Lahy was recognized at the time as the creator of work psychology in France, and one of the European pioneers of the discipline.

Lahy's initial scientific work, conducted in Dr. Toulouse's laboratory, was oriented towards physiology (1901–1905). For example, he did studies on the measurement of blood pressure and respiratory capacity, on the physiology of pleasure, on nutritional changes under the influence of muscular fatigue, and on reaction times under the influence of stimulants. In the field of industrial psychology, Lahy's initial work dates back to 1905 when he began to examine the concept of "professional superiority" and applied it to the case of occupations such as linotypists in 1905, typists in 1905 and tramway conductors in 1906 (see Lahy, 1910; 1913a, 1913b), in which muscular work was less demanding. This research precedes that of Hugo Münsterberg's by five or six years. Lahy's concept of professional superiority would be equivalent to what today is called professional excellence or occupational proficiency. Lahy had four main objectives with these studies. First, to study experimentally the conditions of workers' activity. Second, to determine the usefulness of measurement techniques, to modify them and to create new techniques derived from the working conditions. Third, to design personnel selection systems that would make it possible to select the best candidates. Fourth, to design systems for professional development.

As a continuation of his research into the physiology of work and effort, Lahy tried to find objective signs of fatigue in the occupations studied, but he quickly realized (1) that, already at that time, jobs tended to require more and more intellectual activity, and (2) that, in an increasing number of industries, exclusively physiological methods imperfectly measured variables such as human fatigue, attention, memory and the problems that fatigue caused in intellectual activity. In this area, Lahy's innovative contribution was that along with detailed descriptions of the occupation (distinguishing between functions, tasks, and gestures), he also included measurements obtained by physiological and psychological tests. The tests he used in his research were initially considered unrelated to the occupations examined. For example, he used tests to measure muscular sensibility, tests of visual and auditory reaction time, muscular strength, and tests of memory for letters, attention, and higher intellectual aptitudes, including imagination, abstraction, judgment, and reasoning.

During World War I (WWI), Lahy conducted important research for the French Army, focused on the designing of a system for the selection of machine-gunners. Lahy's report, entitled *Recherches expérimentales sur la psycho-physiologie des mitrailleurs combattants* (Experimental research on the psychophysiology of machine-gunners), was classified as a military secret and never disclosed, and its existence was not known of until 2019 (see Groupe de Recherche e t'Étude sur l'Historire du Travail e de l'Orientation, 2020). To carry out this research, Lahy created an itinerant psychological laboratory and applied the tests at the war front (Argonnne, Verdum, & Somme, 1915–1916). He took with him the typical instruments of the psychological laboratories of the time. For respiration he used the pneumographe and to record circulation he used the sphygmographe, both devices perfected by Marey, and forerunners of what today would be the polygraph. To measure reaction times (RT) he used d'Ansorval's chronoscope and Bull's chronoscope, which measured time in hundredths of a second. The RTs provided information about attention and fatigue. He also employed Binet's motor suggestion apparatus to measure suggestibility. For Lahy, the problem of selecting machine gunners was essentially the same as that of selection in industry: to conduct a psycho-physiological examination to determine which candidates had the aptitudes and characteristics of a good worker in a given profession. Lahy always began a study of this type by obtaining a sufficient number of elite subjects to investigate the characteristics that were common among them. The determination of the common characteristics had to begin with the study of the specific functions of the job, i.e., a study of the tasks. To this end, Lahy established three sets of data: (a) the functions to be performed, (b) a set of movements and actions to be performed for perfect performance of the functions, and (c) the psychophysiological characteristics required for effective performance of the movements and actions. After repeated tests, he found that the average reaction time to visual stimuli was a great deal shorter in elite shooters than in poor shooters. In the case of auditory stimuli, Lahy found a similar result. Through respiratory and circulatory curves (pulse and circulation variations) he determined whether an individual could be considered calm. His results indicated that elite shooters had high stability in their curves versus enormous variability in those of poor shooters.

Starting in 1920, Lahy directed the psychological laboratory for the selection of streetcar and bus drivers for the *Société des Transports en Commun de la Région de Paris* (STCRP) (Lahy, 1924). To classify the candidates (about 4000 per year), he used the following tests: (1) motor suggestibility test, (2) diffuse attention test with visual stimulation and with combined visual and auditory stimulation, (3) reaction time test, measuring regularity and homogeneity. The validity of the methods was established by correlating the test scores and the professional classification made by the company. In particular, the distributed (diffuse) attention test was a breakthrough in its time, since it used electrical control systems and reaction time measurements in combination with projections on a movie screen, all in an environmental situation that closely resembled the one in which the subject would be at work. It can be said that this test was a clear predecessor of the current simulators that are used in various professions for both selection and training (e.g., flight simulators). This method was implemented in psychotechnical laboratories of other French companies (e.g., Citroen, Renault) and in other countries such as Germany, Belgium, Spain, Poland, Switzerland, Italy, and Romania.

Throughout his years of activity, Lahy created numerous tests and evaluative devices that were widely used in the following years, and some of which are still in use today. For example, he developed, among others, a test of logical intelligence, a vision test for drivers, a test of technical intelligence, a fuzzy attention test, a chariot tour (tramway platform), and a chronoscope for measuring reaction times.

Lahy, Münsterberg, and the Origins of IWO Psychology

For years, it was frequently written in works on the history of IWO psychology that Münsterberg was the founder of the discipline and, more recently, Scott and Stern are also mentioned. Lahy and his research is rarely mentioned, for example, as the pioneer of scientific personnel selection and job analysis. However, researchers of those years were aware that Lahy had done his studies on occupational fatigue, occupational analysis, personnel selection, and vocational training years before those of Hugo Münsterberg (e.g., Viteles, 1932). For example, as already indicated, Lahy did his first studies with typists, linotypists, and chauffeurs between 1905 and 1908. For his part, Münsterberg began his studies on ship pilots from 1912 (and they remained unfinished), those on telephonists in 1910, and those on tramway drivers in the winter of 1911. Thus, the primacy of Lahy over Münsterberg in the beginning of industrial psychology and in the psychological selection of personnel is objectively established.

As for the influence of Münsterberg and Lahy on later IWO psychology, there are also differences. For example, Münsterberg's tests were not used in applied personnel selection and research either in the United States or in Europe. On the contrary, the tests and instruments constructed by Lahy were widely used during Lahy's lifetime and continued to be used for many years after his death, both in France and in other European countries (e.g., Belgium, Italy, Poland, Spain, Switzerland). In this sense, Lahy had a much greater influence than Münsterberg on IWO psychology, at least as conducted in Europe.

Conclusion

Lahy can be regarded as one of the founders of IWO psychology. He did pioneer studies in personnel selection, job analysis, test development, fatigue studies, accident studies, among other areas. He was a prolific writer and organizer of numerous psychotechnical laboratories in France. In his time, he was recognized as one of the main forces in the development of the industrial psychotechnics (currently IWO psychology) and was the General Secretary of the International Association of Psychotechnics until his death.

References

Groupe de Recherche e t'Étude sur l'Historire du Travail e de l'Orientation (2020). *Les archives de Jean-Maurice Lahy (1872-1943) à Sainte-Anne*. Octarés editions.

Lahy, J.M. (1910). Recherches sur les conditions du travail des ouvriers typographes composant à la machine linotype. *Bulletin de l'Inspection du* Travail, *1–2*, 45–103.

Lahy, J.M. (1913a). La supériorité professionnelle chez les conducteurs de tramways dans ses rapports avec la consommation d'énergie électrique. *La Technique Moderne, 7*(11), 388–390.

Lahy, J.M. (1913b). Les conditions psycho-physiologiques de l'aptitude au travail dactylographique. *Journal de Physiologie et Pathologie Generale, 15*(4), 826–834.

Lahy, J.M. (1924). La sélection psycho-physiologique des machinistes de la Societé des Transports en commun de la región parisienne. *L'Année Psychologique, 25*(1), 106–172. https://doi.org/10.3406/psy.1924.6140

Turbiaux, M. (1983). J.-M. Lahy (1872–1943) essai de bio-bibliographie. *Bulletin de Psychologie, 36*(362), 969–985. https://doi.org/10.3406/bypsy.1983.12531

Turbiaux, M. (2007). Le mystère de la mort de J.-M. Lahy. *Bulletin de Psychologie, 60*(3), 267–273. https://doi.org/10.3917/bypsy.489.0267

Viteles, M. (1932). *Industrial psychology*. Norton.

Chapter 9

Charles S. Myers (1873–1946)

Geoffrey C. Bunn

Charles S. Myers was arguably the most important British psychologist of the first half of the 20th century. "He, more than anyone else," one obituarist wrote, "has assisted in turning British psychology from a branch of mental philosophy into a branch of experimental science" (Burt, 1947, p. 5). "He passed on to us his own deep and wide love of human studies," his student Frederic Bartlett recalled, "and a complete freedom from that dogmatic theorizing which has been the bane of psychology" (Bartlett, 1948, p. 774). In terms of "his flair for organization" (ibid, p. 769), Myers had a tremendous impact: "He built a laboratory, a society, an institute" (Bartlett, 1965, p. 9): the Cambridge Psychological Laboratory; the British Psychological Society (BPS); and the National Institute of Industrial Psychology (NIIP).

Biographical Overview

"I am exceedingly interested in almost all branches of knowledge," Myers recorded in his undergraduate diary in 1893, "but I feel specially drawn to those subjects which, most directly, bear upon the improvement of mankind. The study of comparative religion, sociology, medicine and kindred studies...will always interest me" (C.S. Myers, Diary, 1893–1894. Transcript, p. 2, July 18, 1893). In 1895, Cambridge anthropologist Alfred Haddon started to plan an anthropological expedition to an archipelago off the Northeastern Australian coast. Haddon's aim was to undertake a comprehensive study of the physiology, linguistics, technology, sociology,

DOI: 10.4324/9781003403258-9

and religion of the Torres Straits islanders (Herle & Rouse, 1998). Myers was well qualified to join the expedition: "My interests in anthropology and psychology, my keen desire for travel, and my ready acquisition of foreign languages bade me accept this invitation" he later recalled (Myers, 1936, p. 218). An expert musician, his task on the expedition was to study auditory perception and indigenous music. Although he successfully recorded the islanders' songs with an Edison Home Phonograph, his experiments on auditory acuity were disrupted by "the constant rustle of the palm-leaves and the beating of the surf on the sea" (Richards, 1998, p. 141).

Settling in Cambridge after qualifying as a medical doctor in 1902, Myers embarked on a period of intense discipline building. He established a laboratory at King's College London, wrote a *Textbook of Experimental Psychology* (Myers, 1909), and lobbied for the replacement of the "damp, dark, and ill-ventilated cottage" that then served as the Cambridge Psychological Laboratory (Myers, 1936, p. 221). He became the editor of the *British Journal of Psychology* in 1914 and was elected a Fellow of the Royal Society the following year. According to Bartlett, the research Myers undertook on musical appreciation prior to the Great War was "probably about the best original work of a purely scientific character that he achieved" (Bartlett, 1948, p. 767).

When war broke out in August 1914, Myers applied to the War Office for service in France. But at 41, he was initially considered too old for active service. Undeterred, he travelled to Paris on his own accord and persuaded the authorities to take him on as the Hospital Registrar at Le Touquet (Myers, 1936, 1940). The following winter, casualties exhibiting unusual symptoms started to arrive at the makeshift hospital. Although not physically wounded, some soldiers were unable to stand; others had lost their memories or their speech. Some men suffered from "the shakes" or couldn't see, smell, or taste properly. The soldiers themselves already had a term for this cluster of symptoms: shell shock (Fueshko, 2016). By the middle of the following year the "Specialist in Nerve Shock" had seen over 2,000 cases. After the war, Myers returned to Cambridge "fired with the desire to apply psychology to medicine, industry and education and becoming increasingly disgusted, after my very practical experience during the war, with the old academic atmosphere of conservatism and opposition to psychology" (Myers, 1936, pp. 224–225).

Contributions to Industrial Psychology

Myers was made Commander of the British Empire and appointed Fellow of his Cambridge College in 1919. He restructured the constitution of the BPS and delivered the inaugural address of the first meeting of the Society's Industrial Section. At a speech he made on the role of psychology in peacetime industry, Myers met Henry J. Welch, a director of a company of East India merchants. The two men co-founded the NIIP in 1921 (Picard, 2018). "For heaven's sake, keep Scientific Management out of it," Sir Robert Hadfield cautioned, "or you'll offend labour" (Picard, 2018, p. 74). Duly distancing themselves from Taylorism, Welch and Myers stated that their ambition was "to promote by systematic scientific methods a more effective application of human energy in occupational life and a correspondingly higher standard of comfort and welfare for the workers" (Welch & Myers, 1932, p. 5).

The Institute would be scientific, impartial, and commercially neutral. As the title of one of Myers' BBC radio talks to the nation had it, industrial psychology was all about "The Human Side of Industry." If the 19th century was the age of mechanism, Myers said, then the 20th century would be characterised as the age of humanism (Myers, 1923). By 1930, the Institute had 50 staff and over 1,600 members, more than twice that of the BPS itself. As late as 1939, there were still only six chairs of psychology in Britain. Yet virtually all the psychologists in the country were associated with the NIIP at some point during the interwar period (Hearnshaw, 1964, p. 208).

As a non-profit-making organization unsupported by central government, the Institute required financial backing and fundraising was paramount. Armed with his manifesto *Mind and Work: The Psychological Factors in Industry and Commerce* (Myers, 1920), Myers set about courting Britain's leading industrialists. Funding promises were received from several enlightened firms including Cadbury Bros., Debenhams, James Pascall & Co., and the Total Broadhurst Lee Co. Substantial grants were secured from the Carnegie United Kingdom Trust and the Rockefeller Trust (Welch & Myers, 1932, p. 5).

One of Myers' first acts was to approach chocolate magnate Seebohm Rowntree for financial help. Having been appointed by Prime Minister Lloyd George to chair the Health of Munitions Workers Committee during the war, Rowntree was an enthusiastic supporter of industrial psychology (Briggs, 1961). Known for its progressive labor policies, the Quaker firm was keen to mobilize expertise in the promotion of those twin ideals of efficiency and welfare (Hollway, 1993). Myers passionately believed that psychology could mediate between these tense polarities, maintaining that the impartial, systematic work of industrial psychology "cannot be begun without the full knowledge and consent and co-operation of all concerned" (Myers, 1920, p. 179).

In 1920, Rowntree wanted someone to give a course of psychology lectures to his workers. Perhaps Myers could suggest someone? Myers countered with a radical suggestion: why not appoint a full-time psychologist at the factory? Myers explained that a factory psychologist "would...give advice to those existing workers who feel they are round pegs in square holes, and would select those suited for particular posts." He would also be an expert adviser in motion study, fatigue study, and the effects of monotony in occupation" (Rowntree & Co. Ltd., Central Works Council Minutes, November 10, 1919.) The greatest hindrance to the pursuit of efficiency was fatigue. Misfit workers tired easily and structural factors like badly designed workshops prevented even well-matched workers from giving their best. "And when such obstacles, such causes of friction, are removed," Myers wrote, "increased output has invariably been found to follow. The new method prepares a smoother path." (ibid.) Rowntree agreed and, in 1922, the company hired Victor Moorrees (1886–1945), the first industrial psychologist in a British company.

Industrial psychology in Britain was positioned between psychology and industry, between capital and labour, and between the laboratory and the factory. Although Myers found himself at the center of these opposing forces, his temperament made him well suited to be able to mediate between them. "He saw most of the leading problems of psychology as forking off in two directions but very nearly always set himself to find middle paths," wrote Bartlett: "His predilections were, in theory, towards a wholly uncompromising spirit of compromise between two extremes" (Bartlett, 1965, p. 8). "Very nearly every specifically psychological paper that he wrote revealed a strong interest in fundamental general problems, and he continued to see two opposed sides and to try to bring them together." (ibid.) If psychology could provide the language to promote harmony, then it could "oil the wheels of industry."

During the interwar years, when there were very few university psychology departments and jobs in applied psychology were scarce, the NIIP was the most significant avenue of employment for psychologists in Britain. "Its service to British psychology was of incalculable importance," the occupational psychologist and historian of psychology Leslie Hearnshaw later asserted, "without which the expansion of psychology in the Second World War and after would have been virtually impossible" (Hearnshaw, 1964, p. 277). "Much of the support the Institute received," the educational psychologist Cyril Burt wrote, "was the direct result of his capacity for communicating to others his own enthusiastic belief in the great part industrial psychology has still to play in the life of the nation" (Burt, 1947, p. 4). Bartlett agreed that Myers had "remarkable social gifts and...charm;" "Nobody could be more popular at conferences and meetings," he wrote, "and all over the world, wherever he went, people are to be found who speak more than anything else of his sympathy, understanding and of the extraordinary way in which he managed a great diversity of social contacts" (Bartlett, 1948, p. 768).

Conclusion

Myers made no significant discoveries, formulated no psychological laws, and articulated no effects or principles. Wary of grand theories, his psychological eclecticism in effect prevented him from leaving a scientific legacy. His ambition was always to see both sides of any conflict and to negotiate a compromise. From Bartlett's vantage point, Myers's compromising character was his fatal flaw: "The very qualities which made him successful in many fields," he wrote, "robbed him of any complete and final personal success in any" (Bartlett, 1948, p. 774). But what his contemporaries perceived as a weakness was in fact a strength. Myers's equanimous and accommodating temperament was crucial to the establishment of industrial psychology in Britain. Without him, British psychology would have become a very different thing altogether.

References

Bartlett, F. C. (1948). Charles Samuel Myers 1873-1946. *Obituary Notices of Fellows of the Royal Society, V*, 767–777. https://doi.org/10.1098/rsbm.1948.0011

Bartlett, F. C. (1965). Remembering Dr. Myers. *Bulletin of the British Psychological Society, 18*, 1–10.

Briggs, A. (1961). *Social thought and social action: A study of the work of Seebohm Rowntree 1871–1954*. Longmans. https://doi.org/10.1111/aehr.31br14

Burt, C. (1947). Charles Samuel Myers, C.B.E., F.R.S. *Occupational Psychology, 11*, 1–6.

Fueshko, T.M. (2016). The intricacies of shell shock: A chronological history of the Lancet's publications by Dr. Charles S. Myers and his contemporaries. *Peace & Change, 41(1)*, 38–51. https://doi.org/10.1111/pech.12171

Hearnshaw, L. S. (1964). A short history of British psychology 1816–1946. Methuen. https://doi.org/10.1192/bjp.111.472.289

Herle, A. & Rouse, S. (Eds) (1998). *Cambridge and the Torres Strait: Centenary essays on the 1898 anthropological expedition*. Cambridge University Press. https://doi.org/10.4000/etudesafricaines.

Hollway, W. (1993). Efficiency and welfare: Industrial psychology at Rowntrees Cocoa Works. *Theory and Psychology, 3*, 303–322. https://doi.org/10.1177/0959354393033002

Myers, C. S. (1909). *A textbook of experimental psychology*. Edward Arnold. https://doi.org/10.1037/13628-000

Myers, C. S. (1920). *Mind and work: The psychological factors in industry and commerce*. University of London Press.

Myers, C. S. (1923). The human side of industry. *The Journal of the National Institute of Industrial Psychology, 1*, 309–312.

Myers, C. S. (1936). Autobiography. In C. Murchison (Ed.), *A history of psychology in autobiography*. Clark University Press. https://doi.org/10.1037/11247-000

Myers, C. S. (1940). *Shell-Shock in France 1914–1918*. Cambridge University Press. https://doi.org/10.1192/bjp.86.365.1093

Picard, D.R. (2018). *Analyzing the human factor in British industrial psychology, 1919–1939*. Dissertation submitted to the Faculty of the Graduate School of Vanderbilt University in partial fulfillment of the requirements for the degree of Doctor of Philosophy, Nashville, Tennessee, USA.

Richards, G. (1998). Getting a result: The expedition's psychological research 1898-1913. In A. Herle and S. Rouse (Eds.), *The Cambridge anthropological expedition to the Torres Straits*. Cambridge University Press. https://doi.org/10.4000/etudesafricaines.

Welch, H. J. & Myers, C. S. (1932). *Ten years of industrial psychology: An account of the first decade of the National Institute of Industrial Psychology*. Sir Isaac Pitman & Sons.

Chapter 10

Lillian Evelyn Moller Gilbreth (1878–1972)

Laura Koppes Bryan and David Devonis

Lillian Evelyn Moller Gilbreth was a tireless advocate of applied psychology in the early part of the 20th century; asserting, researching, and practicing the applications of psychology that are at the forefront of current industrial-organizational (I-O) psychology. She was a consulting pioneer, held academic appointments, and received a plethora of awards and honors for her contributions. Because of her recognized expertise, she was frequently invited to serve on noteworthy committees appointed by United States (US) presidents; after she was selected by Hoover in 1930, she was appointed for additional committees by all succeeding administrations through Lyndon Johnson's. She exemplified the modern I-O psychologist by successfully blending research, practice, service, and a personal life.

Biographical Overview

Lillian Evelyn Moller Gilbreth was born on May 24, 1878, in Oakland, CA. She was raised in the San Francisco Bay area, one of nine children of William Moller and Annie Delger Moller. After high school graduation, she enrolled at the University of California, Berkeley (UC-Berkeley) and majored in English. Gilbreth was asked to be the speaker (the first female speaker at Berkeley) at her commencement in 1900 because of her successful academic accomplishments. In her speech, "Life—A Means or An End?" Gilbreth articulated her early philosophy about life: "human beings should not be treated as mere tools of production; the goal of human life is the fulfillment and happiness of the person" (Kelly & Kelly, 1990, p. 121).

DOI: 10.4324/9781003403258-10

Gilbreth's path to iconic status in psychology was indirect. After graduation at Berkeley, she applied and was accepted to Columbia University but was bluntly rejected from graduate study in literature by the critic Brander Matthews (1852–1929) who saw no place for women in his classroom (Public Broadcasting System, 2020). This rejection was fortunate, since with a background in psychology and literature, she connected with E.L. Thorndike at the beginning of his career as a learning and educational psychologist, a contact that had lasting effects. Illness intervened and she returned to California and Berkeley, completing the MA in 1902. On a post-graduation trip to Europe, in 1903 in Boston she was introduced to Frank Bunker Gilbreth, ten years her senior and already an eminent construction engineer who had independently devised ways of making masonry building far more efficient through the analysis of the motions involved in bricklaying. Gilbreth and F.B. Gilbreth recognized each other as kindred spirits and married in California in 1904. After this Gilbreth began the dual career of starting and raising a family—one that eventually grew to 12 children—and acting as amanuensis and editor to F.B. Gilbreth. The publication of F.B. Gilbreth's treatise on bricklaying (1909) signified a shift from construction engineering to time/motion study, which brought him closer and eventually into conflict with Frederick W. Taylor. Meanwhile, Gilbreth was concurrently finishing a dissertation in psychology at Berkeley on principles of scientific management, informed by Taylor but also containing many novel additions for the revision of all aspects of work.

Although she had been mentored at Berkeley by George Stratton and Knight Dunlap (Grold, 1961) and though the Department of Psychology there was friendly to women, she did not become the first Berkeley psychology PhD because of her move to the east coast with F.B. Gilbreth and of her duties with her family that did not allow her to complete the residence requirement. By 1912, the Gilbreths had become management consultants, becoming well known for their systematization of time/motion study, especially for making film records of their interventions. These films, which captured motion in time-lapse, echoed developments in futurist art at the time. The Gilbreths tried to publish her thesis, but publishers would not print it because it was perceived as being "ahead of its time" and "likely to interest only a few readers" (Gilbreth,

1924, p. 35). Undeterred, Gilbreth, on the strength of an earlier publication in 1912, *Primer of Scientific Management* under F.B. Gilbreth's name (F.B. Gilbreth, 1912), arranged for serialization of her dissertation, *The Psychology of Management: The Function of the Mind in Determining, Teaching, and Installing Methods of Least Waste*, and eventually found a sympathetic publisher for it as a book under her name (L.M. Gilbreth, 1914). At the time, the text was considered to be one of the most influential books on industrial relations (Stevens & Gardner, 1982).Throughout the text, Lillian asserted that managers must know psychology in order to understand their workers. Each chapter included elements of an underlying idea of scientific management that could be subjected to psychological investigation. However, the Gilbreths realized that her credibility would be strengthened with an actual doctoral degree, and since they were then based in Providence, RI, Lillian applied to Brown University to complete the PhD where she had the very good fortune of meeting Stephen Sheldon Colvin (1869–1923), newly arrived from Illinois as the first professor of educational psychology at Brown. Under Colvin's aegis she reconfigured her already-published *Psychology of Management* into a new, 400-page doctoral thesis focusing specifically on promoting efficiency and reducing waste in classroom teaching (L.M. Gilbreth, 1915), for which she was awarded the PhD in 1915 in Education at Brown. (In the same year, Olga Bridgman became the first person awarded the PhD in Psychology at Berkeley.) This seems particularly apt as the rest of her career was divided between consultation and teaching. Coauthored books with F.B. Gilbreth on fatigue (F.B. Gilbreth & L.M. Gilbreth, 1916) and motion study (F.B. Gilbreth & L.M. Gilbreth, 1917) solidified the Gilbreths' presence in what was rapidly coalescing as industrial psychology: Gilbreth's election as the first woman in the Society of Industrial Engineers in 1921 testifies the respect accorded her at that time.

Next, the Gilbreth family moved to a large house in Montclair, NJ. In it the Gilbreths introduced the principles of scientific management into the organization of the household, humorously depicted in the 1950 film of their family life *Cheaper by the Dozen*, based on its novelized version by two of their children, Frank B. Gilbreth Jr. and Ernestine Gilbreth Carey (1949). Frank Gilbreth's sudden death in 1924 compelled precipitate changes in this routine: much of the Gilbreths' consulting work stopped because clients shied from continuing with a woman, and Gilbreth was cast on her own resources. She responded brilliantly, maintaining a consulting practice from home while concurrently branching out into the promotion of efficiencies in a traditional province of women, home economics. Soon Gilbreth was consulting with appliance manufacturers and utility companies, advising them on kitchen design to promote time saving and waste reduction. She is credited, among other things, with the design of the L-shaped kitchen and the foot pedal waste receptacle (Lemelson-MIT, 2024). Along with this, she continued to publish and maintain her professional networks which had become more powerful and influential: her books on home management and childcare (Gilbreth, 1927, 1928) entered the burgeoning mass market for psychological advice.

During the early stages of the Great Depression of 1929–1935, Gilbreth was recruited by US President Herbert Hoover in 1930 for the President's Emergency Committee for Employment, the first of several consultancies with the government (National Academy of Engineering, 2024). Gilbreth consulted and researched applications of psychology for the next 45 years. Additionally, she taught university courses at Bryn Mawr, Newark College of Engineering (Chair, Department of Personnel Relations, 1941–1943), and Rutgers. In 1935, she was appointed on a part-time basis as a full professor of management at Purdue University (the first woman to receive such an appointment) where she remained until her official retirement in 1948. She was appointed as a resident lecturer at MIT in 1964 when she was 86 years of age. She also served on several committees appointed by presidents Franklin Delano Roosevelt, Harry Truman, Dwight Eisenhower, John F. Kennedy, and Lyndon Johnson (Gilbreth, 1970). She died at age 92 in Phoenix, Arizona on January 2, 1972.

Contributions to I-O Psychology

Tireless Advocate for Applied Psychology

During the turn of the century, psychological theory shifted from structuralism to functionalism, and it was a functionalist school of thought that paved the way for a new science, applied psychology (Katzell & Austin, 1992). Gilbreth was among the first psychologists who advocated for general psychology (Perloff & Naman, 1996) as well as the application of psychological principles to the workplace (Koppes, 1997). While searching for the "one best way" to perform every task so the entire system could be more efficient and effective (i.e., scientific management), the Gilbreths realized that scientific management was more than machines, tools, procedures, and inventory control. "It meant, first of all, the *people* who did the jobs" (Gilbreth, 1970, p. 103). As they examined the best motions to improve efficiency, they also wanted to know if those best motions provided the happiest results to those who used them. Gilbreth believed "…nothing could really be 'best' that did not take into account the way those who used them felt about them" (Yost, 1943, p. 107).

The Gilbreths gave up the construction business to establish the Frank B. Gilbreth, Inc., Consulting Engineers, an industrial management and engineering consulting business to pursue their life work: the "Quest for The One Best Way" (L.M. Gilbreth, 1924). They used time and motion studies to determine how worker efficiency could be enhanced and productivity improved while considering the employees' perspectives. They quickly established themselves worldwide as management experts: F.B. Gilbreth, the time and motion study specialist, and Gilbreth, the psychologist who, due to her strong empathy for people and keen insight of human behavior, provided the human element to their system (Gilbreth, 1970).

Following the untimely death of F.B. Gilbreth, Gilbreth continued their work by establishing the Institute for Motion Study, which she operated from her home (Gilbreth, 1970). It was her life-long ambition to heighten awareness of applied psychology by researching and implementing best practices as well as training managers on psychological applications to work. According to Yost (1943),

> At the meetings where she was becoming more and more prominent, and in the smaller groups of which she was often a member, she preached the gospel of what psychology had to offer in the solution of management's problems in industry. (pp. 114–115)

A Consulting Pioneer

By the late 1930s, Gilbreth renamed the consulting firm as Gilbreth, Inc., and she continued to consult a "humanized version of scientific management" (Kelly & Kelly, 1990). One objective of her consulting was to help management and labor accept responsibility for learning how to cooperate rather than creating an atmosphere of conflict (Yost, 1943). Another objective of her consulting was to demonstrate the importance of asking employees for their ideas and suggestions, which she did when she was hired by R.H. Macy and Company department store to analyze and improve their operations for reducing fatigue and increasing job satisfaction. Other examples of consulting included her work for Sears, Roebuck, and Company where she examined personnel relationships and conducted operational analyses (Gilbreth, 1970). She was a management consultant in war plants and military bases. For example, she consulted with the US Navy on a program for the rehabilitation of the disabled. The US Army used the results of her studies on the motions of the disabled to rehabilitate World War II amputees (Gilbreth & Carey, 1950). She also had a leading role on the War Manpower Commission and the Office of War Information (Stevens & Gardner, 1982).

Particularly noteworthy were Gilbreth's consulting skills. For example, Barnum (1962) stated,

> Executives will tell you her greatest gift is as a consultant. Once, after having to refuse an extended assignment to study why a personnel department was not working as the president had hoped, Dr. Gilbreth quietly raised this question, "If your head of manufacturing, engineering, sales, and finance are all vice-presidents reporting directly to you and the head of personnel is placed several layers down the line, is it possible the people in your organization may not understand how highly you value the human relations job?" The next day the president sent Mrs. Gilbreth a check for the full amount of the fee budgeted for the study. With her uncanny knack for cutting through irrelevant details, she had put her finger on the trouble spot and solved the problem in a fifteen-minute talk.
> (p. 186)

Recognition

Beyond her eight books and numerous articles, Gilbreth was known as the "Mother of Scientific Management," the "First Lady of Management," the "World's Greatest Women Engineer" (McKenney, 1952) and the "Mother of Industrial Psychology" (Stevens and Gardner, 1982). She became a fellow of the American Psychological Association in 1921 and was an elected as a member to the Society of Industrial Engineers. She was the first woman to become a member and the second honorary member; Herbert Hoover was the first honorary member. In 1924, she was elected as a member of the American Society of Mechanical Engineers, and during 1927, she was selected as a fellow of The Institute of Management. In 1965, she was the first woman elected to the National Academy of Engineering, and in 1967, she was selected as a fellow for the American Association for the Advancement of Science.

Gilbreth received over 20 honorary degrees including a Doctor of Engineering from Rutgers University and a PhD in Industrial Psychology from Purdue University. She received over 20 awards, primarily in engineering and management. She received the first Gilbreth Medal in 1931 for distinguished contributions to management and received the American Women's Association Award for Eminent Achievement in 1948. In 1966, she was the first woman to receive the Hoover Medal for distinguished public service by an engineer. In 1984, a commemorative US postage stamp was issued in her honor; the first psychologist to receive this honor (Bales, 1984).

Conclusion

Gilbreth was a key thinker who contributed to the development of applied psychology that took shape in the early part of the 20th century by asserting, researching, and practicing the application of psychology to solve industry problems. Yost (1943) noted:

> Mrs. Gilbreth would not want anyone to claim for her too great a part in the changes that have come in industry through the science of psychology. But even she could not name a

> single person who has had a greater influence in this field than she had.
>
> (p. 117)

She was a wife, mother of 12 children, psychologist, engineer, scientist, management expert, consultant to US presidents, educator, and an innovator of her time. While professing that individuals can and should develop their fullest potential, Gilbreth too developed and attained her greatest capacities.

References

Bales, J. (1984, February). Lillian Gilbreth honored on U.S. stamp. *APA Monitor, 15*(2), 2. https://doi.org/10.1037/e529682010-003

Barnum, J. (1962, May-June). The most unforgettable character of all. *Journal of Industrial Engineering, XIII*(3). 26–28.

Gilbreth, F., Jr. (1970). *Time out for happiness*. Thomas Y. Crowell.

Gilbreth, F., Jr. & Carey, E.G. (1949). *Cheaper by the dozen*. Bantam.

Gilbreth, F., Jr. & Carey, E.G. (1950). *Belles on their toes*. Bantam.

Gilbreth. F.B. (1909). *Bricklaying system*. M. C. Clark.

Gilbreth, F.B. (1912). *Primer of scientific management*. D. Van Nostrand.

Gilbreth, F.B. & Gilbreth, L.M. (1916). *Fatigue study: The elimination of humanity's greatest unnecessary waste—a first step in motion study*. Sturgis and Walton.

Gilbreth, F.B. & Gilbreth, L.M. (1917). *Applied motion study: A collection of papers on the efficient method to industrial preparedness*. Sturgis and Walton.

Gilbreth, L.M. (1914). *The Psychology of management: The function of the mind in determining, teaching, and installing methods of least waste*. Sturgis and Walton. https://doi.org/10.1037/10717-000

Gilbreth, L.M. (1915). *Some aspects of eliminating waste in teaching*. Unpublished PhD. Thesis, Brown University.

Gilbreth, L.M. (1924). *The quest for the one best way*. Society of Industrial Engineers.

Gilbreth, L.M. (1927). *The homemaker and her job*. W.W. Norton.

Gilbreth, L.M. (1928). *Living with our children*. W.W. Norton.

Grold, J. (1961). *A history of the University of California Psychology Department at Berkeley*. Typescript online at https://digitalassets.lib.berkeley.edu/edp/history_of_ca_psych_department.pdf

Katzell, R.A. & Austin, J.T. (1992). From then to now: The development of industrial-organizational psychology in the United States. *Journal of Applied Psychology, 77,* 803–835. https://doi.org/10.1037//0021-9010.77.6.803

Kelly, R.M. & Kelly, V.P. (1990). Lillian Moller Gilbreth. In A.N. O'Connell & N.F. Russo (Eds.), *Women in psychology: A bio-bibliographic sourcebook* (pp. 117–124). Greenwood Press. https://doi.org/10.1177/027046769301300340

Koppes, L.L. (1997). American female pioneers of industrial and organizational psychology during the early years. *Journal of Applied Psychology, 82*(4), 500–515. https://doi.org/10.1037//0021-9010.82.4.500

Lemelson-MIT (2024). *Lillian Gilbreth: Kitchen devices.* Lemelson-MIT. mit.edu

McKenney, J.W. (1952). The world's greatest engineer. *CTA Journal, 48,* 9–10, 20–23.

National Academy of Engineering (2024). *Lillian Moller Gilbreth, trailblazer. Engineer Girl.* www.engineergirl.org/123474/Lillian-Moller-Gilbreth#:~:text=During%20the%20Great%20Depression%2C%20President,a%20consultant%20for%20the%20government.

Perloff, R., & Naman, J.L. (1996). Lillian Gilbreth: Tireless advocate for a general psychology. In G.A. Kimble, C.A. Boneau, & M. Wertheimer (Eds.), *Portraits of pioneers in psychology* (Vol. 2, pp. 106–116). American Psychological Association. https://doi.org/10.1037/e412912005-001

Public Broadcasting System. (2020). *American Masters: Lillian Gilbreth, pioneering inventor.* www.pbs.org/video/pioneering-inventor-lillian-gilbreth-e8ylkg/

Stevens, G., & Gardner, S. (1982). *The women of psychology, Vol. 1: Pioneers and innovators.* Schenkman. https://doi.org/10.1002/1520-6696(198607)22:3%3C244::aid-jhbs2300220313%3E3.0.co;2-2

Yost, E. (Ed.) (1943). *American women of science.* Stokes.

Chapter 11

Walter Van Dyke Bingham (1880–1952)

Katrina A. Burch

Many students of industrial-organizational (I-O) psychology may recall first hearing of Walter Van Dyke Bingham and his pioneering work in World War I (WWI) with Walter Dill Scott, developing the first selection tests to be used in military assignments. However, diving below the surface reveals Bingham as a pioneer in merging the science of psychology with that of business, staunchly advocating for the applied focus of the field. Indeed, Bingham spent much of his career supporting the value and application of psychology to the "real world," earning him the label, "the first academic entrepreneur."

Biographical Overview

Walter Van Dyke Bingham was born in Swan Lake, IA, to Lemuel Rothwell and Martha Bingham (Bingham, 1952). Bingham graduated from Estherville High School at the age of 16 with initial career aspirations of teaching mathematics and physics. However, while studying at Beloit College in WI, Bingham met Guy Allen Tawney, who earned his doctorate in psychology under the supervision of Wilhelm Wundt (Benjamin & Baker, 2003; Bingham, 1952). After graduating from Beloit College in 1901, Bingham worked as a teacher for four years in secondary schools prior to seeking additional educational opportunities (Bingham, 1952). Perhaps Tawney's influence inspired Bingham to pursue graduate study in psychology and philosophy at the University of Chicago in 1905, which set Bingham on his inspiring and transformative career path.

DOI: 10.4324/9781003403258-11

While at the University of Chicago, Bingham worked with James Rowland Angell and in the experimental laboratory with John B. Watson (of "Little Albert" fame; Bingham, 1952). Indeed, Bingham's educational mentors read as a "who's who" of the time. In 1907, Bingham went to the University of Berlin to study psychology and philosophy under the influences of Kurt Koffka, Wolfgang Köhler, among others (Bingham, 1952). Because of Bingham's minor in philosophy, upon returning to the United States (US) from his time abroad, Bingham studied under William James and Hugo Münsterberg at Harvard University prior to receiving his doctorate in experimental psychology from the University of Chicago in 1908 (Benjamin & Baker, 2003). Following his graduation, Bingham worked as a research assistant to E.L. Thorndike at Columbia University prior to beginning his academic career as the chair in psychology at Dartmouth College (Benjamin & Baker, 2003).

Historians note that Bingham's impressive list of educational mentors in shaping the man and career he was to have was not by accident. Indeed, they write that Bingham "had a genuine hunger for knowledge; he sought to develop himself broadly and in the acknowledged leaders of his day" (Benjamin & Baker, 2003, p. 142). Two of Bingham's early educational mentors, Angell and Thorndike, likely influenced his adherence to the functionalist school of thought, which seeks to find meaning and purpose in the human experience, with a strong foundation in experimental methods. When reflecting on Bingham's aspirations that led to his arguably illustrious career, his wife, Millicent Todd Bingham, writes that her husband's work was driven by two deep-seated drives: the foundation of experimental psychology to the practical application of his work, and the desire to help people (M. Bingham, 1965).

By all accounts, Bingham did not have any children, having married Millicent when both were in their 40s, in 1920. Bingham died in 1952 in Washington, DC, and is laid to rest in Arlington National Cemetery (Benjamin & Baker, 2003).

Contributions to I-O Psychology

Bridging Academics and Application

During Bingham's tenure at Dartmouth College, he became interested in the measurement of abilities in students (Benjamin & Baker, 2003). Bingham (1952) writes that in 1914, after delivering a talk at the 23rd Annual Meeting of the American Psychological Association (APA) on the norms of college freshmen based on empirical research with students at Dartmouth, he met Arthur A. Hamerschlag who would set the course of Bingham's history-making career. Hamerschlag was the first president of the Carnegie Institute of Technology (CIT), which would later become Carnegie-Mellon University (Benjamin & Baker, 2003). Hamerschlag invited Bingham to provide a report on what, in his opinion, psychology could do for CIT, a newer technical university in Pittsburgh, PA. CIT was founded by Andrew Carnegie, who wanted an institution that blended traditional education in arts and sciences with practical training for jobs, offering affordable education and training to the masses (Carnegie Mellon University, 2024).

Bingham visited CIT in early 1915, and shortly after providing Hamerschlag his report stressing psychology as a practical science, Hamerschlag offered him a position as the director of the Division of Applied Psychology at CIT, a novel program in the US (Bingham, 1952). Bingham's report to Hamerschlag emphasized that psychology be used to identify and match students' talents and abilities to jobs, and that psychology would provide a foundation for students to understand and influence human actions (Benjamin & Baker, 2003). These recommendations were likely a reflection of increased urbanization, industrialization, and immigration in the US in the early 20th century, that was bringing with it new occupations and increased vocational choices. What's more, businesses and organizations focused on efficiency at the time, which indicated businesses needed better advertising, more trained employees, and better selection procedures in order to improve productivity. Bingham, among other notable I-O psychologists of his day, felt that the application of psychology to businesses' needs offered a solution. Indeed, one of Bingham's early educational mentors with whom Bingham remained in contact, Hugo Münsterberg, promoted psychology as the science of human efficiency, with the biggest concern being that of matching the worker's abilities to the requirements of the job (Kraus, 1986).

Bingham's employment at CIT started his highly influential and groundbreaking career in applied research. Indeed, during his tenure at CIT, Bingham developed several successful "Bureaus" of applied research, including the Bureau of Mental Tests, the Research Bureau for Retail Training, and the Bureau of Salesmanship Research, which would later become the Bureau of Personnel Research (Kraus, 1986). The earliest research endeavors of Bingham's work at CIT included the Bureau of Mental Tests, which sought to use data gathered on student abilities to predict success in college and future jobs (Benjamin & Baker, 2003). But perhaps Bingham's most ground-breaking endeavor was the development of the Bureau of Salesmanship Research.

Shortly after starting at CIT, Hamerschlag introduced Bingham to Edward A. Woods, who was the manager of the Pittsburgh office of The Equitable Life Assurance Society of the US, and was concerned that course offerings at colleges were not adequately preparing students for careers in salesmanship (Bingham, 1952). Together, Bingham and Woods developed a plan for a research program on consumer behavior, sales strategies, and the selection and training of salespeople; Bingham proposed that the business community fund this research program through financial investments, as well as the establishment of an advisory board for suggesting research questions (Bingham, 1952). Having developed a talent for communicating the benefits of psychology in supporting business functions, Bingham managed to grow the Bureau of Salesmanship Research to 18 business partners by 1916, including the Heinz Company, Ford Motor Company, and Carnegie Steel, to name a few (Benjamin & Baker, 2003).

In launching the Bureau, Bingham hired Walter Dill Scott as a director, who was well known at the time for his published work bridging psychology and business (Kraus, 1986). Under their joint supervision, the Bureau produced products for participating organizations, such as *Aids in the Selection of Salesman* booklet (Scott, 1916). This booklet contained, among other things, a personal history record for job candidates to complete, an interviewers scale for rating candidates' traits and abilities, a range of interest form for assessing candidate's knowledge, and a paper-and-pencil intelligence test. Participating businesses were tasked with completing the forms and returning them to CIT to aid in the development of valid predictors of successful salesmanship. Indeed, it was Bingham and Scott's work with the Bureau that lead to the development of the selection tests used during WWI.

World War I (1917–1918)

American psychologists serving in WWI were primarily tasked with two objectives: the assessment of intelligence in recruits and selection testing for military assignments. A committee of seven psychologists, including Bingham, and chaired by then APA president, Robert Yerkes, headed the assessment of intelligence task that would eventually develop what would be known as the Army Alpha and Army Beta (Bingham, 1952). During this time, Bingham also served on the Committee on the Classification of Personnel in the Army, chaired by Scott, who had advocated for selection testing for military recruits, convincing the Secretary of War at the time to authorize the development and implementation of a training program (Benjamin & Baker, 2003; Bingham, 1952). To accomplish this feat, Scott and Bingham modified the selection tests they developed for salespeople as part of the Bureau of Salesmanship Research. Through the course of WWI, Bingham, Scott, and the committee members developed selection tests for 80 military jobs and had screened more than 3.5 million military personnel (Benjamin & Baker, 2003). When reflecting on his life and career, Bingham (1952) indicated that his time at CIT supporting applied psychology and test measurement served as a "rehearsal for the enormous task of military classification and assignment" (p. 15). Indeed, Bingham's efforts, along with the efforts of his many colleagues, helped to garner public awareness and appreciation for the role of psychology in supporting business efforts, which led to expanded opportunities for applied psychology in the post-war era.

From Academic to Applied Psychologist

Bingham returned as director for the Division of Applied Psychology at CIT following his war efforts, and continued to lead the field in applied psychology. In fact, between 1916 and 1921, the Division received more than $235,000 (which, when adjusted for inflation constitutes approximately $5.8 million US dollars today) from businesses in support of research and training (Kraus, 1986). Impressively, by 1920, the Division had grown to include departments of psychology, vocational education, educational psychology, and personnel administration, which housed the Research Bureau for Retail Training and the Bureau of Personnel Research (formerly the Bureau of Salesmanship Research; Kraus, 1986). Between 1916 and 1924, the Division of Applied Psychology experienced incredible growth; the Division's published research heavily dominated the field and the Division trained more than 65 graduate students (Benjamin & Baker, 2003).

However, all good things must end, as the saying goes. Regardless of the success of the Division of Applied Psychology, which included, among other things, research institutes largely funded by business partnerships (the first of its kind in the field of psychology), which serves as a model for university-based research institutes today, the Division was dissolved in 1924. Some attribute this to the change in CIT presidency from Hamerschlag to Thomas Baker, whose agenda, along with the Board of Trustees, included enhancing engineering research (Benjamin & Baker, 2003).

Following his time at CIT, Bingham became the director of the Personnel Research Federation (PRF), which he helped to found in 1921 (Kraus, 1986). While at PRF, Bingham spent time in the field, engaging with and interviewing employees and managers in a variety of occupational settings. He also spent time consulting with academia and government, ultimately viewing his work as bridging the science of psychology with personnel questions (Bingham, 1952). Between 1926 and 1937, Bingham authored three books, *Procedures in Employment Psychology* (Bingham & Freyd, 1926), *How to Interview* (Bingham & Moore, 1931), and *Aptitudes and Aptitude Testing* (Bingham, 1937), which is largely considered to be Bingham's most important contribution to the literature as it bridged theory, method, and scope of interpretation to a wide audience, making the information contained within highly accessible. Indeed, Bingham's post-academic career held a number of accomplishments, including publishing in the popular press promoting applied industrial psychology, organizing radio lectures for *Psychology Today* (a national radio program), and becoming the first and only industrial psychologist to lead the American Association of Applied Psychology in 1942, which would later merge with the APA (Benjamin & Baker, 2003).

World War II (1941–1945)

In April 1940, following the invasion of Poland by Germany, the Adjutant General formed a committee of psychologists to advise on the classification of military personnel; Bingham served as the chair of that committee. Work by the committee included, among other things, the Army General Classification Test, aptitude testing, selection procedures for officers, and interview procedures (Benjamin & Baker, 2003). By August 1940, Bingham was appointed chief psychologist in the Adjutant General's Office of the War Department, a position he held until June 1947 (Benjamin & Baker, 2003). During his tenure as chief psychologist, Bingham supported the integration of psychology with the war effort, including the use of clinical psychologists in training officers to provide exit interviews for soldiers leaving military service.

Bingham's Legacy

Until his death in 1952, Bingham served as a consultant to the Army General Staff and to the Secretary of Defense. Bingham dedicated his life to advocating for, and pioneering, the value of applied psychology in bridging science and business. Bingham's work led to improved selection procedures and valid, accessible selection tests. Indeed, Bingham has been credited as the single, greatest influence on the field of personnel psychology in the 20th century (Kraus, 1986). Bingham rests at Arlington National

Cemetery in Washington, DC, with his tombstone bearing the inscription "architect of the classification system of the army, 1940–1947." While this inscription is accurate, it does not do justice to the legacy that Bingham left on the field of psychology. Indeed, Bingham's legacy is that of the true scientist-practitioner, who led the way for generations to come.

Conclusion

Walter Van Dyke Bingham's early education in mathematics and physics pivoted to psychology under the influence of mentors like Guy Allen Tawney, James Rowland Angell, E.L Thorndike, James B. Watson, and Hugo Münsterburg. Bingham's career in psychology began at Dartmouth College, focusing on student abilities, and which offered a natural transition to applied psychology at the CIT. There, he established several influential research bureaus, including the Bureau of Salesmanship Research, which contributed significantly to military personnel selection during WWI. Bingham's work at CIT set the foundation for his contributions during WWII, where he served as chief psychologist in the War Department. His legacy includes pioneering valid selection procedures and being a major influence in 20th century personnel psychology, with his innovative approach laying the legacy of bridging academic psychology and practical business applications.

References

Benjamin, Jr., L.T., & Baker, D.B. (2003). Walter Van Dyke Bingham: Portrait of an industrial psychologist. In G.A. Kimble & M. Wertheimer (Eds.), *Portraits of pioneers in psychology* (vol. 5, pp. 141–157). Psychology Press. https://doi.org/10.4324/9781410607638-15

Bingham, M.W.V. (1965). Presentation of citations. *American Psychologist, 20*(9), 721–722. https://doi.org/10.1037/h0021471.

Bingham, W.V.D. (1937). *Aptitudes and aptitude testing.* Harper.

Bingham, W.V.D. (1952). Walter Van Dyke Bingham. In E.G. Boring, H.S. Langfield, H. Werner, & R.M. Yerkes (Eds.), *A history of psychology in autobiography* (vol. 4, pp. 1–26). Clark University Press. https://doi.org/10.1037/11154-001

Bingham, W.V.D., & Freyd, M. (1926). *Procedures in employment testing*. Shaw.

Bingham, W.V.D., & Moore, B.V. (1931). *How to interview*. Harper.

Carnegie Mellon University. (2024). *Andrew Carnegie*. www.cmu.edu/about/history.html

Kraus, M.P. (1986). *Personnel research, history and policy issues: Walter Van Dyke Bingham and the Bureau of Personnel Research*. Garland Publishing.

Scott, W.D. (1916). *Aids in the selection of salesmen*. Carnegie-Mellon University Archives, Bingham Papers.

Chapter 12

Harry Levi Hollingworth (1880–1956)

Stephanie C. Payne and Fan Yang

Harry Levi Hollingworth clearly deserves a place in this book as a pioneer of scientific research studies funded by organizations to solve industry-related problems. Some of his most notable accomplishments were partnering with multiple corporations to carefully conduct true experiments involving pharmacological tests on human behavior, testifying in court regarding those studies, and writing extensively about psychology (25 books and over 100 journal articles). In this brief biography of Hollingworth's contributions to applied psychology, we describe three studies funded by organizations and thus some of the earliest applied psychological research supported by corporate America.

Biographical Overview

Harry Levi Hollingworth was born on May 26, 1880 in the small town of Dewitt on the eastern side of NE and raised in a relatively poor family. Sadly, his mother died when he was an infant. His father soon remarried. At the age of eight, he started school and soon began working to help his family. He worked many jobs such as carpenter, church janitor, and grave digger. He originally planned to pursue missionary work, but he was drawn to philosophy and psychology after reading books by Aristotle, Plato, and others. In his biography, he explained his choice of psychology and realization of his intellectual gifts, "I seem to have been born that way and have persisted in it in spite of obstacles" (Poffenberger, 1957, p. 136). In 1906, Hollingworth earned a Bachelor of Arts degree at the University of Nebraska. During that time, he was mentored by Thaddeus Bolton, as reflected in his later work, "Judgements of the Comic," (Hollingworth,

DOI: 10.4324/9781003403258-12

1911) which was subsequently labeled as having an early influence on attitude scaling. Hollingworth then worked as a principal of a high school in Nebraska for a few months, before being offered an assistantship to work with James McKeen Cattell at Columbia University in New York City. After earning his PhD in psychology in 1909, Hollingworth joined the psychology faculty at Barnard College, where he spent his entire career. He published the first textbook on *Vocational Psychology* (Hollingworth, 1916) and dedicated it to Bolton. He achieved a career by age 40 and was a strong mentor to A. T. Poffenberger, Jr., who achieved substantial eminence in the first half of the 20th century.

In 1908, Hollingworth married Leta Stetter (1886–1939) whom he met at the University of Nebraska. She moved to New York City with him and earned her PhD in psychology from Columbia in 1916. Soon after, she became a professor of Education and Psychology at Columbia Teachers College. Leta's choice to stay at Columbia likely determined Harry's decision to remain at Barnard since he was deeply committed to her. Similar to other partnerships in psychology (e.g., Kenneth and Janet Spence; Muzafer and Carolyn Sherif), the Hollingworths were devoted to each other and their careers and did not have any children. Leta dedicated her career to research on the education of highly intelligent and gifted children. She contributed a chapter on the vocational aptitudes of women to Hollingworth's *Vocational Psychology* textbook. Devastated by Leta's death, Hollingworth was moved to write not only his own autobiography but her biography as well. On September 17, 1956 at the age of 76, Hollingworth died of a heart attack at his home in Montrose, NY.

Although he was more interested in theory, Hollingworth's contributions to applied psychology warrant acknowledgement. Ironically, Hollingworth did not perceive his studies as applied psychology; instead he believed them to be more basic science (Poffenberger, 1957). He conducted several applied psychology studies funded by companies, including a somewhat famous Coca-Cola study, an alcohol study, and a chewing gum study, which are described in more detail below. As more of a generalist, Hollingworth's contributions extend beyond applied psychology to include experimental studies of taste (Hollingworth &

Poffenberger, 1917) to verbal tasks (Hollingworth, 1938), to fatigue (Hollingworth, 1939). His laconic prose reflects a patient methodological scientist and a self-effacing demeanor.

Over the course of his career, Hollingworth published extensively – 25 books and over 100 journal articles. He published several books on advertising psychology, vocational psychology, business psychology, and applied psychology. Dr. Ludy T. Benjamin, Jr. has written extensively about Hollingworth's contributions to psychology, from which we relied heavily to write this biography (Benjamin, 1975; 2000; 2004). For an even deeper dive into Hollingworth's writings, there are nine boxes of Hollingworth's published and unpublished papers at the Cumming Center for the History of Psychology at the University of Akron.

Coca-Cola Study

Arguably, the most famous study conducted by Hollingworth in the area of applied psychology was a study of the effect of caffeine found in the Coca-Cola beverage on human behavior. Under the Pure Food and Drug Act, the Coca-Cola Company was accused by the United States (US) federal government of including a dangerous ingredient, caffeine, in their beverage. In the spring of 1911, Coca-Cola hired Hollingworth to conduct an experiment to examine the influence of caffeine on mental and motor processes (Benjamin & Barton, 2016). Although Hollingworth was fully aware that the results of experiments funded by private companies would be greatly questioned, he still accepted this opportunity because he needed the money, and he was confident that he could conduct this experiment without bias (Benjamin et al., 1991).

Hollingworth wrote in his autobiography:

> With me there was a double motive at work. I needed money, and here was a chance to accept employment at work for which I had been trained, with not only the cost of the investigation met, but with a very satisfactory retaining fee and stipend for my own time and services. I believed I could conscientiously conduct such an investigation, without prejudice

> to the results, and secure information of a valuable scientific character as well as answer the practical questions raised by the sponsor of the study (p. 62).

Hollingworth recruited 16 participants (male students and wives of graduate students) to perform mental and motor tasks in the laboratory. The study took place over the course of 40 days, organized into three sections with experimental and control groups differing in the daily schedule (when), amount (how much in each dose), and frequency (how many doses) of caffeine administration. Small amounts of caffeine (1-3 grains; 1 grain = 15.43 grams) were contrasted with large amounts of caffeine (4-6 grains). To reduce any possible effects caused by the study being sponsored by Coca-Cola, Hollingworth conducted a double-blind experiment (neither the experimenters nor the participants were privy to the conditions to which the participants were assigned). All participants were required to report about their previous experience with caffeine consumption.

Nine tests organized into three sets were administered to investigate the effects of caffeine on mental and motor abilities. Perception and association tests included a color-naming test, an opposites test, and a simple mathematical calculation test. Sensory discrimination, attention, and judgment tests included a size-weight test (selecting one out of 14 cylindrical weights that is equal in weight to a standard block), a cancellation test (time required to cross out some numbers on a sheet containing hundreds of numbers), and a discrimination and choice reaction test (using left or right hand to press a telegraph key to react to the appearance of either a red or a blue disc). A steadiness test (standing without support and holding a metal rod for one minute), a speed tapping test (tapping a solid metal base 400–500 times as fast as possible using a metal rod), and a coordination three-hole test (insert a rod in three holes sequentially as fast as possible to achieve a total of 100 insertions) were administered to measure motor abilities.

Hollingworth and his team found that caffeine did not have any adverse effects on general health or cognitive and behavioral performance. For the color-naming test, opposites test, and calculation test, caffeine had a stimulating effect regardless of the size of the dose. For the rest of the tests, the size of the effect was highly correlated with the size of the dose. Specifically, for coordination, discrimination, motor performance, and typing speed, small amounts of caffeine were stimulating and large amounts were inhibiting. However, the effect of caffeine on the cancellation test was the opposite. Small doses of caffeine did not influence sleep but large doses did. They also found that nervousness and unsteadiness ensued after the administration of caffeine, but this result could be influenced by the time of day the caffeine was consumed. Hollingworth presented these results in court in a Chattanooga courtroom and the charges against Coca-Cola were subsequently dismissed on a technicality. Despite this, Hollingworth's study influenced popular opinions about caffeine in Coca-Cola and led to additional requests from companies to conduct applied psychological studies.

The Alcohol Study and the Chewing Gum Study

Two additional Hollingworth studies funded by corporations are worthy of note which are described in detail in Benjamin and Barton (2016).

During prohibition in 1919–1920, Hollingworth and his colleagues Prof. Woodworth, Dr. G. S. Gates, and Dr. F. E. Carothers were invited by the brewing industry to investigate the effects of alcohol on mental and motor performance (Benjamin & Barton, 2016). Earlier work by Dodge and Benedict (1915) had documented numerous negative effects of alcohol. Hollingworth and colleagues implemented many of the same techniques and tests that he used in his caffeine experiments. Six male participants performed various tests under the influence as well as not under the influence of alcohol. The researchers found that similar to the effects of caffeine, the influence of alcohol is largely dependent on the amount consumed with larger amounts having more adverse effects. These results had implications for future drug experiments. The researchers also explored individual differences (e.g., learning ability) in susceptibility to alcohol. They confirmed a previous claim that introverts and extroverts differ in their susceptibility to toxic substances. They also found that intelligent participants were more immune to the effects of alcohol. The results were published in two articles in the *Journal of Abnormal and Social Psychology* (Hollingworth, 1923, 1924). This study convinced Hollingworth once again that the validity of studies sponsored by commercial parties can be guaranteed if the results can be published regardless of the consequences. Since this alcohol study was conducted during prohibition, it also contributed to the science behind current social issues, broadening the reach of applied psychology beyond industry.

The chewing gum study began in December of 1934 (Benjamin & Barton, 2016). Once again Hollingworth applied some of the same experimental design techniques that he used in the Coca-Cola caffeine study, but this time he added self-ratings of tension and strain. The Beech Nut Gum Company was curious about the growing popularity of gum and wanted to determine if there were any possible adverse effects of its use. Male participants were required to wear a confining respiration helmet which helped to measure metabolism rate by collecting exhaled air. Strain and relaxation were measured by utilizing a rating scale at the end of each segment of work performed during the study. Hollingworth and his team found that the motor activity of chewing produced relaxation and reduced tension in participants. The results were published as the article entitled "Psycho-Dynamics of Chewing," thus drawing a brief mention in the *Psychoanalytic Quarterly* (Grotjahn, 1939). This study combined Hollingworth's own scientific interests with industry's interests of selling their product and providing another example of applied research with practical implications for industry.

Substantial Contributions to Industrial-Organizational (I-O) Psychology

Because of the Coca-Cola study, Hollingworth was a forerunner of scientific research funded by organizations to solve problems in industry. Before this study, research funded by a vested party was regarded as a taboo. Hollingworth proved that research funded by organizations can be free of bias. He also conducted studies on the accuracy of perceptual judgments (Hollingsworth, 1913) which remain the primary way we assess job performance in research and practice today. Initially motivated by a request from a college debate club, Hollingworth ultimately wrote a book summarizing research to date on how to appeal to various audiences. This 1935 *Psychology of the Audience* book was reviewed by Dr. Forrest H. Kirkpatrick (1936), who was influential in the steel industry (Hollingsworth, 1935). His 1917 (revised in 1920 and 1923) *Applied Psychology* (Hollingworth & Poffenberger, 1917/1920/1923) book coauthored with Poffenberger contained multiple work-related topics that are still relevant today including but not limited to the effects of environmental conditions on night work, optimum duration of work periods, importance of rest and sleep, substance use at work, selection of employees based on intelligence, and motivational incentives. Although he was not that passionate about applied research, Hollingworth's experimental approach gave early I-O research needed scholarly cachet, making him a pioneer of I-O psychology.

References

Benjamin, L. T., Jr. (1975). Psychology at the University of Nebraska, 1889-1930. *Nebraska History, 56,* 375–387. www.neb raskahistory.org /publish/publicat/history/fulltext/NH1975UNPsych.pdf

Benjamin, L. T., Jr. (2000). A platform disaster: Harry Hollingworth and the psychology of public speaking. *Nebraska History, 81*(2), 67–73.

Benjamin, L. T., Jr. (2004). Science for sale: Psychology's earliest adventures in American advertising. In J.D. Williams, W.N. Lee, & C.P. Haugtvedt (Eds.), *Diversity in advertising: Broadening the scope of research directions* (pp. 21–39). Lawrence Erlbaum.

Benjamin, L. T., Jr., & Barton, L. R. (2016). *From Coca-Cola to Chewing Gum: The Applied Psychology of Harry Hollingworth, Vol II*. University of Akron Press.

Benjamin, L. T., Jr., Rogers, A. M., & Rosenbaum, A. (1991). Coca-Cola, caffeine, and mental deficiency: Harry Hollingworth and the Chattanooga Trial of 1911. *Journal of the History of the Behavioral Sciences,* 27(1), 42–55. https://doi.org/10.1002/1520-6696(199101)27:1%3C42::AID-JHBS2300270105%3E3.0.CO;2-1

Dodge, R., & Benedict, F. G. (1915). *Psychological effects of alcohol: An experimental investigation of the effects of moderate doses of ethyl alcohol on a related group of neuro-muscular processes in man.* Carnegie Institute of Washington.

Grotjahn, M. (1939). Psycho-dynamics of chewing: H. L. Hollingworth. *Archives of Psychology*, No. 239, July 1939. *Psychoanalytic Quarterly* 11:144.

Hollingworth, H. L. (1911). Experimental studies in judgment: Judgments of the comic. *Psychological Review, 18,* 132–156. https://brocku.ca/MeadProject/Hollingworth/Hollingworth_1911a.html

Hollingworth, H. L. (1913). Perceptual criteria of judgments of efficiency. In H. L. Hollingworth & R. S. Woodworth (Eds.), *Experimental studies in judgment* (pp. 17–26). Science Press. https://doi.org/10.1037/13783-002

Hollingworth, H. L. (1916). *Vocational psychology: Its problems and methods.* D. Appleton. www.loc.gov/item/16015686/

Hollingworth, H. L. (1923). The influence of alcohol. *Journal of Abnormal and Social Psychology, 18*(3), 204–237. https://doi.org/10.1037/h0066385

Hollingworth, H. L. (1924). The influence of alcohol (Part II). *Journal of Abnormal and Social Psychology*, 18(4), 311–333. https://doi.org/10.1037/h0071117

Hollingworth, H. L. (1935). *The psychology of the audience.* American Book Company. https://doi.org/10.1037/11245-000

Hollingworth, H. L. (1938). Verbal Gestalt experiments with children. *Journal of Experimental Psychology, 23(1),* 90–95. https://doi.org/10.1037/h0057076

Hollingworth, H. L. (1939). Perceptual fluctuation as a fatigue index. *Journal of Experimental Psychology, 24(5),* 511–519. https://doi.org/10.1037/h0059663

Hollingworth, H. L., & Poffenberger, A. T., Jr. (1917). *The sense of taste.* Moffat, Yard, and Company. www.gutenberg.org/files/59082/59082-h/59082-h.htm

Hollingworth, H. L., & Poffenberger, A. T., Jr. (1917/1920). *Applied psychology.* D. Appleton. https://archive.org/details/appliedpsycholog00holluoft

Kirkpatrick, F. H. (1936). Review of H. L. Hollingworth's *Psychology of the audience. Psychological Bulletin, 33*(2), 132–133. https://doi.org/10.1037/h0050581

Poffenberger, A. T., Jr. (1957). Harry Levi Hollingworth: 1880-1956. *The American Journal of Psychology, 70*(1), 136–140. www.jstor.org/stable/1419250?seq=1

Chapter 13

Otto Lipmann (1880–1933) and Walther Moede (1888–1958)

David Devonis

Otto Lipmann and Walther Moede arguably represent the full range of development of the concept and movement in Weimar-era Germany known as Psychotechnik (psychotechnics). Both Lipmann and Moede are typically treated individually and separately in histories of applied and industrial psychology. Here, abstracting from their individual biographies and considering them together reveals not only the main forces shaping applied and industrial psychology in Germany but also the contrasts and antipathies in the field in Germany at that time.

Biographies and Careers I: Convergence

Taken together, the biographies of Otto Lipmann and Walther Moede are representative of the development of German applied psychology before and during the Weimar period and typify the career trajectories of German academic psychologists of their time. Both were born in the eastern part of the recently unified German Empire—Lipmann in Breslau (now Wrocław, Poland) in 1880, Moede about a hundred miles away in Sorau (Now Żary, Poland) in 1888—and both came of age during the Wilhelminian period. Both entered psychology as part of the second generation after Wundt and both were mentored by individuals committed to developing an autonomous discipline of psychology separate from philosophy. Lipmann's mentor and future close colleague was William Stern at the University of Breslau, who evolved a comprehensive systematic personalistic psychology emphasizing the role of individual differences and who is credited with coining the term 'Psychotechnik' circa 1900 (Weinberger, 2021). Moede's

DOI: 10.4324/9781003403258-13

was Ernst Meumann at the University of Leipzig, his doctoral preceptor in 1911, a bearer of Wundtian experimental tradition but also an early exponent of the experimental psychology of education, one of the elements of Psychotechnik as it developed during the first decade of the 20th century.

Lipmann's and Moede's dissertations were both planted firmly in the soil of German experimental psychology and dealt with aspects of memory. Lipmann's (1904) employed the nonsense-syllable technique of his mentor Hermann Ebbinghaus; Moede's more expansive effort (Moede, 1911) took a monistic and realistic approach to the concept of memory, seeking to generalize it across several fields of science. Both Lipmann and Moede were swept up into World War I, which in Germany enlisted earlier than other countries a greater number of psychologists advising on military technology. The historical record is indistinct regarding actual military service for Lipmann and Moede. Franziska Baumgarten (1934) noted that Lipmann 'served on the Eastern Front' but apparently his main activity during the period took place in Berlin. Lipmann, an independent scholar, already had established an extensive presence as a disseminator of information relating to general applied psychology. He was a cofounder with Stern in 1906 of the *Zeitschrift fur angewandte Psychologie und psychologische Sammelforschung* (*Journal of Applied Psychology* and *Associated Psychological Research*) and, after Stern departed for Hamburg in 1916 after Meumann's chair there became vacant, became the sole editor and manager of its associated Institute for Applied Psychology at his home in Berlin. Moede appears to have had closer ties to the military. Along with Curt Piorkowski he established, in 1915, a system for testing and evaluating chauffeurs and truck drivers which ultimately operated in seventeen centers supervised by Moede. Between 1915 and 1917 he also investigated rehabilitation of brain injured individuals and the value of French tests for aircraft pilots. Both Lipmann and Moede were extensively involved in developing methods evaluating aptitude and placement for a variety of professions during the war, supporting the need for replacements in industry for individuals called to front service. Activity during the war apparently provided both Lipmann and Moede momentum for transitioning to postwar psychotechnical activity.

Lipmann was involved in the calling together of an Ausschuss fur Psychotechnik (Committee for Psychotechnics) in 1918 for various industries. At the same time, Moede, under the aegis of the engineering professor Georg Schlesinger, established an Institute for Industrial Psychotechnics at the Technisches Hochschule in Berlin-Charlottenburg, which became Moede's base of operations in subsequent years. As Privatdozent there he published, in January 1919, his first extensive monograph on industrial psychotechnics, *Die Experimentalpsychologie im Dienste des Wirtschaftslebens* (*Experimental Psychology in Service of Economic Life*) (Moede, 1919). Moede, along with Piorkowski, established and published the journal *Praktische Psychologie* in 1919 which was succeeded by *Industrielle Psychotechnik* in 1924. In the 1920s, Lipmann and Moede were often found together in professional settings. As an early example, Lipmann co-moderated, in September 1920, along Schlesinger and Moede, a conference explaining psychotechnical testing methods to officials of the newly reorganized Reichsbahn (Gundlach, 2002). In the extensive bibliography (885 entries) on vocational counseling and professional aptitude compiled by Franziska Baumgarten and Lipmann in 1922 (Baumgarten & Lipmann, 1922), Moede, with 10 citations, ranks among the most prolific contributors in the area, after Lipmann himself with 33 citations, Jean-Maurice Lahy and Erich Stern with 12 each, and William Stern with 11.

In Morris Viteles's (1923) survey of business psychology in Europe, Moede's Psychotechnical Institute and Lipmann's Institute of Applied Psychology lead the list of psychotechnical institutes in Germany, and Moede supplied the optimistic evaluation of the future of industrial psychology with which Viteles's account closed. Moede provided significant assistance in organizing German participation in the Fourth International Conference of the International Association of Applied Psychology in Paris in 1927 (Carpintero & Lafuente, 2021): a photograph of the conference provides a rare view of both Stern and Lipmann together (Rostane, 2022). Between 1926 and 1930, Lipmann and Moede both published substantial summative texts: Lipmann's *Grundriss der Arbeitswissenschaft und Ergebnisse der arbeitswissenschafliche Statistik* (*Outline of the Science of Work* and *Related Statistical Results*) in 1926 (Lipmann, 1926); Moede's

Lehrbuch der Psychotechnik (*Textbook of Psychotechnics*) in 1930 (Moede, 1930).

Biographies and Careers II: Contrasts and Conflict

From the foregoing one might construct a picture of two vigorous and prolific individuals working together, or at least in parallel, toward the full realization of a comprehensive science and technology of psychology applied to industry, a picture encountered in recent histories of modern psychology (e.g. Rutherford & Pickren, 2010). This, however, smooths over consequential differences between them. The first of these differences are generational and locational. Although only eight years of age separated them, and though each returned precisely or nearly to his birthplace to complete his education, in a period in which developments in art and science were rapidly accelerated, eight years and a hundred miles' separation could be a chasm. Sommer (2012, 2014) describes a division at the time of psychology's splitting off from philosophy in Germany between those psychologists willing to admit psychical research as a subject for psychological consideration and those excluding it from consideration on materialist grounds. Along with Hermann Ebbinghaus, Lipmann cited, in the *Lebenslauf* of his dissertation, his time studying with Max Dessoir during Lipmann's brief period in Berlin. Dessoir, who coined the term 'parapsychology' in 1889 but later came to reject it, was a prime representative of the former group of psychologists in Germany circa 1900 (Devonis, 2023). He founded a discipline of theoretical and experimental aesthetics and established a journal in that area, and exemplified the eclecticism of psychologists still connected to the historical, philological, and philosophic aspects of the field, an eclecticism that characterized Lipmann's scholarly activity as well. Lipmann not only superintended the journal and Institute of Applied Psychology and the many pamphlets in the series *Schriften zur Psychologie der Berufseignung und des Wirtschaftslebens* (*Literature on the Psychology of Career Aptitudes and Economic Life*) but also found time to author influential treatises on school psychology, sex differences in ability, naïve physics, and lying. Moede also sojourned as a student in Berlin before returning to Meumann and Leipzig. The only individual specifically mentioned by Moede in his dissertation was Alois Riehl, to whom that work was dedicated 'with honor.' Riehl was the leading proponent of realism in German philosophy and an exponent of modernism. The first commission for the modernist architect Mies Van Der Rohe was Riehl's house in Potsdam in 1907. Materialist and modernist influences were reflected in Moede's persona as a 'Mann der Tat,' a professor in an engineering college focused on the rationalization of work through a focus on experiment and the delivery of results to corporations to increase their efficiency and productivity. Moede's streamlined approach to theory favored engineering solutions to problems of management and efficiency: his primary models, expressed in his *Arbeitstechnik* (Moede, 1935) were Frederick Taylor and Henri Fayol. The core difference between Lipmann and Moede was more than in their styles of approach. Lipmann was committed to a psychotechnics as originated by Stern, and wanted to construct a synthesis of all aspects of working and present them in systematic way as Stern wanted to do for personality. But more than this, Lipmann along with Stern valued individuals in all their complexity and difference: work was part of a wholistic context of life, a transcendent human activity. In contrast, Moede's vision centered on national economic concerns. In the preface to his 1919 *Die Experimentalpsychologie im Dienste des Wirtschaftslebens* (*Experimental Psychology in the Service of Economic Life*) he expressed this vision as follows:

> Die industrielle Psychotechnik bildet aber auch einen wichtige Bestandteil der Volkswirtschaftslehre, da die rationelle Bewirtschaftung der Arbeitskrafte der Nation eine wichtige Angelegenheit der Volkswirtschaft ist, zumal in einer Zeit, wo die grosste Sparsamkeit mit allen werteschaffenden Kraften des Volkes auf lange hinaus dringend geboten ist. (s. III, 1919) ('Industrial psychotechnics form an important component of economic study, since the rational employment of the national workforce is an important matter for the national economy, especially at a time when conservation of all productive aspects of the people is acutely demanded far into the future.')

This contrast between individual psychology and a psychology linked to the needs of state power came to a public head in 1930 in a highly publicized incident spurred by Moede's suggestion that measurements of aptitude and productivity be used to triage workers (Rabinbach, 1995). Publication of this plan engendered, in the highly volatile economic and political environment at that time, vociferous public resistance, and drew also a direct, measured rebuttal from Lipmann against a merely expedient approach to psychotechnics. However, by this time the die was cast for Lipmann's and Moede's very different fates. Simply expressed, Lipmann was a socialist, Moede a National Socialist. Lipmann's 1932 appointment to a teaching position at the University of Berlin was blocked in February 1933. Eight months later at the beginning of October, Lipmann and Stern (who had already fled into exile) were removed from their positions with the *Zeitschrift der angewandte Psychologie*, and Lipmann's home, with all the records of the Institute for Applied Psychology which was based there, was invaded and demolished by Nazi gangs. Accounts differ on whether Lipmann, a few days after this invasion, suffered a sudden heart attack or committed suicide. Franziska Baumgarten expressed it thus: 'His life-work torn from him, his heart would beat no more' (Baumgarten, 1934, p.327). In 2019, the documentary film tracing Lipmann's great-granddaughter's search for the lost past of her family centering on Lipmann's still-standing Berlin villa, *The House on Wannsee Street*, premiered (Jewish Film Review, 2024). Moede continued in his career at the Technische Hochschule, promoted to full professor in 1940. A senior member of the community of newly professionalized psychologists in Germany, he was one of the German delegates to a psychological conference in Rome in 1941 directed at improving the methods of Italian psychology in service of military ends (Gundlach, 2010). He continued to teach and publish *Industrielle Psychotechnik* through 1944, when most German journals curtailed publication due to the worsening conditions of war. In autumn 1945, Moede was removed from his academic position on several grounds, including past Nazi party membership, by the orders of the British occupying forces. His appeal of this decision failed and he was severed from the Technisches Hochschule in February 1946. Ultimately, he returned to teaching at the Humboldt University in Berlin in 1950 and in the Verwaltungsakademie in West Berlin from 1951 until his death (TU Berlin, 2024).

References

Baumgarten, F. (1934). Otto Lipmann—Psychologist. *Personnel Journal, 12*, 324–327.

Baumgarten, F. & Lipmann, O. (1922). Bibliographie zur psychologischen Berufsberatung, Berufseignungsforschung und Berufskunde. In O. Lipmann & W. Stern (Eds.), *Schriften zur Psychologie der Berufseignung und des Wirtschaftslebens*. Johann Ambrosius Barth.

Carpintero, H. & Lafuente, E. (2021). Max Möller and the foundation of the IAAP: An epistolary history. *Revista de Historia de la Psicologia, 42(2)*, 2–16.

Devonis, D. C. (2023). Max Dessoir, 1867-1947. In J. Shook (Ed.), *Bloomsbury Encylopedia of Philosophers*. Online via Bloomsbury Digital Resources. DOI: 10.5040/9781350962217.0004

Gundlach, H. (2002). *Psychologie und Psychotechnik bei der Eisenbahn*. https://doi.org/10.23668/psycharchives.10257

Gundlach, H. (2010). Psychology and its professionalization in times of war: The convention of German and Italian psychologists in Rome in 1941. *Physis, XLVII*, 319–337.

Jewish Film Review (2024). The house on Wannsee Street. *Jewish Film Review* (online review). https://jewishfilmreview.com/p-r/the-house-on-wannsee-street, accessed March 5, 2024.

Lipmann, O. (1904). *Der Einfluss der einzelnen Wiederholungen auf verschieden Starke und verschieden alte Associationen*. Verlag Johann Ambrosius Barth.

Lipmann, O. (1926), *Grundriss der Arbeitswissenschaft und Ergebnisse der arbeitswissenschafliche Statistik*. Verlag Gustav Fischer.

Moede, W. (1911). *Gedächtnis in Psychologie, Physiologie und Biologie: Kritische Beitrage zum Gedächtnisproblem*. Wilhelm Engelmann.

Moede, W. (1919). *Die Experimentalpsychologie im Dienste des Wirtschaftslebens*. Verlag Julius Springer.

Moede, W. (1930). *Lehrbuch der Psychotechnik* (2 vols.). Verlag Julius Springer.

Moede, W. (1935). *Arbeitstechnik: Die Arbeitskraft—Schutz, Erhaltung, Steigerung*. Ferdinand Enke Verlag.

Rabinbach, A. (1995) Entre psychotechnique et politique: la psychologie industrielle dans l'Allemagne de Weimar. In Y. Cohen and R. Baudouï

(Eds.), *Les Chantiers de la Paix Sociale, 1900–1940* (pp. 127–150). ENS Editions.

Rostane, P. (2022). *Der IV. Internationale Kongress fue Psychotechnik in Paris 1927.* Fernuniversität in Hagen, Fakultät fur Psychologie. www.fernuni-hagen.de/psychologie/forschung/schaufenster/DerIVInternationaleKongressfuerPsychotechnikinParis1927.shtml, accessed March 2, 2024.

Rutherford, A. & Pickren, W. E. (2010). *A history of modern psychology in context.* Wiley.

Sommer, A. (2012). Psychical research and the origins of American psychology. *History of the Human Sciences, 25(2)*, 23–44.

Sommer, A. (2014). Psychical research in the history and philosophy of science: An introduction and review. *Studies in History and Philosophy of Science Part C: Studies in History and Philosophy of Biological and Biomedical Sciences, 48 Part A*, 38–45.

TU Berlin (2024). Walther Moede—Charakterliche Prüfung im Zuge der Entnazifizierung. In *Die TH Berlin in Nationalsozialismus* (online). https://geschichte-tu-berlin.projekte.tu-berlin.de/moede.html, accessed March 6, 2024.

Viteles, M. (1923, November). Psychology in business—in England, France, and Germany. *The Annals of the American Academy of Political and Social Science, 110(1)*, 207–220.

Wenninger, G. (2024). Psychotechnik. In G. Wenninger (Ed.), *Lexicon der Psychologie. Heidelberg: Spektrum Akademischer Verlag.* www.spektrum.de/lexikon/psychologie/psychotechnik/12201

Chapter 14

Elton Mayo (1880–1949)

Jessica J. Sim and Jennifer Feitosa

Elton Mayo, originating from Adelaide in Australia, stands as a key thinker in the field of industrial-organizational (I-O) psychology for his pioneering contributions and work with the Hawthorne studies. More specifically, the studies laid the groundwork for the Human Relations Movement and shifted the field's focus to social factors and the employee experience. Despite criticisms, the Hawthorne studies set new methodological standards and underscored the profound impact of employees' emotional states within organizational contexts. Mayo's legacy continues to shape research and practice in areas such as employee motivation, leadership styles, and organizational culture. Stated simply, Mayo's enduring contributions influence and enrich our understanding of organizational dynamics.

Biographical Overview

(George) Elton Mayo was born on December 26, 1880, in Adelaide, Australia (Myors, 2005). In 1911, he received a BA in Philosophy and Psychology from the University of Adelaide. Mayo's academic career began at the University of Queensland, where he held the position of Lecturer (1911–1918) followed by Professor (1918–1922; Baker Library, 1998b).

In 1923, Mayo immigrated to the United States and served as a research associate at the University of Pennsylvania's Wharton School before joining Harvard Business School in 1926 as the Head of the new Department of Industrial Research. He was an Associate Professor (1926–1929) then Professor (1929–1947) before retiring in 1947. Mayo remained Professor Emeritus and

DOI: 10.4324/9781003403258-14

industry advisor to the British government until his death in Guilford, England on December 9, 1949 (Baker Library, 1998b).

Mayo's Contributions to I-O Psychology

Mayo engaged in private practice in the 1920s (Buchanan, 2012; Baker Library, 2007). He applied analytic techniques with soldiers returning after the war and conducted research on World War I shell shock patients from 1914 to 1922 (Baker Library, 1998b; Erez et al., 2017). While in Australia, he developed the view that psychological research could inform issues of industrial and social unrest. Disliking Australia's system of politicized unionism and compulsory arbitration, he became particularly interested in destructive *revery*—mental or physical fatigue caused by repetitive and monotonous work (Griffin et al., 2002). For most of his career, Mayo integrated social and clinical psychological principles to understand the emotional and psychological factors that affected employee performance and retention (Roethlisberger, 2011).

The Hawthorne Studies

Mayo is most well-known as the chief spokesperson of the Hawthorne experiments (Myors, 2005). He popularized the studies conducted in the manufacturing arm of AT&T at their Western Electric plant in Hawthorne, IL (now Cicero, IL). Initially influenced by scientific management principles, the company studied various factors affecting worker productivity. With support from the National Research Council of the National Academy of Sciences, Massachusetts Institute of Technology, and the Rockefeller Foundation (Baker Library, 2007), Western Electric conducted the Illumination Studies from 1924 to 1927 (Franke, 1979). Contrary to expectations, changes to the physical working conditions did not translate to consistent changes in production (Koppes Bryan & Vinchur, 2012); productivity increased regardless of whether the illumination level increased, decreased, or stayed the same (Zickar & Austin, 2018).

In 1928, Western Electric sought Mayo's guidance. He and Fritz Roethlisberger—leveraging their combined knowledge of anthropology, engineering, and sociology—investigated additional factors affecting worker output. From 1927 to 1932, they ran the Relay Assembly Test Room to examine the effects of rest breaks, working hours, and wage incentives on the performance of a small group of women assembling telephone relays. Similar to the earlier studies, productivity increased regardless of the variation used.

In its first appearance, the "Hawthorne effect" was used to describe increased productivity due to "special social position and social treatment" (French, 1953, p. 101). Since then, however, multiple, often contradictory definitions of the term have proliferated (e.g., placebo effect, demand characteristics; Chiesa & Hobbs, 2008). The studies have also been criticized for their methodology and conclusions (Bramel & Friend, 1981; McCambridge et al., 2014). Described as a "glorified anecdote" (Kolata, 1998), secondary analyses of the original data suggest that the research lacked scientific rigor and experimental control (Kompier, 2006). Further criticisms include the work's managerial bias, weak theoretical grounding, and tendency to downplay the significance of pay. Nevertheless, it should be noted that Mayo did not design the original studies but provided insights to generate new hypotheses (Muldoon et al., 2019).

Despite these criticisms, the studies were unique in their use of mixed, quantitative and qualitative methods within organizational contexts. A hallmark of the scientist-practitioner approach, Mayo and colleagues introduced new paradigms by systematically examining employees' experiences through field research, observational studies, and employee interviewing (Austin & Davies, 2017; Baker Library, 1998a; Griffin et al., 2002). Furthermore, the presence of confounding variables in the Hawthorne studies highlight the importance of both internal and external validity in quasi-experimental research, which have shaped current methodological standards (Cook, 1962; Grant & Wall, 2009; Parsons, 1974; Wickström & Bendix, 2000).

Human Relations Movement

The various Hawthorne experiments as well as interviews with over 21,000 employees are described in Mayo's (1933) *The Human Problems of Industrial Civilization* and Roethlisberger and Dickson's (1939) *Management and the Worker*. Mayo's interpretation of the Hawthorne experiments shifted the field's focus to social factors and group dynamics (Adair, 1984). For instance, Mayo and colleagues observed that a group of men working in Hawthorne's Bank Wiring Room restricted their output due to normative pressures, despite the financial incentives (Busse & Warner, 2017; Koppes Bryan & Vinchur, 2012).

The Hawthorne studies are credited for the emergence of the Human Relations Movement (Austin & Davies, 2017; Busse & Warner, 2017; Cook, 1962). According to the human relations school of management, scientific management ignored the subjective, socioemotional side of workers in favor of strict efficiency. As an example, human relations theorists argue that participative leadership styles (e.g., the freedom and respect accorded in the Relay Assembly Test Room) would boost worker productivity and job satisfaction, in contrast to the traditional styles of command and control (Baker Library, 1998b).

Mayo applied social science to organizational life, viewing organizations as complex social systems. This laid the foundation for the nascent field of organizational behavior and the birth of organizational psychology (Feitosa & Sim, 2021; Kozlowski, 2012; Muldoon et al., 2019). In 1973, organizational psychology achieved formal recognition when APA Division 14 changed its name from "Industrial Psychology" to "Industrial and Organizational Psychology."

Enduring Legacy

Elton Mayo has had a lasting influence on the field of I-O psychology (Koppes Bryan & Vinchur, 2012). His legacy continues to inform current research on organizational culture and organizational development (Kozlowski, 2012). The Hawthorne studies led to increased awareness of employee attitudes, work motivation, and job satisfaction (Adair 1984; Hesketh et al., 2018; Parsons, 1974). The findings paved the way for research on worker well-being including the effect of working conditions, psychological needs such as autonomy and recognition, and group processes on the quality of work life (Baker Library, 2007; Roethlisberger, 2011; Sonnefield, 1985; Stagner, 1982).

The Human Relations Movement promoted a humane approach to management, emphasizing worker beliefs and feelings (Roethlisberger, 2011). The movement further influenced work design and job enrichment programs for meaningful work (e.g., vertical job loading; Herzberg, 2003) and research on employee-centered leadership styles (e.g., leader–member exchange, Theory Y; McGregor; 1960; Cardy & Selvarajan, 2001). Mayo's emphasis on the human factor, which led to several books and articles (Baker Library, 1998b), continues to shape the science and practice of organizational dynamics.

References

Adair, J. G. (1984). The Hawthorne effect: A reconsideration of the methodological artifact. *Journal of Applied Psychology, 69*(2), 334–345. https://doi.org/10.1037/0021-9010.69.2.334

Austin, J., & Davies, S. (2017). Hawthorne studies/Hawthorne effect. In S. G. Rogelberg (Ed.), *The SAGE encyclopedia of industrial and organizational psychology* (2nd ed., pp. 600–602). SAGE Publications. https://doi.org/10.4135/9781483386874

Baker Library. (1998a). *Western Electric Company*. Harvard Business School. https://hollisarchives.lib.harvard.edu/repositories/11/resources/462

Baker Library. (1998b). *Mayo, Elton, 1880-1949*. Harvard Business School. https://hollisarchives.lib.harvard.edu/agents/people/2991

Baker Library. (2007). *The human relations movement: Harvard Business School and the Hawthorne experiments (1924-1933)*. Harvard Business School. www.library.hbs.edu/hc/hawthorne

Bramel, D., & Friend, R. (1981). Hawthorne, the myth of the docile worker, and class bias in psychology. *American Psychologist, 36*(8), 867–878.

Buchanan, R. D. (2012). Australia. In D. B. Baker (Ed.), *The Oxford handbook of the history of psychology: Global perspectives* (pp. 19–33). Oxford University Press. https://doi.org/10.1093/oxfordhb/9780195366556.013.0002

Busse, R., & Warner, M. (2017). The legacy of the Hawthorne experiments: A critical analysis of the human relations school of thought. *History of Economic Ideas, 25*(2), 91–114.

Cardy, R. L., & Selvarajan, T. T. (2001). Management interventions. In N. Anderson, D. S. Ones, H. K. Sinangil, & C. Viswesvaran (Eds.), *Handbook of industrial, work, and organizational psychology* (pp.

346–376). SAGE Publications. https://doi.org/10.4135/9781848608368

Chiesa, M., & Hobbs, S. (2008). Making sense of social research: How useful is the Hawthorne effect? *European Journal of Social Psychology, 38*(1), 67–74. https://doi.org/10.1002/ejsp.401

Cook, D. L. (1962). The Hawthorne effect in educational research. *The Phi Delta Kappan, 44*(3), 116–122.

Erez, M., Chhokar, J. S., Nair, E., Wood, R., & Griffin, M. (2017). History of industrial and organizational psychology in other parts of the world. In S. G. Rogelberg (Ed.), *The SAGE encyclopedia of industrial and organizational psychology* (2nd ed., pp. 643–647). SAGE Publications. https://doi.org/10.4135/9781483386874

Feitosa, J., & Sim, J. (2021). I-O psychology around the world: A snapshot of historical roots. In L. Koppes Bryan (Ed.), *Historical perspectives in industrial and organizational psychology* (2nd ed., pp. 63–82). Routledge. https://doi.org/10.4324/9780429052644-4

Franke, R. H. (1979). The Hawthorne experiments: Re-view. *American Sociological Review, 44*(5), 861–867. https://doi.org/10.2307/2094534

French, J. R. P. (1953). Experiments in field settings. In L. Festinger & D. Katz (Eds.), *Research methods in the behavioral sciences* (pp. 98–135). Dryden Press.

Grant, A. M., & Wall, T. D. (2009). The neglected science and art of quasi-experimentation: Why-to, when-to, and how-to advice for organizational researchers. *Organizational Research Methods, 12*(4), 653–686. https://doi.org/10.1177/1094428108320737

Griffin, M. A., Landy, F. J., & Mayocchi, L. (2002). Australian influences on Elton Mayo: The construct of revery in industrial society. *History of Psychology, 5*(4). 356–375. https://doi.org/10.1037/1093-4510.5.4.356

Herzberg, F. (2003). One more time: How do you motivate employees? *Harvard Business Review*. https://hbr.org/2003/01/one-more-time-how-do-you-motivate-employees

Hesketh, B., Neal, A., & Griffin, B. (2018). Industrial, work and organizational psychology in Australia and New Zealand. In D. S. Ones, N. Anderson, H. K. Sinangil, & C. Viswesvaran (Eds.), *The SAGE handbook of industrial, work and organizational psychology* (pp. 76–90). SAGE Publications. https://doi.org/10.4135/9781473914964

Kolata, G. (1998, December 6). Scientific myths that are too good to die. *New York Times*. https://archive.nytimes.com/www.nytimes.com/library/review/120698science-myths-review.html

Kompier, M. A. (2006). The "Hawthorne effect" is a myth, but what keeps the story going? *Scandinavian Journal of Work, Environment & Health, 32*(5), 402–412. https://doi.org/10.5271/sjweh.1036

Koppes Bryan, L. L., & Vinchur, A. J. (2012). A history of industrial and organizational psychology. In S. W. J. Kozlowski (Ed.), *The Oxford handbook of organizational psychology* (pp. 22–76). Oxford University Press. https://doi.org/10.1093/oxfordhb/9780199928309.013.0002

Kozlowski, S. W. J. (2012). The nature of organizational psychology. In S. W. J. Kozlowski (Ed.), *The Oxford handbook of organizational psychology* (pp. 3–21). Oxford University Press. https://doi.org/10.1093/oxfordhb/9780199928309.013.0001

Mayo, E. (1933). *The human problems of industrial civilization*. Macmillan.

McCambridge, J., Witton, J., & Elbourne, D. R. (2014). Systematic review of the Hawthorne effect: New concepts are needed to study research participation effects. *Journal of Clinical Epidemiology, 67*(3), 267–277. https://doi.org/10.1016/j.jclinepi.2013.08.015

McGregor, D. (1960). *The human side of enterprise*. McGraw-Hill.

Muldoon, J., Bendickson, J., Bauman, A., & Liguori, E. W. (2019). Reassessing Elton Mayo: Clarifying contradictions and context. *Journal of Management History, 26*(2), 165–185. https://doi.org/10.1108/JMH-05-2019-0033

Myors, B. (2005). Oz I-O. *The Industrial-Organizational Psychologist, 43*(2), 85–88. https://doi.org/10.1037/e579152011-014

Parsons, H. M. (1974). What happened at Hawthorne? *Science, 183*(4128), 922–932. https://doi.org/10.1126/science.183.4128.922

Roethlisberger, F. J. (2011). The Hawthorne experiments. In W. E. Natemeyer & P. Hersey (Eds.), *Classics of organization theory* (pp. 158–166). Waveland Press. (Reprinted from *Management and morale*, pp. 7–26, by F. J. Roethlisberger, 1941, Harvard University Press).

Roethlisberger, F. J., & Dickson, W. J. (1939). *Management and the worker*. Harvard University Press.

Sonnenfeld, J. A. (1985). Shedding light on the Hawthorne studies. *Journal of Organizational Behavior, 6*(2), 111–130. https://doi.org/10.1002/job.4030060203

Stagner, R. (1982). Past and future of industrial/organizational psychology. *Professional Psychology, 13*(6), 892–903. https://doi.org/10.1037/0735-7028.13.6.892

Wickström, G., & Bendix, T. (2000). The "Hawthorne effect"—what did the original Hawthorne studies actually show? *Scandinavian Journal of Work, Environment & Health, 26*(4), 363–367. https://doi.org/10.5271/sjweh.555

Zickar, M. J., & Austin, J. T. (2018). History of industrial, work and organizational psychology in North America. In D. S. Ones, N. Anderson, H. K. Sinangil, & C. Viswesvaran (Eds.), *The SAGE handbook of industrial, work and organizational psychology* (pp. 3–42). SAGE Publications. https://doi.org/10.4135/9781473914964

Chapter 15

Edward K. Strong, Jr. (1884–1963)

Janet L. Kottke

What are vocational interests and how should we measure them? This question formed the basis for a lifetime of study for Edward K. Strong, Jr. Of course, Strong's professional life was more than vocational research, but his Interest Inventory is still among the most widely used and is arguably his most notable contribution to psychological science. This brief biography will describe the early life and education of Strong, his work in advertising, his contribution to the war effort in World War I (WWI), his research of second-generation Japanese in California, and his enduring legacy of vocational interest measurement.

Biographical Overview

Early Life and Education

Edward Kellogg Strong, Jr. was born in Syracuse, NY, August 18, 1884. His father was a Presbyterian minister and his mother an English college major and avid reader. In Strong's childhood, the family moved several times to follow his father's ministry, eventually settling in northern CA in 1902. During his childhood, Strong was very active in outdoor activities, an interest that persisted throughout his lifetime (Hansen, 1987).

Strong earned a bachelor's degree in biology from the University of California at Berkeley in 1906. During a short stint working for the United States (US) Forestry Service, Strong built trails and solidified his love of the outdoors. Returning to Berkeley, he earned a master's degree in psychology in 1909[1] (Darley, 1964).

DOI: 10.4324/9781003403258-15

Initially intending to teach in China, he found the needed clearances were slow in coming, and applied to Columbia University to continue his graduate education (Hansen, 1987). Columbia, at the time, was a developing bastion of functionalism (Vinchur, 2018). Strong was a lab assistant for Harry Hollingworth who suggested a dissertation topic comparing advertising stimuli (Hansen, 1987); James McKeen Cattell supervised the dissertation (Vinchur, 2018).

Early Professional Career

Columbia

After being awarded his PhD in 1911, Strong worked at Columbia for three years in advertising, marketing, and business research. He received a research fellowship sponsored by the New York Advertising Men's League and Association of National Advertisers. During this era, he conducted experiments that tested repetition of presentation, use of white space, size, and number of ads in securing a reader's attention, accurate recognition, and "pulling power" (persuasiveness) (Strong, 1914).[2]

George Peabody

In 1914, he became a professor at George Peabody College for Teachers (now merged with Vanderbilt). There he published reviews of the causes and effects of fatigue (Strong, 1916), as well as a guide for instructors teaching introductory psychology (Strong, 1922a).

World War I Military Service

Strong left Peabody for military service in 1917, serving on the Committee on Classification of Personnel in the Army. This committee conducted research on and provided advice about how best to place military men into the positions in which they could be most effective. Along with Strong, the roster of the active members of the committee included a who's who of notable psychologists of the era: Walter Dill Scott, Edward Thorndike,

Walter Van Dyke Bingham, James Angell, John Watson, and Robert Yerkes. In addition to placing nearly a million Army inductees into specialties, the committee developed trade skill tests, identified occupational sets needed by military divisions, and indexed existing skills among the men in the Army. Strong authored the committee report published in the *Journal of Applied Psychology*[3](Strong, 1918).

Carnegie Institute of Technology

In 1919, Strong joined the faculty of the Carnegie Institute of Technology (CIT) as head of the Bureau of Educational Research, where he first became involved – indirectly – with interest measurement. During 1919–1920, Clarence Yoakum held a graduate seminar focused on developing survey questions about interests that yielded a 1000-item pool. Multiple inventories measuring vocational interests tapped this pool, the first of which was the Carnegie Interest Inventory (Harrington & Long, 2013). Though Strong's attention was focused elsewhere (Bingham, 1923), he had a cognate connection to the substance of the seminar because of his prior association with Hollingworth and Edward Thorndike at Columbia. Hollingworth published one of the first books in the area (Hollingworth & Hollingworth, 1916), and Thorndike was developing measures of intellect, interest, and learning (Donnay, 1997). The evidence of these connections would come full bloom later, at Stanford.

At CIT, Strong conducted job analyses of Pittsburgh industry managers and executives with the intent to develop training curricula for these positions – a key mission of CIT (Bingham, 1923). According to Tarbell (1937), the newly appointed CIT president liquidated the then Division of Cooperative Research, formerly the Division of Applied Psychology, in June 1923. All of the division's programs had disappeared by the summer of 1924 (Benjamin & Baker, 2003). Fortunately for the history of vocational interest measurement, the renowned intelligence researcher, Lewis Terman, who had worked with Strong during WWI, invited Strong to join the faculty at Stanford. Shortly thereafter, Strong joined the business faculty at Stanford but continued an affiliation with the psychology department (Hansen, 1987).

Stanford

In 1924, Strong instructed his graduate student, Karl Cowdery, to compare occupational groups by their interests. Cowdery wrote nearly 200 items for the Interest Report Blank (IRB) with which he successfully differentiated lawyers, engineers, and physicians (Cowdery, 1926). When Cowdery elected not to pursue these studies (Donnay, 1997), Strong did. In his 1927 article, Strong presented the Vocational Interest Blank (SVIB) and the logic behind its development. In 1933, Strong published the Vocational Interest Blank for Women (SVIB-W) (Strong, 1933).

Strong's work on interest measurement became key to his involvement in another project in the 1930s. Stanford's president, Ray Lyman Wilbur, asked Strong to investigate the so-called Japanese "problem;" that is, why first generation Japanese-Americans were unable to secure jobs worthy of their talent. Reportedly, Strong was reluctant to accept this assignment (Hansen, 1987), but ultimately wrote two Stanford series monographs, *Vocational Aptitudes of Second-Generation Japanese in the United States*, and *Japanese in California*. A third monograph by Reginald Bell, *Public School Education of Second-Generation Japanese in California*, was incorporated with Strong's monographs into the book, *The Second-Generation Japanese Problem* (Strong, 1934). Strong reported data from interviews with over 9,000 Japanese – a number representing nearly 10% of the Japanese in California in 1933. Strong detailed significant challenges for second-generation Japanese – anti-immigrant sentiment, laws proscribing immigration quotas, racial prejudices, segregated schools, and segregated public accommodations; Strong noted many of these issues were true for all immigrant groups. A key conclusion was that Japanese-Americans with IQs equivalent to whites achieved better grades in school and were more honest, law-abiding, and trustworthy. The book concluded by questioning whether whites could change their prejudices towards Japanese-Americans and, if so, how this could best be accomplished.

During his more than 25 years at Stanford, Strong conducted laborious research, collecting data from thousands of men and women in an array of occupations. Strong's daughter, Fran, recalled that work on the SVIB was a family affair – scoring SVIB forms that came by mail to earn fees to sustain her father's research. Strong's wife, Margaret, served as a primary editor for him and frequently rewrote his papers! Strong retired from Stanford in 1949, but continued researching and publishing articles and books about his eponymous inventory, with his last paper appearing posthumously in 1964 (Hansen, 1987).

In 1955, Strong was invited to the University of Minnesota (UM), which held a symposium about the SVIB (Layton, 1960). Strong began collaborating on an SVIB revision with Ralph Berdie, Director of the Student Counseling Bureau, and his son-in-law. Because he believed UM researchers were most likely to continue his work, Strong laid plans to have the corpus of his research materials transferred to UM. Upon his death in 1963, what had not already been shipped, was sent to the care of a young David Campbell,[4] Director of the newly established Center for Interest Measurement Research (Donnay, 1997).

E. K. Strong, Jr. died December 4, 1963, in Menlo Park, CA.

Evolution of the Strong Interest Inventory

As already noted, Strong picked up where others had begun work on vocational interests. For example, Progressive era *bricoleur* Frank Parson (1909) proposed people should be matched to jobs based on their interests and aptitudes. In 1919, Yoakum's seminar at CIT addressed how paper and pencil surveys could differentiate people by occupation. Cowdery's IRB – itself a modification of the Carnegie Interest Analysis Blank – contained 263 items that asked respondents their preferences for jobs, school subjects, hobbies, types of people, pets, and other miscellaneous activities (Cowdery, 1926).

Once Cowdery passed the baton to his thesis advisor, Strong (1927) collected additional data and refined the contrast groups method. Strong compared the responses of people in each occupation (the criterion group) with people in general (i.e., in other, diverse occupations). Items that best differentiated the criterion group were used to create a similarity score for the respondent to any given occupation. Strong (1935) established predictive validity for the SVIB through longitudinal data collected from Stanford graduates; he would follow this study with another in 1951, with both showing good predictive "hit" rates. Strong had proposed interests are very stable – virtually over a lifetime – an assertion that has been borne out with vocational interest profiles taken decades apart.[5]

The SVIB has been updated several times with most revisions expanding the number of occupations and adding new scales. The SVIB Men's form indexed 34 occupations in the 1938 revision[6] whereas the 1966 revision used 54 occupations. The SVIB-W revisions in 1946 and 1968 created parallel forms to the SVIB-M. Further changes in the 1960s added basic interest scales to both forms. These scales measure interest in general areas such as mathematics or writing.

After considerable public controversy in the 1970s regarding separate forms for men and women – they were printed on blue and pink paper, respectively – the two were merged into one and renamed the Strong–Campbell Interest Inventory (SCII), acknowledging Campbell's contributions to that revision. Controversy erupted again in 1983 when Stanford University Press and Campbell disagreed on the rights to future development of the SCII. After a protracted court battle, Campbell withdrew his name (Campbell, 2002).[7]

E. K. Strong Jr.'s Legacy

Today, it is virtually impossible to speak of vocational testing or guidance without considering Strong's work. Though other inventories are readily available, the Strong Interest Inventory (SII) is one of the most widely used vocational tests in the world (Nye, 2022). Strong's wish that young men and women searching for a satisfactory career would have a suitable resource for guidance appears to have been well met. Even if aspiring seekers of career advice do not complete the SII, Strong's work laid a solid foundation for the past century of vocational measurement.

The method of contrasted groups championed by Strong is still used to revise occupational scales (Donnay, 1997). Further, this method was adopted by the developers of other measures such as the Minnesota Multiphasic Personality Inventory and the

California Personality Inventory, demonstrating its applicability (Gough, 1956; Hathaway & McKinley, 1943).

During a period when ability testing was predominant, Strong promoted interests as critical in career development. Using a boat metaphor, he wrote: "The motor (abilities) determines how fast the boat can go, the rudder (interests) determines which way the boat goes" (Strong, 1943, p. 17). This assertion has stood the test of time – meta-analyses (Nye et al., 2012) show that interests, when added to traditional aptitude measures – improve prediction of career success. When congruence between interests and chosen occupation are considered, correlations are stronger, a finding consonant with current studies in industrial-organizational (I-O) psychology that assess person-job fit (Van Vianen, 2018). Strong thus laid a foundation for this important area of I-O research.

Although Strong himself was not personally interested in developing a theory of occupational interests, his empirical work was eventually merged with the career theory developed by John Holland (Campbell & Holland, 1972). In Holland's model, six personality types – Realistic, Investigative, Artistic, Social, Enterprising, and Conventional – and their combinations are predicated on vocational interests. The Holland hexagon is relevant for guiding people in their career decision making and has been shown to be related to job satisfaction (Hoff et al., 2020) and performance (Nye et al., 2012).

Conclusion

Edward Strong accomplished much during his lifetime – researching how best to advertise, supporting the military in WWI through personnel activities, and assessing the experiences of a targeted minority group. Strong's most enduring legacy, however, is borne of his vocational interest research. Countless career aspirants have been helped by this work – and the legacy continues.

Notes

1 Strong's thesis, "The effect of various types of suggestion upon muscular activity," was published in 1910 in the *Psychological Review* under the banner of the University of California Psychological Laboratory. His advisor, George Malcolm Stratton, founded the lab

in 1896 with brass instruments carried from Leipzig where he earned his PhD with Wundt (MacFarlane, 1952).

2 Strong continued publishing books on selling (1922b) after leaving Columbia.
3 Strong became a consulting editor of the *Journal of Applied Psychology* in 1917, a role he held until 1955.
4 In a 1962 letter to Ralph Berdie, Strong identified David Campbell as a "man really interested in such a project" should Campbell be willing to "devote his time to such an enterprise." Cited in Donnay (1997).
5 From Strong (1951), *r* of .75 over 22 years; Rottinghaus et al. (2007), median rho of .54 over 30 years.
6 A copy is enshrined in the National Museum of American History of the Smithsonian as exemplar of a psychological test. https://americanhistory.si.edu/collections/nmah_1213691
7 Stanford retained rights to the inventory. Campbell subsequently developed the Campbell Interest and Skill Survey.

References

Benjamin, L. T., Jr., & Baker, D. B. (2003). Walter Van Dyke Bingham: Portrait of an industrial psychologist. In G. A. Kimble & M. Wertheimer (Eds.), *Portraits of pioneers in psychology* (Vol. 5; pp. 141–157). Lawrence Erlbaum. https://doi.org/10.4324/9781410607638-15

Bingham, W. (1923). Psychology applied. *The Scientific Monthly*, *16*, 141–159.

Campbell, D. (2002). The history and development of the Campbell Interest and Skill Survey. *Journal of Career Assessment, 10*(2), 150–168. https://doi.org/10.1177/1069072702010002002

Campbell, D. P., & Holland, J. L. (1972). A merger in vocational interest research: Applying Holland's theory to Strong's data. *Journal of Vocational Behavior,* 2(4), 353–376. https://doi.org/10.1016/0001-8791(72)90012-7

Cowdery, K. (1926). Measurement of professional attitudes. *Journal of Personnel Research*, *5*(4), 131–141.

Darley, J. G. (1964). Edward Kellogg Strong, Jr. *Journal of Applied Psychology, 48*(2), 73–74. https://doi.org/10.1037/h0047064

Donnay, D. A. C. (1997). E. K. Strong's legacy and beyond: 70 years of the Strong Interest Inventory. *The Career Development Quarterly*, *46*(1), 2–22. https://doi.org/10.1002/j.2161-0045.1997.tb00688.x

Gough, H. G. (1956). *California Psychological Inventory*. Consulting Psychologists Press.

Hansen, J.-I. (1987). Edward Kellogg Strong, Jr.: First author of the Strong Interest Inventory. *Journal of Counseling and Development, 66*(3), 119–125. https://doi.org/10.1002/j.1556-6676.1987.tb00815.x

Harrington, T., & Long, J. (2013). The history of interest inventories and career assessments in career counseling. *The Career Development Quarterly, 61*(1), 83–92. https://doi.org/10.1002/j.2161-0045.2013.00039.x

Hathaway, S. R., & McKinley, J. C. (1943). *The Minnesota Multiphasic Personality Inventory* (Rev. ed., 2nd printing). University of Minnesota Press.

Hoff, K. A., Song, Q. C., Wee, C. J. M., Phan, W. M. J., & Rounds, J. (2020). Interest fit and job satisfaction: A systematic review and meta-analysis. *Journal of Vocational Behavior, 123*, 1–16. https://doi.org/10.1016/j.jvb.2020.103503

Hollingworth, H. L., & Hollingworth, L. S. (1916). *Vocational psychology: Its problems and methods*. D. Appleton. https://doi.org/10.1037/10729-000

Layton, W. L. (Ed.). (1960). *The Strong Vocational Interest Blank: Research and uses*. University of Minnesota Press. https://doi.org/10.1177/001316446102100454

MacFarlane, J. (1952). *Preliminary notes on the history of the Psychology Department, University of California, 1896–1951*. https://psychology.berkeley.edu/sites/default/files/macfarlane_p1-4.pdf

Nye, C. D. (2022). Assessing interests in the twenty-first-century workforce: Building on a century of interest measurement. *Annual Review of Organizational Psychology and Organizational Behavior, 9*, 415–440. https://doi.org/10.1146/annurev-orgpsych-012420-083120

Nye, C. D., Su, R., Rounds, J., & Drasgow, F. (2012). Vocational interests and performance: Quantitative summary of over 60 years of research. *Perspectives on Psychological Science, 7*(4), 384–403. http://doi.org/10.1177/1745691612449021

Parson, F. (1909). *Choosing a vocation*. Brousson Press.

Rottinghaus, P. J., Coon, K. L., Gaffey, A. R., & Zytowski, D. G. (2007). Thirty-year stability and predictive validity of vocational interests. *Journal of Career Assessment, 15*(1), 5–22. https://doi.org/10.1177/1069072706294517

Strong, E. K., Jr. (1914). The effect of size of advertisements and frequency of their presentations. *Psychological Review, 21*(2), 136. https://doi.org/10.1037/h0072562

Strong, E. K., Jr. (1916). Fatigue, work, and inhibition. *Psychological Bulletin, 13*(11), 430–433. https://doi.org/10.1037/h0070048

Strong, E. K., Jr. (1918). Work of the committee on classification of personnel in the army. *Journal of Applied Psychology*, *2*(2), 130–139. https://doi.org/10.1037/h0074881

Strong, E. K., Jr. (1922a). *Brief introductory psychology for teachers*. Warwick & York.

Strong, E. K., Jr. (1922b). *The psychology of selling life insurance*. Harper & Brothers.

Strong, E.K., Jr. (1927). A vocational interest test. *Educational Record*, *8*, 107–114.

Strong, E. K., Jr. (1933). *Vocational Interest Blank for Women*. Stanford University Press.

Strong, E. K., Jr. (1934). *The second-generation Japanese problem*. Stanford University Press.

Strong, E. K., Jr. (1935). Predictive value of the vocational interest test. *Journal of Educational Psychology*, *26*(5), 331–349. https://doi.org/10.1037/h0062498

Strong, E. K., Jr. (1943). *Vocational interests of men and women*. Stanford University Press.

Strong, E. K., Jr. (1951). Permanence of interest scores over 22 years. *Journal of Applied Psychology*, *35*(2), 89–91. https://doi.org/10.1037/h0054643

Tarbell, D.A.W. (1937). *The story of Carnegie Tech: Being a history of Carnegie Institute of Technology from 1900 to 1935*. Carnegie Institute of Technology.

Van Vianen, A. E. M. (2018). Person–environment fit: A review of its basic tenets. *Annual Review of Organizational Psychology and Organizational Behavior*, *5*, 75–101. https://doi.org/10.1146/annurev-orgpsych-032117-104702

Vinchur, A. J. (2018). *The early years of industrial and organizational psychology*. Cambridge University Press. doi: 10.1017/9781107588608

Chapter 16

Franciszka Baumgarten-Tramer (1883–1970)

Sharon Glazer and Jonna Williams

Franciszka Baumgarten-Tramer was a trailblazing Jewish female psychologist, who was drawn to bridging science and practice. She was a prescient scholar studying topics such as personality traits, source error in testing, leadership, morality, and justice, to name a few. She approached topics that her contemporaries would not dare think of studying, which cost her dearly, as she was never appointed to a professorial role, although she was bestowed an honorary title after her retirement. Baumgarten always made a point to remember those who are voiceless and contextualized most of the works she published. Her contributions to industrial-organizational (I-O) psychology, therefore, reach farther than in her works on personality, aptitude testing, and managerial practices; her works remind us of the fragility of our place in the world and the importance of situating all human conditions in the environment.

Biographical Overview

Franciszka Baumgarten-Tramer, born in Lødz (in Poland) on November 26, 1883, was a pioneering psychologist whose scholarship was "remarkable, sometimes uncomfortable and courageous considering the time" (Daub, 2011, p. 232; google translate). As a woman, a Jew, and an independent thinker, she was a "lone fighter," blazing her own trail in the science and practice of psychology, including I-O psychology (Sprung & Sprung, 1996, p. 188), through to her death in Berne, Switzerland on March 1, 1970.

DOI: 10.4324/9781003403258-16

In this chapter we honor Baumgarten's scholarly approach of contextualizing her writing. Baumgarten grew up experiencing discrimination and oppression by Russians and Polish nationalists because she was Jewish and then, in World War II (WWII), 46 family members, not to mention dozens of academic colleagues, perished in Nazi death camps (Daub, 2011). This loss was the backdrop for Baumgarten-Tramer's (1959) chapter on Jews in psychology who, in the field's first 80 years, had made a profound impact, but whose lives were cut short. Now, 80 years after WWII, Jews are again facing intense antisemitism globally and many lessons can be gleaned from Baumgarten's (1948) piece in which she admonishes German psychologists for their immoral roles in the Shoah. Yet, her astute accounts began even before the Shoah, when she fearlessly raised awareness of those oppressed.

Also not lost on us is that for Baumgarten (1937) "biographies...serve...for finding out any special peculiarities of the mental structure" (p. 147). Indeed, we encountered "special peculiarities." For example, as a child, she was often reprimanded for her inability to focus on her studies; instead, she was curious and observant of her environment. As an adult she also followed her curiosities, taking many interests, whether in human development, international relations, ethics/morality, political and social psychology, or industrial psychology (Baumgarten, 1975; Canziani, 1975). This chapter depicts the life and career of a psychologist who persevered through adversity to bridge psychological theory with practice in I-O psychology.

Early Years

Baumgarten was the eldest of four children in an upper-middle class well-educated family that spoke Polish, Russian, and German (Daub, 2011). Her father owned a glassworks factory (Baumgarten, 1975). Growing up in an industrial city, surrounded by factories, made a strong impression on her. An avid reader, but also a hyperactive child, some referred to Baumgarten as a prodigy (Baumgarten, 1975), a topic she would later study as a scholar. Engrossed in political-revolutionary literature as a teenager, she hoped to enlighten people about improving political conditions and social institutions.

Becoming a Scholar

In 1905, Baumgarten began her studies at the University of Kraków where she learned of psychology and claimed her calling. In 1906, she entered the Sorbonne in Paris for one year, exploring more scientific disciplines (Baumgarten, 1975). Upon her return to Kraków in 1907, Baumgarten worked under Władysław Heinrich, founder of the first experimental psychology laboratory in Poland (Zeidler, 2018). She then (in 1908) also decided to pursue a doctorate at the University of Zurich, Switzerland (Daub, 2011), studying history, philosophy, anthropology, and psychology, because women could not earn doctorates in Poland. In winter 1910/1911, Baumgarten moved to Berlin to study under visiting Harvard professor Hugo Münsterberg (Baumgarten, 1975; Baumgarten-Tramer, 1959). It was then that Baumgarten began to contemplate on the injustices "inflicted" on factory workers "through overwork and low pay" (Baumgarten, 1975, p. 490). Her doctoral dissertation, on Maine de Biran, a French psychologist, under the supervision of Gustav Störring (Daub, 2011; Zeidler, 2018) also inspired her works on the phenomenon of freedom (Baumgarten-Tramer's, 1947). Baumgarten completed her doctoral studies April 1911, graduating magna cum laude (Zeidler, 2018).

Returning to Lødz in 1911 for three years, she co-founded the Polish Society for the Study of Children, but during a holiday in Berlin in 1914, World War I erupted, and she did not return to Poland (Daub, 2011). In Germany, she worked with Otto Lipmann, Curt Piorkowski, and William Stern (Zeidler, 2018) studying, among other topics, how one wins a war. In 1917, she transitioned her research to focus on applied psychology, as influenced by Swiss psychologist Édouard Claparède.

In 1924, Baumgarten moved to Switzerland to marry Moritz Tramer. She affiliated with the University of Bern but struggled to earn the respect of the faculty (Canziani, 1975). By staying connected with her colleagues in Germany, as well as with the International Association of Psychotechnology (IAP, which became the International Association for Applied Psychology in 1955), Baumgarten continued contributing to scientific knowledge. Having firmly established herself as an independent researcher in a male-dominated field, in 1929, she passed her habilitation—the second woman to do so at the university (Daub, 2011)—and became a privatdozent (permitted to teach and examine without a professional appointment; Baumgarten, 1934) of applied psychology in the university's Department of Philosophy (Baumgarten-Tramer, 1934). From then through to her 1953 retirement, Baumgarten offered two-to-three seminars per semester. She also served as head of the psychotechnical department from 1929 to 1953 (Baumgarten-Tramer, 1959). Prior to her retirement, in a July 1952 letter to her department Dean, Baumgarten expressed her frustration over being discriminated against for her approach to research, despite having published at least 140 journal articles, conference proceedings, and monographs, with many translated into 14 languages (Daub, 2011). Although she never had a professional appointment, Baumgarten-Tramer was awarded the title of honorary professor in 1954. Even after retiring, Baumgarten-Tramer contributed to applied psychology by chronicling the scientific contributions of applied psychology and writing on balancing one's own morality in the face of societal pressures (Canziani, 1975).

Contributions to Scientific Research

Baumgarten's research interests in I-O psychology were ahead of her time, by decades. She was among the first to consider sex differences in work experiences, as well as among the first to address mentoring, vocational interests, and professional development of youth (Canziani, 1975). She also inaugurated research on empathetic or sympathetic intuition and later social sensitivity—precursors to emotional intelligence. Her research addressed justice, motives, and attitudes, perspective-taking, psychotechnics, character traits, aptitude testing, job satisfaction, democracy, prejudice, conflict, friendships, obedience, moral education, climate, and professional ethics (Baumgarten, 1952; Baumgarten-Tramer, 1938, 1948; Zeidler, 2018).

Personality Traits and Aptitude Testing

Baumgarten's interest in personality traits at work began in the early 1920s through the 1930s with her studies on child prodigies. Baumgarten-Tramer (1938) lamented on researchers' reticence to conduct experimental research on personality traits, but she forged ahead and linked gratefulness with happiness. Those works were predecessors to positive psychology and emotional labor. She also developed a typology of workers (Canziani, 1975): the work-bound type and life-bound type (akin today to the concept of work centrality). Baumgarten (1952) was among the first to assess a worker's attitude toward work. In her doctoral dissertation, Baumgarten noted that occupational success is not merely a function of job skills and abilities (i.e., suitability), but also how much a person is motivated to fulfill the responsibilities of the occupational role (i.e., inclination). Complementing this revelation, she developed assessments of inclination (Baumgarten, 1959) or, in today's vernacular, vocational interest.

Over time, Baumgarten (1937) included "qualities of character," though she questioned the subjectiveness of assessments of people's character. Baumgarten (1935) designed a technique for evaluating applicants' behaviors while they are preparing and taking a test. In this technique, evaluators are presented a list of potential applicant behaviors and a list of possible interpretations of those behaviors. For example, an applicant's slow approach to a test may be interpreted as the applicant being apathetic, lacking interest in the task, or both. Baumgarten (1948, 1959) also recognized that the work environment and context influence worker behaviors and could adversely affect the reliability of aptitude tests. She recommended increasing rigor and reducing source error in psychological assessment of job applicants, employment testing, selection, and job placement, focusing on worker "qualifications and propensities" (Baumgarten-Tramer, 1934, p. 618) and advocating for alignment between people's vocational interests and their professional aptitudes (Baumgarten, 1948, 1952).

Leadership Behaviors

Other areas Baumgarten (1952, 1959) opined on were goal-setting (e.g., ensuring subordinates serve supervisors' interests), goal acceptance (i.e., ensuring workers internalize employers' interests), and effort (i.e., ensuring workers skills and abilities are fully utilized), while recognizing that good working and psychological conditions influence subordinate performance. Her deliberation on conflicting interests (between person and management) resulting in tension, foreshadowed research on person-organization fit. Fit was thematic in *Democracy and Character* (1947) too, as Baumgarten-Tramer examined democracy from a psychological perspective, asserting that a nation's character and its citizens' characters are mutually dependent.

In *The Psychology of Human Relations in Industry* (1959; 2nd edition), Baumgarten wrote about worker incompliance with management's needs and its consequential "diminution of output, lack of punctuality, and minor damage to tools and manufactured articles" (p. 2; i.e., in present terms: performance, tardiness, and sabotage). She advocated for hiring the right workers and treating them well. Baumgarten's ideas parallel many contemporary topics on leadership, performance management, reward and recognition, interactional justice, and organizational climate. Still, Baumgarten (1959) cautioned that "there is no magical system that is equally valid for all situations and for all kinds of human beings" (pp. 187–188).

Service to Teaching and Profession

In addition to being a scholar, Baumgarten-Tramer was an educator and contributor to professional service (Daub, 2011). She spearheaded an effort to standardize psychology curriculum and "in 1931 [she laid] the foundation of a 'Union for Applied Psychology'" (Canziani, 1975, p. 484). In service to the profession, Claparède, co-founder of the IAP) and its inaugural president (1920 and 1921), invited Baumgarten to join its leadership board in 1922. She served as the secretary from 1947 to 1951 and was the only woman to serve as an officer until 1990 (https://iaapsy.org/about/historyofiaap/).

Humanitarian Injustices

Unfettered by the pressures of her peers during a dark period of antisemitism, Baumgarten used her position as an independent scholar to criticize other psychologists for their immoral behaviors. In her write-up of the 8th International Psychotechnic Congress (of the IAP), held September 1934 in

Prague, Baumgarten-Tramer (1934) addressed injustices Jewish faculty of universities in Germany were enduring, resulting in the IAP creating a new membership category for "representative of world science" (p. 618). She also called for psychologists not to be swayed by trending philosophies of the masses (Baumgarten, 1952; Baumgarten-Tramer, 1934). Unfortunately, in her account of German psychologists during WWII, she found that most who supported National Socialisim were complicit in discrediting Jewish scholars, and "did nothing to oppose Hitler" (Baumgarten-Tramer, 1948, p. 465). She observed that words were manipulated until their "logical meaning...evaporate[d] while at the same time the emotional intensity, the feeling tone, increase[d] tremendously" (Baumgarten-Tramer, 1948, p. 452). Today we see such word manipulations again being used against the Jewish people.

As with humanitarian work psychology today, Baumgarten gave voice to the voiceless. She further leveraged her leadership in the IAP to rebuild it, organizing the Bern conference in 1949, after a 15-year hiatus. Baumgarten (1947) also edited, *Progress of Psychotechnics*, with contributions from colleagues around the world. Paying homage to the past, reflecting on psychologist lives lost and others' country displacements, and looking toward the future, Baumgarten presented the state of the field in the intervening 15 years. Her thoughtfulness over others' experiences is further reflected in her publications on coping with conflict, human tragedies, prejudice, distress, and in her advocacy for use of practical case studies to address ethical and moral work practices (Canziani, 1975).

Legacy

Although, Baumgarten self-proclaimed her work was of little value, we see her as an audacious rule-breaker who did not cower to the norms of society or academia. Instead, she studied people's real experiences within various contexts. She also aimed never to forget those whose voices were dimmed, whether children, workers working in harsh factory conditions, or her colleagues whose lives were cut short. Baumgarten was a trailblazer, not only in her research, but in her treatment of people and issues of the day.

References

Baumgarten, F. (1935). Approach in taking tests: A technique for studying the examinee's behavior. *Occupations: The Vocational Guidance Journal, 14*(2), 115–122.

Baumgarten, F. (1937). Character traits derived from biographies. *Journal of Personality, 6*(2), 147–149.

Baumgarten, F. (Ed.). (1947). *Progress de la psychotechnique*, 1939-1945 [*Progress of psychotechnics, I. 1939–1945*]. A. Francke.

Baumgarten, F. (1948). Le caractère et la psychotechnique [Character and psychotechnique]. *Le Travail Humain* [*Human Work*], *11e*(3/4), 153–163. www.jstor.org/stable/40658826

Baumgarten, F. (1952). A proverb test for attitude measurement. *Personnel Psychology, 5*(4), 249–261. https://doi.org/10.1111/j.1744-6570.1952.tb01017.x

Baumgarten, F. (1959). *The psychology of human relations in industry*. Pitman.

Baumgarten, F. (1975). II. Autobiographical notes: Prof. Dr. Franziska Baumgarten. *Perceptual and Motor Skills, 41*(2), 487–490.

Baumgarten-Tramer, F. (1934). The Eighth International Psychotechnics Congress, Prague, September 11–15, 1934. *Journal of Applied Psychology, 18*(5), 617–618, 656, 695–696.

Baumgarten-Tramer, F. (1938). "Gratefulness" in children and young people. *Journal of Genetic Psychology, 53*, 53–66.

Baumgarten-Tramer, F. (1947). Democracy and character. *British Journal of Psychology, 38*, 20–22.

Baumgarten-Tramer, F. (1948). German psychologists and recent events. Translated by Wyatt, F., & Wyatt, G. *Journal of Abnormal and Social Psychology, 43*, 452–465. https://doi.org/10.1037/h0062777

Baumgarten-Tramer, F. (1959). Psychologie [Psychology]. In S. Kaznelson (Ed.), *Juden im deutschen Kulturbereich; ein Sammelwerk*. [*Jews in the German cultural area: A collection*] (pp. 282–292). Jüdischer Verlag.

Canziani, W. (1975) Contributions to the history of psychology: XXIII. I. Franziska Baumgarten-Tramer (11/26/86-3/1/70). *Perceptual and Motor Skills, 41*, 479–486.

Daub, E. (2011). Franziska Baumgarten-Tramer: Für die Wissenschaftlichkeit praktischer Psychologie. [For the scientific nature of practical psychology]. In S. Volkmann-Raue, & H. E. Lück (Eds.), *Bedeutende Psychologinnen des 20. Jahrhunderts* [*Important Psychologists of the 20th Century*] (pp. 223–234). VS Verlag. https://doi.org/10.1007/978-3-531-93064-0_17

Sprung, L., & Sprung, H. (1996). Women in psychological and women's lecturing activities at German psychology Congress 1904-1978. *Revista de Historia de la Psicología, 17*(1–2), 185–202.

Zeidler, W. (2018). *Psychologia i Psychotechnika w Twórczości Franciszki Baumgarten. [Psychology and psychotechnics in the works of Franciszka Baumgarten*]. Liberi Libri.

Chapter 17

Bernard Muscio (1887–1926)

Mengting (Rachel) Xia and Mark Griffin

Bernard Muscio was a distinguished philosopher and pioneering industrial-organizational (I-O) psychologist. Despite his significant contributions, he is often forgotten in the field of I-O psychology due to his strong footprint in philosophy. His groundbreaking publication, *Lectures of Industrial Psychology*, marked the earliest statement on the aims and value of I-O psychology in Great Britain and Australia. His work has left an indelible mark in the history of I-O psychology, cementing his legacy as an influencing figure in the field.

Biographical Overview

Bernard Muscio, an Australian I-O psychologist, was born in 1887 in New South Wales. He married Florence Mildred Fry in 1915 and passed away at his Potts Point home in Sydney in 1926 (O'Neil, n.d.). Muscio's career spanned Sydney and Cambridge, involving both philosophy and psychology. He was acknowledged as a seminal figure in the development of I-O psychology throughout the British Empire by C. S. Myers, the first British psychologist to specialize in I-O psychology (Anderson, 1926).

Muscio's journey into psychology and philosophy began with a solid foundation in logic and mental philosophy. Graduating with first-class honours with both bachelor's and master's degrees from the University of Sydney, he then pursued postgraduate studies at Cambridge University, under the supervision of James Ward in philosophy and C. S. Myers in psychology. At Cambridge, he earned his research degree and won the Burney Prize for the thesis "Idealism and the Neo-realism." A pivotal shift in his career occurred during the outbreak of World

DOI: 10.4324/9781003403258-17

War I (WWI) – rejected for military service, Muscio served as a Demonstrator in Experimental Psychology at Cambridge University from 1914 to 1916. As later recognized by James Ward, the distinguished Cambridge philosopher, "circumstances – partly due to the war – have diverted him to working at experimental psychology, and there he has certainly made his mark." (Anderson, 1926, p. 158).

In the next five years, from 1916 to 1921, Muscio made significant contributions to I-O psychology. He inherited the empiricist approach from British philosophy, which manifested in his commitment to statistical and psychometric techniques to measure individual differences. In 1916, he published his first psychological paper in the *British Journal of Psychology*, entitled "The Influence of the Form of a Question" (Muscio, 1916), a long experimental report on the study of questioning. From 1916 to 1919, Muscio returned to Sydney and acted as a Lecturer in Psychology and Philosophy at the University of Sydney[1] (Anderson, 1926). He delivered lectures on developments in applied psychology in the United States (U.S.), Britain, and Europe and published *Lectures on Industrial Psychology* (Muscio, 1917), a pioneering work that became the earliest statement that emphasized the aims and value of I-O psychology for practical industrial problems in the British Empire.

In 1919, he returned to Cambridge as the Organizing Secretary and Lecturer for the Industrial Fatigue Research Board (Anderson, 1926). In 1921, he joined the newly formed National Institute of Industrial Psychology, conducting investigations and serving on the Institute's Scientific Committee (Landauer & Cross, 1971). Over this period from 1919 to 1921, Muscio established a strong association with I-O psychology. He contributed nine research reports for the Board, incorporating surveys, experimental studies, and fieldwork analyses, some of which were published in the *British Journal of Psychology*. His work significantly advanced the field of I-O psychology, challenging prevailing notions of fatigue, exploring mental fatigue, and unravelling the multifaceted nature of fatigue (Muscio, 1921a, 1921b, 1922b; Muscio & Brooke, 1922). He also investigated the use of psychological tests in vocational guidance for both factory occupations and office occupations (Muscio, 1921c, 1922a, 1922c; Muscio &

Eyre, 1922; Muscio & Sowton, 1923), some of the earliest studies within this field.

In 1922, Muscio accepted the Challis chair of philosophy at the University of Sydney, returning to his roots as a Professor of Philosophy. Despite this shift, his interest in I-O psychology persisted; he believed in the development of psychological theory and the philosophical basis of Realism (Muscio, 1923), leading him to co-found and serve as the inaugural president of the Australasian Association of Psychology and Philosophy in 1923 (Anderson, 1926).

Contributions to I-O Psychology

Bernard Muscio's contributions to I-O psychology encompassed a diverse range of endeavours, from advancing empirical approaches and establishing the early views on the aims and value of I-O psychology to reshaping perspectives on fatigue and efficiency in the workplace.

The Earliest to Address the Value of I-O Psychology

Muscio's groundbreaking work in I-O psychology began with his influential series of lectures on industrial psychology in 1916 and 1917. In these lectures, he integrated recent empirical work from the US, Britain, and Europe, covering topics such as work methods, motion study, fatigue, and vocational selection. These lectures were later compiled into a seminal book, *Lectures on Industrial Psychology*, published in Sydney in 1917 (Muscio, 1917) and reprinted in London in 1920. This publication was the first book in the world to include "Industrial Psychology" in the title and advocated for the application of psychology in industry, education, law, and medicine (Salgado, 2001).

In his lectures, Muscio (1917) emphasized the nature of I-O psychology as an applied science. He urged the implementation of empirical approaches, which involve the precise application of psychological knowledge within the framework of experimental psychology, stressing the importance of observation, hypothesis formulation, and systematic testing. He also stated the aim of I-O psychology is the utilization of psychological knowledge in "selecting workers on the basis of natural fitness and creating methods of work, for purposes of obtaining from any expenditure of human energy or effort a maximum production" (Muscio, 1917, p. 26).

Central to Muscio's vision of I-O psychology was his recognition of the mutual benefits of I-O psychology for both employer and employee. His work reshaped the landscape of practical applications of psychology in the early 20th century[2], redirecting the focus from mechanical efficiency to the conservation of human energy. Muscio (1917) not only highlighted individual self-assessment as essential for creating an efficient workforce while minimizing wasted human energy but also argued that attempts to increase productivity through simplistic "speed-up" incentives alone were futile without concurrent improvements in work methods.

Overall, Muscio's lectures laid the groundwork for I-O psychology in Great Britain and Australia, emphasizing its nature of applied science, consideration of individual differences, and the interconnectedness of employer and employee well-being.

Conceptual and Empirical Approach to Fatigue and Fatigue Tests

Muscio's work was among the first to systematically define aspects of fatigue and propose fatigue tests (Landauer & Cross, 1971). While on the Industrial Fatigue Research Board at Cambridge University, Muscio advocated for a nuanced understanding of fatigue that considers both mental and physiological dimensions, making significant theoretical and experimental contributions to future research on fatigue and associated topics such as information overload and optimal stress.

Theoretically, Muscio's work challenged the prevailing belief that fatigue was solely physio-chemical, cautioning against the detrimental effects of overworking in the pursuit of efficiency. Muscio defined fatigue as "a condition caused by activity in which output produced by that activity tends to be relatively poor and the degree of fatigue tends to vary directly with the poorness of output" (1921b, p. 40). He highlighted a nuanced interplay between mental and physiological factors and advocated for the understanding of conservation of human energy and the limitations of individual energy consumption.

Experimentally, Muscio explored fatigue tests but questioned their precision, suggesting that the term "fatigue" should be avoided in scientific discussions. He believed that fatigue was a complex phenomenon, and the characteristic expression of fatigue (diminished capacity) was vague and ambiguous (Muscio, 1921b). His views on fatigue significantly influenced later researchers and aligned with conclusions regarding behavioural fatigue in contemporary psychology.

Conclusion

Bernard Muscio's work ignited a paradigm shift in the understanding of the human element in industrial settings. His groundbreaking contributions – from his influential lectures and pioneering publications to his empirical studies and innovative approaches to fatigue and vocational selection – significantly advanced the development of I-O psychology in Great Britain and Australia. Muscio's empirical rigor, commitment to holistic well-being, and vision of I-O psychology as an applied science continue to influence the field of I-O psychology today.

Notes

1 In most early 20th Australian universities, psychology grew up within departments of philosophy, with many individuals involved in both inquiries (Turtle, 1995).
2 Influenced by World War I, this was a time of a zest for the efficiency movement in industrial practices.

References

Anderson, F. (1926). In memoriam – Bernard Muscio. *Australasian Journal of Psychology and Philosophy*, *4*(3), 157–159. https://doi.org/10.1080/00048402608540795

Landauer, A. A., & Cross, M. J. (1971). A forgotten Australian: Muscio's contribution to industrial psychology. *Australian Journal of Psychology*, *23*(3), 235–240. https://doi.org/10.1080/00049537108254617

Muscio, B. (1916). The influence of the form of a question. *British Journal of Psychology*, 1904-1920, *8*(3), 351–389. https://doi.org/10.1111/j.2044-8295.1916.tb00138.x

Muscio, B. (1917). *Lectures on industrial psychology*. Angus & Robertson.

Muscio, B. (1920). *Lectures on industrial psychology* (2nd ed.). Routledge.

Muscio, B. (1921a). Feeling-tone in industry: A report to the Industrial Fatigue Research Board. *British Journal of Psychology. General Section*, *12*(2), 150–162. https://doi.org/10.1111/j.2044-8295.1921.tb00047.x

Muscio, B. (1921b). Is a fatigue test possible? *British Journal of Psychology. General Section*, *12*(1), 31–46. https://doi.org/10.1111/j.2044-8295.1921.tb00036.x

Muscio, B. (1921c). Vocational guidance: A review of the literature. *Industrial Fatigue Research Board Reports*, *12*, 5–57.

Muscio, B. (1922a). Motor capacity with special reference to vocational guidance. *British Journal of Psychology. General Section*, *13*(2), 157–184. https://doi.org/10.1111/j.2044-8295.1922.tb00091.x

Muscio, B. (1922b). On the relation of fatigue and accuracy to speed and duration of work. *Industrial Fatigue Research Board Reports*, *19*, 18–37.

Muscio, B. (1922c). The psycho-physiological capacities required by the hand compositor. *Industrial Fatigue Research Board Reports*, *16*, 5–37.

Muscio, B. (1923). The meaning of philosophy (I.). *Australasian Journal of Psychology and Philosophy*, *1*(4), 235–240. https://doi.org/10.1080/00048402308540643

Muscio, B., & Brooke, R. S. C. (1922). An investigation into the packing of chocolates (II). *Journal of National Institute of Industrial Psychology*, *1*, 68–75.

Muscio, B., & Eyre, A. (1922). Measurements of physical strength with reference to vocational guidance. *Section B, Report of* Industrial Fatigue Research Board London, 38–73.

Muscio, B., & Sowton, S. C. M. (1923). Vocational tests and typewriting. *British Journal of Psychology. General Section*, *13*(4), 344–369. https://doi.org/10.1111/j.2044-8295.1923.tb01162.x

O'Neil, W. M. (n.d.). Muscio, Bernard (1887–1926). In *Australian dictionary of biography* (pp. 1–18). National Centre of Biography, Australian National University. Retrieved September 15, 2023, from https://adb.anu.edu.au/biography/muscio-bernard-7714

Salgado, J. F. (2001). Some landmarks of 100 years of scientific personnel selection at the beginning of the new century. *International Journal of Selection and Assessment*, *9*(1–2), 3–8. https://doi.org/10.1111/1468-2389.00159

Turtle, A. M. (1995). The forerunners and foundation of the *Australian Journal of Psychology*. *Australian Journal of Psychology*, *47*(3), 123–127. https://doi.org/10.1080/00049539508257512

Chapter 18

Louis Leon Thurstone (1887–1955)

Nathan T. Carter

> Thurstone was forever interested in applying psychological methods to practical problems...
>
> (Wolfe, 1956)

Louis Leon Thurstone pioneering work in psychometrics and factor analysis reshaped psychology. He challenged prevailing notions with innovations like the Law of Comparative Judgment, which quantified subjective evaluations. His work introduced statistical techniques to measuring attitudes, influencing fields from job satisfaction to personality assessment to performance measurement. As president of the American Psychological Association (APA) and the Psychometric Society, Thurstone advocated for rigorous, quantitative methods in psychology. His legacy includes advancing factor analysis, advocating for subfactors beyond a general intelligence factor, and emphasizing complex structures in data interpretation. Thurstone's later career at the University of Chicago and University of North Carolina underscored his commitment to integrating theory and practice. His impact on industrial-organizational (I-O) psychology remains profound, which is evident in our field's contemporary assessment tools and methodologies. Thurstone's contributions continue to resonate across psychological disciplines, exemplifying a lifelong dedication to scientific rigor and the practical application of our scientific understanding of human behavior.

DOI: 10.4324/9781003403258-18

Biographical Overview

Early Life and Engineering Career

Louis Leon Thurstone was born in Chicago, IL on May 29, 1887, to Sophie (née Ströth) and Conrad Thurstone, who would later change the family name from the original Thunström. The family emigrated to the United States (US) from Sweden, where Conrad had been an instructor in the Swedish military. Later, Conrad would take up occupation as a Lutheran minister, newspaper editor, and publisher, while Sophie was interested in music, teaching Louis and his younger sister Adele piano. The family moved several times during his elementary education years, settling in Jamestown, NY. While in Jamestown, Thurstone was awarded a prize for geometry, perhaps foreshadowing his novel use of geometric expressions of psychological constructs. With this prize money of $30, Thurstone purchased a Kodak camera, beginning his lifelong interest in photography. His next feat was his first publication in the *Scientific American* as a high school sophomore titled "How to Save Niagara" (Thunström, 1905).

Louis would enroll at Cornell University and study engineering, where he would learn to write out a method for trisecting any angle into an equation that he would later publish, again in *Scientific American* (Thurstone, 1912). But perhaps the most impactful influence on a young Thurstone was his machine design class, in which he began to recognize the importance of understanding the human element of machine design. In particular, he was interested in how humans' limitations interfere with their use of machines. This led to an interest in the progression of human learning, and at Cornell, Thurstone attended lectures in psychology, notably one by Edward Titchener, a leading thinker in the area of the psychology of learning at the time. Thurstone noted about Titchener "I remember being interested in his lecture, but curious about his extremely formal and pompous nature" (Thurstone, 1952a, p. 298).

While at Cornell, Thurstone had invented a method for eradicating flickering from motion picture films, which was a major problem at the time. He later presented the model to Thomas

Edison's lab in East Orange, NJ. Although they declined to utilize his model, Thurstone was offered an apprenticeship, and worked on similar problems for Edison until 1912, when he accepted a lecturer position in engineering at the University of Minnesota. Thurstone's interests continued to lean toward human learning, and in 1914 he moved to the University of Chicago to pursue graduate education in psychology.

The Engineer Becomes Psychologist

Thurstone had some interesting observations regarding his first year, including that graduate students seemed to be able to "... talk fluently, even when they clearly knew nothing about the subject," that upon taking an "advanced" educational psychology course it made him wonder "what the elementary course could be like," and that "One of my accomplishments during that year was to learn how to carry five soup plates over my head through the swinging doors of the University Commons," where Thurstone worked as a waiter (Thurstone, 1952a, p. 300). Thurstone's intellectual fortune would soon turn when in 1915 Walter Bingham from Carnegie Institute of Technology (CIT) – now Carnegie Mellon – interviewed graduate students to be assistants with the goal of establishing the first applied psychology laboratory in the US. In addition to graduating from the University of Chicago in 1917, while at Carnegie Mellon Thurstone would work on test development for the US Military in World War I. In addition, he wrote the monograph *The Nature of Intelligence* (Thurstone, 1924). The Division of Applied Psychology at CIT, according to Thurstone, fell out of favor with the university, and in 1923 he spent a year in Washington, D.C., writing test manuals for civil service positions at the Institute for Government Research.

In 1924, Thurstone returned to his birthplace of Chicago and married Thelma Gwinn, whom he met as a fellow graduate student at the University of Chicago when he would return from the Carnegie Institute to teach. During his time as a faculty member at Chicago he would conduct the majority of his most influential work. His work on understanding the scaling of intelligence in a scientific manner, including the problem of the "mental age" concept inherent to the Stanford-Binet (Thurstone, 1926), and the identification of an absolute zero began (Thurstone, 1952a; Thurstone, 1928a).[1] He also began to attempt to correct the dearth of comprehensive theory on psychological measurement, more generally, particularly in his foundational article "A Method for Scaling Educational and Psychological Tests" (Thurstone, 1925), which he considered to be among his best work. However, just before his death, Thurstone was still bemoaning the fact that little in the way of comprehensive texts on measurement theory had been produced (Thurstone, 1952a), other than Gulliksen (1950). Thurstone also made major advances in psychophysics as well which he called "psychological measurement proper" (Thurstone, 1952a, p. 306), including a law of comparative judgment (Thurstone, 1927). Rather than physical attributes – such as lifting of weights – Thurstone utilized the cases of social judgments – such as the relative seriousness of certain crimes. Thus, his theories were generalizable to many applications areas such as decision-making, and attitude measurement.

Attitude Measurement and Factor Analysis

In 1928, Thurstone published an article with the audacious but appropriate title "Attitudes Can Be Measured" (1928b). Critics claimed social attitudes by their nature were unmeasurable. That did not stop Thurstone. He utilized his technique – which involved asking hundreds of subjects to place statements on an attitude continuum ranging between the extremes of the attitude level they reflected. Items with high variability in raters' scale assignments were discarded. Armed with median estimates on a scale of say 0–9 that reflected the extremity of the statements themselves, one can then administer those statements, asking persons to agree or disagree. If you agree with a statement, it is added to your score average, and if you disagree, it is ignored. Thus, someone whom – for example – agrees with moderately-worded statements is moderate in the attitude. Thurstone indeed created many attitude scales on a variety of topics to study social psychological issues. For example, he and his students showed that viewing of *A Birth of a Nation*, a film which portrays the Ku Klux Klan as heroes, made high school students have less favorable attitudes toward African Americans. Moreover, he was able to demonstrate a "summation effect" in that if viewing such films does not have a noticeable impact on one viewing, that multiple views will generally show an effect on attitude levels (Peterson & Thurstone, 1932). As he notes in his autobiography, this is a vital concept to understanding the operation and effects of propaganda campaigns (Thurstone, 1952a).

In the 1930s, Thurstone began work on what is perhaps his most enduring legacy: factor analysis. As noted by Guilford (1955), although Thurstone did not invent factor analysis, the method as contemporary psychologists know it was developed at least in part by Thurstone. Thurstone would argue for and develop methods for uncovering multiple "group" factors of intelligence – i.e., factors comprising of "groups" of observed scores that he believed cannot be ignored – rather than focusing only on a general factor. Indeed, he invented methods as foundational as the communality, uniqueness, and the rotation of factors with the goal of simple structure, including oblique factor rotation, which allows for factors to intercorrelate. Indeed, the idea that general intelligence is likely a second-order factor with unignorable first-order factors originated with Thurstone, and one that resonates in most intelligence tests to date.

In 1932, Thurstone became the President of the APA, where his address (see Thurstone, 1934) was largely focused on factor analysis and the dimensions of intelligence. In 1936, he was named President of the Psychometric Society. It was this later address in which he laid out his vision of psychology as a "quantitative, rational science" (see Thurstone, 1937). In the 1940s he continued to apply and extend his factor analytic and scaling methods, including the publishing and application of tests in vocational and educational settings. Thurstone's productivity at this time was likely aided by the Wednesday research talks he and Thelma held in their home's comfortable study, where Swedish pastry and coffee were served. In attendance were invited colleagues and graduate students, including visiting speakers (Wolfe, 1956).

Retirement and Legacy

In 1948–1949, Thurstone and his wife Thelma were appointed as visiting professors at the University of Frankfurt to – in his own words – "help, even in a very small way, to repair what is left after the physical and moral destruction in Europe" (Thurstone, 1952a, p. 319). Notably, the Thurstones were told the books they brought with them were the first to reach their laboratory from outside the country since the beginning of World War II. Thurstone's international legacy was further cemented by hosting students from around the world, including China, Spain, and South Africa (Thurstone, 1952a). In 1952, Thurstone retired from the University of Chicago, and moved to the University of North Carolina at Chapel Hill, where he was appointed a Research Professor and Director of the Psychometric Laboratory. Thurstone passed away on September 29, 1955.

Thurstone's legacy for psychology can be found all throughout his career. As a graduate student, he worked on early military applications of intelligence testing, and later worked as a practitioner in writing technical manuals for civil service examinations. His theoretical work on intelligence would have far-reaching effects on many subfields of psychology, but few were more affected than I-O psychology, and the field continues to be affected by his work. As Cortina et al. (2017) noted, Thurstone's 1919 article in the *Journal of Applied Psychology* regarding the relationship between dimensions of intelligence and telegraphy speed produced results that are mirrored in the contemporary literature. Thurstone (1922) investigated a curious trend among intelligence test scores of police, in which it was found in Detroit that officers showed considerably lower scores than those on patrol, whereas those in Cleveland showed no discernable difference between ranks (his analyses suggested it was likely due to those with high intelligence leaving the career early enough that they did not have the chance at promotion). As noted by Guion (2004), Thurstone and Chave's (1929) method of equal-appearing intervals for attitude measurement was the basis for Behaviorally Anchored Ratings Scales (BARS) (Smith & Kendall, 1963), a method of performance measurement ubiquitous within I-O psychology. His methods of attitude scaling were also instrumental to the development of early job satisfaction measures, including seminal works by Kornhauser (1933), Hoppock and Stiegler (1938), and later influenced the Job Descriptive Index (Smith et al., 1969), a hallmark in the measurement of job satisfaction. Late in his career, Thurstone (1952b) edited a book entitled *Applications of Psychology*, which contained book chapters regarding testing in the military, attitude measurement in personnel settings, and creative talent.

Although Thurstone did not do much in the way of studying personality (Thurstone, 1952a), his most recent impact has been in the area of personality assessment, particularly in I-O psychology circles. Item response models inspired by his method of attitude scaling (see Roberts et al., 2000) – in which statements are distributed all across the continuum rather than extreme statements reflecting high and low attribute levels – have been shown to better capture how persons respond to personality self-reports, resulting in articles suggesting "75 Years After Likert: Thurstone Was Right!" (Chernyshenko & Stark, 2010), to allow for precision of measurement high enough to reliably detect nonlinear personality-performance links (Carter et al., 2014), and have been the basis for Army testing via the Tailored Adaptive Personality Assessment System (TAPAS; Drasgow et al., 2023).

Conclusion

Thurstone's legacy in I-O psychology – and in the social sciences more broadly – has been enormous. In addition to his direct contributions to I-O psychology listed above, the more indirect impacts have been innumerable. For example, any time a factor is rotated, or a second-order factor is proposed and estimated, Thurstone is invoked, be it explicitly or implicitly. With the aid of his contributions, I-O psychology continues to evolve toward the goal of being a quantitative, rational science. In doing so, Thurstone always placed great emphasis on the practicality of a solid theoretical bedrock, mirroring the ideal of the scientist-practitioner duality.

Note

1 Thurstone (1928a) specified absolute zero as the level of test performance in an age group wherein variability in test scores vanishes; that is, in plotting a linear relation between mean test scores and the absolute deviation in those same scores, one can indirectly extrapolate the

mean test score at which variability would be equal to 0 for a given age group.

References

Carter, N.T., Dalal, D.K., Boyce, A.S., O'Connell, M.S., Kung, M-C., & Delgado, K.M. (2014). Uncovering curvilinear relationships between conscientiousness and job performance: How theoretically appropriate measurement makes a difference. *Journal of Applied Psychology*, *99*, 564–586. https://doi.org/10.1037/a0034688

Chernyshenko, O.S., & Stark, S. (2010). 75 years after Likert: Thurstone was right! *Industrial and Organizational Psychology: Perspectives on Science and Practice*, *3*, 465–476. https://doi.org/10.1111/j.1754-9434.2010.01273.x

Cortina, J.M., Aguinis, H., & DeShon, R.P. (2017). Twilight of dawn or of evening? A century of research methods in the *Journal of Applied Psychology*. *Journal of Applied Psychology*, *102*, 274–290. https://doi.org/10.1037/apl0000163

Drasgow, F., Chernyshenko, O.S., Stark, S., & Nye, C. (2023). *Tailored adaptive personality assessment system (TAPAS) pre-implementation documentation* [Technical report]. U.S Air Force.

Guilford, J.P. (1955). Louis Leon Thurstone. *Psychometrika*, *20*, 263–265. https://doi.org/10.1007/bf02289032

Guion, R.M. (2004). Validity and reliability. In S.G. Rogelberg (Ed.), *Handbook of research methods in industrial-organizational psychology* (pp. 57–76). Blackwell. https://doi.org/10.1002/9780470756669.ch3

Gulliksen, H. (1950). *Theory of mental tests*. Wiley. https://doi.org/10.1037/13240-000

Hoppock, R., & Spiegler, S. (1938). Job satisfaction: Researches of 1935–1937. *Occupations*, *16*, 636–643. https://doi.org/10.1002/j.2164-5892.1938.tb00348.x

Kornhauser, A. (1933). The technique of measuring employee attitudes. *Personnel Journal*, *9*, 99–107.

Peterson, R. C. & Thurstone, L. L. (1932). The effect of motion pictures on the attitudes of high school children, In R. C. Peterson & L. L. Thurstone (Eds.), *Motion pictures and the social attitudes of children* (pp. 62–63). Macmillan. https://doi.org/10.1037/14715-000

Roberts, J.S., Donoghue, J.R., & Laughlin, J.E. (2000). A general item response theory model for unfolding unidimensional polytomous response models. *Applied Psychological Measurement*, *24*, 3–32. https://doi.org/10.1177/01466216000241001

Smith, P.C., & Kendall, L.M. (1963). Retranslation of expectations: An approach to the construction of unambiguous anchors for rating scales. *Journal of Applied Psychology*, *47*, 149–155. https://doi.org/10.1037/h0047060

Smith, P.C., Kendall, L.M., & Hulin, C.L. (1969). *The measurement of satisfaction in work and retirement: A strategy for the study of attitudes*. Rand-McNally.

Thunström, L.L. (1905). How to save Niagara. *Scientific American*, *93*, 27.

Thurstone, L.L. (1912). A curve which trisects any angle: A modern solution of a classical problem. *Scientific American*, *73*, 259.

Thurstone, L.L. (1919). The learning curve equation. *Psychological Monographs*, *26*, 1–51. https://doi.org/10.1037/h0093187

Thurstone, L.L. (1922). The intelligence of policemen. *Journal of Personnel Research*, *1*, 64–74.

Thurstone, L.L. (1924). *The nature of intelligence*. Harcourt Brace & Company. https://doi.org/10.1037/11388-000

Thurstone, L.L. (1925). A method of scaling psychological and educational tests. *Journal of Educational Psychology*, *16*, 433–451. https://doi.org/10.1037/h0073357

Thurstone, L.L. (1926). The mental age concept. *Psychological Review*, *33*, 268–278. https://doi.org/10.1037/h0072344

Thurstone, L.L. (1927). A law of comparative judgment. *Psychological Review*, *33*, 268–278. https://doi.org/10.1037/h0070288

Thurstone, L.L. (1928a). The absolute zero in intelligence measurement. *Psychological Review*, *35*, 175–197. https://doi.org/10.1037/h0072902

Thurstone, L.L. (1928b). Attitudes can be measured. *American Journal of Sociology*, *33*, 529–554. https://doi.org/10.1086/214483

Thurstone, L.L. (1934). The vectors of mind. *Psychological Review*, *41*, 1–32. https://doi.org/10.1037/h0075959

Thurstone, L.L. (1937). Psychology as a quantitative, rational science. *Science*, *85*, 227–232. https://doi.org/10.1126/science.85.2201.227

Thurstone, L. L. (1952a). L. L. Thurstone. In E. G. Boring, H. Werner, H. S. Langfeld, & R. M. Yerkes (Eds.), *A history of psychology in autobiography*, Vol. 4 (pp. 295–321). Clark University Press. https://doi.org/10.1037/11154-014

Thurstone, L.L. (1952b). *Applications of psychology*. Harper & Brothers.

Thurstone, L.L., & Chave, E.J. (1929). *The measurement of attitude*. University of Chicago Press. https://doi.org/10.1037/11574-000

Wolfe, D. (1956). Louis Leon Thurstone (1887-1955). *American Journal of Psychology*, *69*, 131–134.

Chapter 19

Marion Almira Bills (1889–1970)

Laura Koppes Bryan

As a scientist-practitioner throughout her career, Marion Almira Bills identified organizational needs, conducted empirical research in business settings, and recommended specific changes to improve organizational processes. Her research primarily focused on selection, classification methods, compensation, and job permanency, cutting edge topics of the time. Bills was a leading advocate for psychologists in industry and played a critical role in bringing together individuals who were applying psychology in industry during the early years of industrial and organizational (I-O) psychology.

Biographical Overview

Marion Almira Bills was born in Allegan, MI, on July 5, 1889; her parents were Martha Rood and Walter H. Bills. She earned a bachelor's degree in 1908 from the University of Michigan and then enrolled in the experimental psychology doctoral program at Bryn Mawr College, where she completed her PhD in 1917 (Bills, 1920). After completing her doctorate, she was a professor at Miami University (Oxford, Ohio) from 1917 to 1918, and an associate professor of psychology at the University of Kansas from 1918 to 1919. Shortly thereafter, Bills began a successful career in business using psychological research methods to study industry issues (Koppes, 1997; Koppes & Bauer, 2006; Vinchur & Koppes Bryan, 2021). Walter Van Dyke Bingham hired Bills as a research assistant for the Bureau of Personnel Research (BPR), a unit of the Division of Applied Psychology (DAP) that was established in 1915 with Bingham as the director to promote

DOI: 10.4324/9781003403258-19

applied psychology at the Carnegie Institute of Technology (CIT) (now Carnegie-Mellon University) (Hilgard, 1987). From 1919 to 1923, Bills was an associate director to consult businesses on office management, selection, training, and supervision. She continued to work as a consultant between 1922 and 1925 when the BPR became the Life Insurance Sales Research Bureau and relocated to Hartford, Connecticut.

In 1926, Bills joined Aetna Life Insurance Company (later known as Aetna Life Affiliated Companies) as an assistant secretary only if she were made a voting officer (Patricia Cain Smith, personal communication, June 14, 1996). After a long and successful 30-year career with Aetna (retirement in 1955), Bills was diagnosed with Parkinson's disease and passed away in 1970 in Hartford. She did not marry (Patricia Cain Smith, personal communication, June 14, 1996).

Contributions to I-O Psychology

Based on previous work (Koppes, 1997; Koppes & Bauer, 2006), I highlight three areas for which Bills is recognized.

Research Pioneer in Industry

Bills advocated that a scientific approach would improve each person's work and thus, believed in using empirical research methods to solve business and industry problems. Her research samples were typically large, the measures were of top quality for the time period, the analyses were suitable, and her discussions were thoughtful and reasoned (Austin & Waung, 1994). While working for the BPR, Bills researched three primary areas: selection, job permanency, and compensation. She conducted extensive selection research of clerical and sales personnel for the life insurance industry throughout her career at Aetna; this research was considered one of the first congenial collaborations between business individuals and psychologists (Ferguson, 1952).

One frequently cited study was about the selection of comptometer (a calculating machine) operators and stenographers (Bills & Yoakum, 1921). This study had two purposes. One purpose was to determine whether tests could be used to select applicants for technical school courses in stenography and comptometer operation. The second purpose was to examine whether successful comptometer and stenographic operators could be selected from this applicant group. Bills discovered that it was best to select successes and eliminate failures from a battery of tests rather than from a single examination. Particularly noteworthy was that Bills studied multiple predictors for selection decisions and examined the use of critical scores for assessing the validity of tests in selection, not typical practices of the time.

Another example of Bills' selection research was a study on selection predictors, including scores on the Strong Vocational Interest Blank, the Bernreuter Personality Inventory, a personal history blank, and a mental alertness test (Bills, 1941). These scores were compared to managers' ratings of productivity, ranging from outstanding, probably successful, to probably failure. Bills determined that a predictor's utility will vary by the variable of interest. As an example, items on the Strong Vocational Interest Blank were worse predictors for younger groups and better predictors for individuals over 30 years of age.

The focus of Bills' research on "permanency," which she labeled and is now known as retention or turnover, was the identification of factors that predicted length of service in a job (e.g., Bills, 1923a). Some factors that she studied included gender, age at employment, social status, mental alertness, and achievement orientation. Similar to her selection research, Bills applied the results of the job permanency studies; she used job difficulty level and mental alertness scores when selecting clerical employees because she found these variables to be related to job permanency, for example. Austin and Waung (1994) noted that the breadth and depth of Bills' influence at Aetna was strengthened because of her perseverance to rely on empirical data for understanding tenure and retention, especially with regard to gender differences.

Bills also studied classification methods and compensation. For example, she developed a standardized process for rating employee performance, a process to classify 300 clerical jobs, and equitable employee salaries based on this information (Bills, 1923b). The classification model included variables ranging from supervisory responsibilities, decision making, and manual dexterity to knowledge of a large number of rules and regulations. Bills then conducted internal and external salary reviews in order to set the salary limits for each clerical pay grade. Additionally, she developed a graphic rating scale with differentially weighted items to measure employee efficiency. Based on the managers' ratings of employee efficiency, salaries were adjusted.

Bills recognized the challenges of conducting research in industry. She noted a "disconnect" between psychologists working in university settings and those working in private industry (1953). One explanation was the lack of recognition of applied contributions because of the paucity of publications and reports produced by psychologists in industry. She noticed that psychologists in industry were hesitant to report results of their research because most of their research was conducted in organizations with less control of potential confounds, as compared to a laboratory experience. What was noteworthy according to industry standards may not have been statistically significant. Bills recalled that statisticians could have shot holes in her statistical analyses; however, such skeptics would miss the real point of her studies—the use of quasi-experimental data for solving business problems. She believed that workable solutions completed in a timely fashion are more valuable than publishing. As a trained scientist, however, Bills pondered her contributions to a scientific discipline. She questioned, "Would our publications in this less rigid field (management) add anything to the fundamental knowledge of psychology?" (Bills, 1953, p. 145).

Psychologists in Industry

During the early years of industrial psychology, Bills was a significant person in bringing together colleagues who were working in industry and applying psychology. For example, she was the founder of the Psychologists Employed Full-Time in Industry, an informal group that met at American Psychological Association (APA) meetings. Over the years, membership expanded from eight individuals to over 200 (Crissey, 1957), and several additional groups evolved from this first group (e.g., the Dearborn and Mayflower Groups; Meyer, 2007). Bills served on the newly formed Board of Governors of the American Association of

Applied Psychology as the recording secretary of the Industrial and Business Section during 1939. She was then an active participant in the committee that formed the original APA Division 14 (also known as the Society for Industrial and Organizational Psychology).

In a 1944 article, Bills defined three types of psychological services that are typically rendered by organizations: consultant, psychologist hired for a particular job, and staff psychologist. She further discussed the range of contributions provided by psychologists within the spectrum of office personnel, such as a classification/job evaluation scale for clerical work, selection tests such as mental alertness and work samples, and recommendations for the effects of noise on work efficiency. Later, Bills noted that management turned to psychologists for problems because psychology was a new science. She stated,

> What are these principles that we carry over? I believe one of the most important is the principle of 'Stop, look and listen' that as scientists has been ground into us in all of our training. (Bills, 1953, p. 143)

She (1953) advocated that the primary role of psychologists in industry is to serve as a liaison between scientists and management:

> ...psychologists in private industry are only about 100 strong and we need the advice of our consulting friends and especially of our academic ones to help us to see clearly where our greatest contribution to a young but fast growing science lies. (p. 145)

Major Publications

Bills wrote publications read by executives such as the *American Management Association Office Executive Series, American Management Association Office Management Series, American Management Association Marketing Series*, and *Life Office Management Association* (e.g., Bills, 1926, 1927). She published extensively in scientific journals on her research in industry, including the *Journal of Applied Psychology, Journal of Personnel Research* (later *Personnel Journal*), *Personnel, Psychological Bulletin, Psychological Monographs*, and *Journal of Consulting Psychology* (e.g., Bills, 1920, 1933), and contributed chapters to the *Annals of the American Academy of Political and Social Science* (Yoakum & Bills, 1923), the *Handbook of Applied Psychology* (Bills, 1950), and *Applications of Psychology: Essays to Honor W.V. Bingham* (Bills, 1952). Topics included job analysis, selection, job permanency, compensation, measurement of office work, and fair personnel policies, and all her publications consistently exhibited a practical perspective or orientation.

Recognition

Bills was frequently recognized by other professional psychological organizations on a state and national level. At the state level, she was a founder of the Connecticut Valley Association of Psychologists and its successor, the Connecticut State Psychological Society, for which she was the second president in 1945–1946. She helped create the Connecticut Certified Psychologists Act and facilitated the development of the Connecticut Board for Certification of Psychologists, serving as a charter member of the board, and as its secretary from 1945 to 1950.

Bills was a charter trustee for the American Board of Examiners in Professional Psychology. She served on the APA Council of Representatives (1945) and was a member of the Policy and Planning Board (1945–1947), the Committee on Academic Freedom and Conditions of Employment (1952), and the Conference of State Psychological Associations. Particularly noteworthy is that Bills served as the seventh president of the APA Division 14, the first woman, and one of three women to be elected in 50 years. She was included in *American Men of Science* (Cattell & Brimhall, 1921), and in 1940, she received the Leffingwell Medal from the National Office Management Association for her work with personnel management.

Conclusion

As a scientist and practitioner, Bills identified organizational needs, conducted empirical research on employees, and recommended specific changes to improve organizational processes. The use of scientific research methods and psychological theory to examine typical as well as novel concepts within work settings, a prominent role in the DAP at CIT, an influential contributor in industry, and substantive involvement with professional organizations distinguish Bills as a key thinker of I-O psychology.

References

Austin, J. T., & Waung, M. P. (1994, April). Dr. Marion A. Bills: Allegan to Aetna. In L. Koppes (Chair), *The founding mothers: Female I/O psychologists in the early years*. Symposium conducted at the Ninth Annual Conference of the Society for Industrial and Organizational Psychology, Inc., Nashville, TN. https://doi.org/10.1037/e579632009-001

Bills, M. A. (1920). The lag of visual sensation in its relation to wave lengths and intensity of light. *Psychological Monographs, 28*, 101. https://doi.org/10.1037/h0093154

Bills, M. A. (1923a). Relation of mental alertness test score to positions and permanency in company. *Journal of Applied Psychology, 7*, 154–156. https://doi.org/10.1037/h0072305

Bills, M. A. (1923b). A method for classifying the jobs and rating the efficiency of clerical workers. *Journal of Personnel Research, 1*, 384–393.

Bills, M. A. (1926). The status of measuring office work. *American Management Association, Office Executive Series* (No. 16), 3–12.

Bills, M. A. (1927). An application of principles of the individual bonus plan to home office clerical work. *Life Office Management Association, 192*, 153–159.

Bills, M. A. (1933). Rate of promotion of clerical forces. *Psychological Bulletin, 30*, 731–732.

Bills, M. A. (1941). Selection of casualty and life insurance agents. *Journal of Applied Psychology, 25*, 6–10. https://doi.org/10.1037/h0057158

Bills, M. A. (1944). Psychology applied to problems of office personnel. *Journal of Consulting Psychology*, *8*, 160–164.

Bills, M. A. (1950). Field salesmen. In D. H. Fryer & E. Henry (Eds.), *Handbook of applied psychology* (Vol. 1, pp. 212–215). Rinehart. https://doi.org/10.1037/11520-000

Bills, M. A. (1952). A tool for selection that has stood the test of time. In L. L. Thurstone (Ed.), *Applications of psychology: Essays to honor Walter V. Bingham* (pp. 131–138). Harper.

Bills, M. A. (1953). Our expanding responsibilities. *Journal of Applied Psychology, 37*, 142–145. https://doi.org/10.1037/h0053475
Bills, M. A., & Yoakum, C. S. (1921). Methods for the selection of comptometer operators and stenographers. *Journal of Applied Psychology, 5*(3), 275–283. https://doi.org/10.1037/h0069600
Cattell, J. McKeen, & Brimhall, D. R. (1921). *American men of science: A biographical directory* (3rd ed.). Science Press. https://doi.org/10.5962/bhl.title.3786
Crissey, O. L. (1957, October 19). [Letter to M. A. Bills]. Marie Crissey Collection, Box M2054, Folder 4; Industrial psychologists employed full-time in industry. University of Akron, Archives of the History of American Psychology, Akron, OH.
Ferguson, L. W. (1952). A look across the years 1920 to 1950. In L. L. Thurstone (Ed.), *Applications of psychology: Essays to honor Walter V. Bingham* (pp. 1–17). Harper.
Hilgard, E. R. (1987). *Psychology in America: A historical survey*. Harcourt Brace Jovanovich.
Koppes, L. L. (1997). American female pioneers of industrial and organizational psychology during the early years. *Journal of Applied Psychology, 82*, 500–515. https://doi.org/10.1037//0021-9010.82.4.500
Koppes, L. L., & Bauer, A. (2006). Marion A. Bills: Industrial psychology pioneer bridging science and practice. In D. A. Dewsbury, L. T. Benjamin, & M. Wertheimer (Eds.), *Portraits of pioneers in psychology: Vol. VI* (pp. 103–116). American Psychological Association. https://doi.org/10.4324/9781315822464
Meyer, H. H. (2007). Influence of formal and informal organizations on the development of I-O psychology. In L. L. Koppes (Ed.), *Historical perspectives in industrial and organizational psychology* (1st ed., pp. 139–168). Erlbaum. https://doi.org/10.4324/9780429052644-5
Vinchur, A., & Koppes Bryan, L. (2021). Early contributors to the science and practice of industrial psychology. In L. Koppes Bryan (Ed.), *Historical perspectives in industrial-organizational psychology* (2nd ed., pp. 21–41). Routledge Press/Taylor & Francis. https://doi.org/10.4324/9780429052644-2
Yoakum, C. S., & Bills, M. A. (1923). Tests for office occupations. *Annals of the American Academy of Political and Social Science, 110*, 1–14. https://doi.org/10.1177/000271622311000107

Chapter 20

Kurt Lewin (1890–1947)

Rebecca Grossman

"There is nothing as practical as a good theory" (Lewin, 1943–1944/1951, p. 169). Most who have been educated within the field of industrial-organizational (I-O) psychology have heard this quote, and some may even associate it with the renowned Kurt Lewin, to whom it is indeed attributed. Beyond basic familiarity, however, many do not know what made Lewin renowned, and are unacquainted with his body of work. Previous scholars have speculated about this contradiction, citing his unfocused and interdisciplinary research endeavors, ideas that were too innovative for his time, and challenging writing style, as reasons why his work is missing from curricula and often gets forgotten (Endrejat & Burnes, 2022). Whether we realize it or not, however, Lewin had a profound impact on the field of I-O, and his work continues to be foundational to many of the core areas we focus on today.

Biographical Overview

Lewin was born in 1890 in present-day Poland, where he received an Orthodox Jewish education and later went on to pursue his doctoral degree in philosophy and psychology at the University of Berlin (Burnes & Bargal, 2017). After serving and getting wounded in World War I, he returned to complete his studies and became a researcher and professor at the Psychology Institute of the University of Berlin from 1926 to1932 (Burnes & Bargal, 2017; Wheeler, 2008). During this time, he conducted a series of highly regarded psychological experiments on topics such as needs, motivation, learning, and tension states.

DOI: 10.4324/9781003403258-20

Escaping the rise of fascism, Lewin and his family immigrated to the United States (US) in 1933 (Burnes & Bargal, 2017). He eventually landed at the University of Iowa and established a research center which became the site of some of the first classical experiments in social psychology. During his time there (1935–1945), he also took his research out of the lab and into the real world, exploring various social and organizational interventions – this work became the foundation of modern organizational development (OD) approaches (Burnes, 2007; Burnes & Bargal, 2017). In what turned out to be his final years, Lewin took a position at MIT in 1945 and developed the Research Center for Group Dynamics, where he and his collaborators conducted both laboratory and applied social psychology research, spanning topics such as group dynamics, leadership, conflict, and discrimination. He also contributed to launching the journal *Human Relations,* produced major scholarly articles, and began working with the American Jewish Congress and the Connecticut State Commission to address community concerns related to minority group bias and intergroup relations (Wheeler, 2008). When Lewin had a heart attack and died in 1947, his varied efforts were culminating, and he had much left to contribute.

Major Contributions

Lewin's contributions were shaped by his life and scholarly experiences. The discrimination he faced as a Jew in both Germany and the US, for instance, sparked his motivation to improve the human condition by resolving social conflict (Endrejat & Burnes, 2022). He brought humanitarian and democratic perspectives to much of his research endeavors. Additionally, his education in both philosophy and psychology, as well as his exposure to early Gestalt psychologists at the University of Berlin (Wheeler, 2008), affected his approach to studying and changing human behavior. Lewin's work was far-reaching, spanning everything from housewives' food habits to memory in children. While being 'all over the place' can make his impact hard to pin down (Endrejat & Burnes, 2022), one way to understand his influence on I-O psychology is by considering his research approach, the topics he pursued, and his continuous commitment to bettering society.

Research Approach

Underlying everything Lewin did was field theory, the idea that behavior is a function of both the person and their environment (Wheeler, 2008). This meant that to understand the individual, the total field or surrounding context must be taken into account. Like much of his work, field theory was interdisciplinary – it built on concepts from physics, philosophy, and psychology. While these approaches were not commonplace at the time, they are arguably foundational to the field of I-O today. For example, by definition, I-O is the study of human behavior within a context (i.e., the workplace), and models often incorporate a range of individual, group, and organizational factors that influence outcomes. Likewise, I-O is interdisciplinary at its core, drawing from various branches of psychology (e.g., cognitive, social), as well as business and management. Lewin was thus one of the first to adopt some of I-O's primary practices.

Lewin's other major approach was action research, the idea that applied research should entail cooperation between researchers and practitioners, where an iterative process of research, action, and evaluation is performed until the objective is achieved (Burnes, 2020). Inherent to this was Lewin's devotion to taking his research out of the lab and into the real world – something quite rare for psychologists at a time when laboratory research ruled. His first major implementation of action research occurred in the Harwood studies, which were arguably as groundbreaking and impactful on I-O as the Hawthorne experiments, though less recognized due to there being less information about them on record (Burnes, 2007). What began as an effort to address turnover within a pajama manufacturing organization transformed into over 30 years of research on topics such as decision-making, leadership, and resistance to change, much of it in the early years (1939–1947) spearheaded or otherwise influenced by Lewin. Alex Bavelas and John R. P. French, two of Lewin's graduate students at the University of Iowa who he recruited to the Harwood studies, conducted a great deal of the day-to-day research, yet Lewin played a heavy role in guiding their efforts (Burnes, 2007). Lewin's work in this context has been described as the first real use of science to understand how to manage people in industry (Marrow, 1972). Over the course of his research, he even suggested the company should hire a full-time psychologist, perhaps initiating the early concept of an internal I-O consultant! Lewin was thus one of the first to embody the core purpose of our field – to use science to acquire knowledge about human behavior within organizations and apply such knowledge to address workplace issues. His adherence to the scientist-practitioner model was further exemplified in his argument for, 'No research without action, no action without research' (Marrow, 1972, p. 90).

Research Topics

A comparison between the many topics Lewin pursued and a current I-O textbook would yield considerable overlap. His research spanned a range of workplace issues, such as leadership style, group dynamics, conflict resolution, group decision-making, affect, and motivation (Burnes, 2007; Wheeler, 2008). Importantly, many of these topics were considered outside of the scope of psychology research or had not yet been studied at the time. Lewin's work is hence a foundation for much of the field's research that is still being conducted today. Two topics he is perhaps most well-known for are the three-step model of change, and T-groups. Lewin argued the change process consisted of three stages – 'unfreezing' current practices, 'moving,' or implementing the change, and 'refreezing,' or adopting the new behavior or practice (Burnes, 2020). Though not without criticism, it went on to become the most influential model of organizational change and is still utilized. Related is Lewin's practice of using T-groups, which primarily involved providing feedback and engaging in discussion with groups undergoing leadership training (Wheeler, 2008). This approach became central for implementing OD interventions of all kinds (Burnes & Bargal, 2017), and remains relevant (Highhouse, 2002). Lewin therefore has impacted many domains of I-O but particularly organizational change and OD.

Commitment to Bettering Society

All of Lewin's efforts were rooted in a commitment to bettering society by promoting democratic values and addressing social conflicts (Burnes & Bargal, 2017). Much of his work focused on reducing prejudice and discrimination in the broader community, but this was apparent in his efforts specific to the workplace as well. For example, in a study of discrimination in the community, the largest disparities were observed in employment contexts, where Black employees were earning less than White employees (Marrow, 1969). Lewin was interested in not only uncovering the discrepancies but also fighting to address them. Many of his interests were concerned with how work processes could become more humane (Endrejat & Burnes, 2022), and his major approach, action research, was driven by democratic and humanistic values that supported the freedom, dignity, and welfare of every person participating in an organizational intervention (Burnes & Bargal, 2017). These are noteworthy points because Lewin was arguably ahead of his time in this regard. Much of the early work in I-O pertained to maximizing productivity and other outcomes beneficial to the organization, while today, we also see a heavy emphasis on factors beneficial to the individual. For example, the Top 10 Work Trends identified by the Society for Industrial and Organizational Psychology in 2023 included employee mental health, psychological safety, work-family balance, and diversity, equity, and inclusion, all topics that align with Lewin's humanistic values. Lewin brought a unique perspective to the study of behavior in the workplace which helped lay the groundwork for I-O to become a field that values the well-being of both people and organizations.

Conclusion

Whether it is always recognized or not, Kurt Lewin has clearly had a fundamental and lasting impact on I-O psychology. Just as recently as 2017, a special issue of the *Journal of Change Management* demonstrated the continued relevance of his work, showing how it is being applied in different ways by scholars around the world (Burnes & Bargal, 2017). Beyond his well-known quote about the practical value of theory, Lewin should be recognized as one of the field's key thinkers.

References

Burnes, B. (2007). Kurt Lewin and the Harwood studies: The foundations of OD. *Journal of Applied Behavioral Science*, *43*(2), 213–231.

Burnes, B. (2020). The origins of Lewin's three-step model of change. *Journal of Applied Behavioral Science*, *56*(1), 32–59.

Burnes, B., & Bargal, D. (2017). Kurt Lewin: 70 years on. *Journal of Change Management, 17*(2), 91–100.

Endrejat, P. C., & Burnes, B. (2022). Kurt Lewin's ideas are alive! But why doesn't anybody recognize them? *Theory & Psychology*, *32*(6), 931–952.

Highhouse, S. (2002). A history of the T-group and its early applications in management development. *Group Dynamics: Theory, Research, and Practice*, *6*(4), 277–290.

Lewin, K. (1943–1944/1951). Problems of research in social psychology. In D. Cartwright (Ed.), *Field theory in social science: Selected theoretical papers by Kurt Lewin* (pp. 155–170). Harper and Row.

Marrow, A. J. (1969). *The practical theorist: the life and work of Kurt Lewin.* Basic Books.

Marrow, A. J. (1972). The effects of participation on performance. In A. J. Marrow (Ed.), *The failure of success* (pp. 90–102). Amacom.

Society for Industrial and Organizational Psychology (2023). Top 10 work trends. www.siop.org/Business-Resources/Top-10-Work-Trends

Wheeler, L. (2008). Kurt Lewin. *Social and Personality Psychology Compass*, *2*(4), 1638–1650.

Chapter 21

Bruce V. Moore (1891–1977)

Mengting (Rachel) Xia and Mark Griffin

Bruce V. Moore is a pivotal figure in the evolution of industrial-organizational (I-O) psychology. He made significant contributions to occupational interests and personnel interviews and greatly improved graduate education in applied psychology. Moore served as the first chair of the Department of Psychology at Penn State University and during his tenure, he committed to a scientist-practitioner model and cultivated an environment rich in applied research. The current Penn State psychology building is still named after Bruce V. Moore today, honoring his lasting contributions to the field and the institution.

Biographical Overview

Early Days and Education

Bruce V. Moore was born on September 9, 1891, near Kokomo, IN (Bernreuter, 1979). He completed both a bachelor's degree and a master's degree at Indiana University where he worked as a graduate assistant in psychology and wrote his thesis in the field of vocational education (Farr & Tesluk, 1997). Moore received a graduate scholarship to Columbia University for his PhD and enrolled in 1917, planning to study under Robert L. Thorndike. After spending a semester at Columbia, Moore enlisted in the United States Army, becoming part of Psychological Company Number 1 within the Army Medical Corps in 1918. He received training at Camp Greenleaf, Georgia, focusing on applying psychological assessments to military personnel issues and classification problems. His duties led him to Walter Reed Hospital in Washington, DC, and Army Hospital Number 20 in Prescott, AZ.

DOI: 10.4324/9781003403258-21

This experience spurred Moore's interest in applying psychology in work settings and prompted him to search for graduate programs. He was awarded a fellowship in the Bureau of Personnel Research at Carnegie Institute of Technology's (presently known as Carnegie Mellon University) Division of Applied Psychology and began his doctoral work in September 1919. For his doctoral thesis, he developed an effective strategy for assigning engineers to either design or sales positions at Westinghouse Corporation (Moore, 1921). In 1921, Moore received his PhD in industrial psychology (now known as I-O psychology), becoming one of the first two graduates of the first graduate program uniquely tailored to educate researchers and practitioners in the field of industrial psychology (Bernreuter, 1979; Farr & Tesluk, 1997; Vinchur, 2018).

Academic Career

Moore began his professional career as an assistant professor of psychology in the College of Education and Psychology Department[1] at Pennsylvania State College (now University) in September 1920 (Bernreuter, 1979). Moore quickly gained recognition for his hard work and was promoted to the head of the psychology faculty in 1928 (Zak, 2020). During his early days at Penn State, Moore was requested by Dean of Engineering Robert L. Sackett to develop a comprehensive curriculum in general and applied psychology for first-year engineering students. Due to the lack of existing textbooks, Moore consulted Louis Thurstone[2] and decided to include topics on group behavior and dynamics, motivation, and work satisfaction—elements that presaged the later merger of I-O psychology (Moore, 1962). This collection of mimeographed readings later became *Readings in Industrial Psychology* (Moore & Hartmann, 1931).

By 1945, Moore had successfully advocated for the division of the Education and Psychology Department into two separate entities, focusing respectively on education and psychology (Bernreuter, 1979). As the head of the newly formed Psychology Department, Moore was instrumental in shaping its direction, emphasizing research and the practical application of psychological principles in industrial settings. He maintained this position until his retirement in 1952.

Moore's contributions to psychology, particularly in test construction and industrial consulting, earned him the first presidency of Division 14 of the American Psychological Association (APA),[3] dedicated to Industrial and Business Psychology (Farr & Tesluk, 1997). Following his retirement, Moore continued to contribute to the field of psychology as the APA's Executive Officer for the Education and Training Board for seven years and later as a visiting professor at the University of Miami, where he aided in expanding their graduate program. Bruce Moore passed away in State College, Pennsylvania, on November 14, 1977.

Personal Life

Beyond his notable contributions to the field of I-O psychology and his significant role at Pennsylvania State University, Moore embraced a vibrant and engaged lifestyle marked by a blend of leisure activities and community involvement. He enjoyed hunting and bowling (Zak, 2020).

Moore's life was filled with love, security, and family (Farr & Tesluk, 1997). He married Elsie Kohler in 1924, and together, they welcomed a daughter, Mary Ellen Moore Kinnaird. After Kohler's death in 1967, he married Winona Morgan, a fellow psychologist specializing in childhood development, in 1969. The Moores resided in State College, where Winona Moore continued to live after Bruce Moore's passing in 1977.

Contributions to I-O Psychology

Dr. Bruce V. Moore made pioneering contributions to I-O psychology, primarily through developing psychometric tests, advocating the objective use of interviews, and fostering the development of graduate education.

Psychometric Assessment

Early in Moore's career, he worked for the Westinghouse Electric and Manufacturing Company as part of his graduate fellowship for his PhD studies at Carnegie Tech. There, he utilized psychometric tests for the selection and placement of 300 newly hired engineers per year in a variety of functions, significantly improving the process (Moore, 1962). He challenged existing unvalidated selection methods, introducing a framework that differentiated technical information and knowledge and social information and intelligence for engineering functions. This innovative approach enabled him to devise two tests: one measuring technical and the other measuring social knowledge. He validated these tests using a sample of recently hired design and sales engineers, leading to a successful classification system that linked engineers' performance with their test scores, where the tests were designed for the particular abilities required for the job functions (Moore, 1921).

In addition to the knowledge tests, Moore was an early pioneer in developing vocational interest tests. He created a simple checklist method for assessing the interests of sales and design engineers, based on Westinghouse's belief that an engineer's interests should factor into the placement decision (Moore, 1921). His dissertation laid the groundwork for subsequent instruments in vocational psychology, influencing the creation of the Strong Vocational Interest Blank for Men by E. K. Strong, Jr. (Farr & Tesluk, 1997).

Following his dissertation, Moore (1923) found that combining the knowledge tests with the interests questionnaire was more effective in predicting success after approximately two years on the job than using either test alone. This combination of both ability and interest measures in the prediction of job success was one of the first empirical studies in this field.

In 1941, Moore used his colleague's personality test, the Bernreuter Personality Inventory, along with the Strong Vocational Interest Blank to analyze engineering students' personality traits, vocational interests, and engineering aptitude (e.g., arithmetic reasoning, physical aptitude) (Moore, 1941a). This study further advanced the selection and placement of engineering functions by combining personality traits and occupational interests and distinguishing different engineering aptitudes. The Psychological Corporation later published and distributed two Moore-developed tests: the Test of Arithmetic Reasoning (Moore, 1941b) and the Engineering and Physical Science Aptitude Test (Moore et al., 1951).

Moore also devised a college aptitude test for incoming students, shaping the university's admissions practices and the academic psychology department at Penn State for many years. This program, which utilized personality tests to help students identify suitable career paths, lasted into the 1990s (Zak, 2020).

Interviews

Bruce V. Moore significantly advanced the interviewing methodology in I-O psychology research, addressing skepticism about its reliability and advocating for standardized techniques to enhance its practical application.

During his sabbatical leave in 1928–1929, supported by a Social Science Research Council grant, Moore produced an annotated bibliography of interviews and conducted empirical studies to test the validity of information gained by interviews. Moore (1929) described the interviewing process as involving both the exchange of information and the observation of the interviewee's behavior and environment. He argued that interviews, like any psychological process, could be systematically analyzed and refined. He also highlighted the importance of question formulation, the potential influence of biases, and the need for accuracy in interview responses. Moore (1930) introduced 'objectivity methods' for interviews to transcend subjective biases and reveal reliable, factual insights about workers' attitudes and vocational interests. He advocated for careful discrimination between fact and inference and the use of objective tools such as rating scales and record sheets.

These efforts resulted in a co-authored book with Walter V. Bingham, entitled *How to Interview*, (Bingham & Moore, 1931), which laid out foundational principles for conducting effective interviews.

Graduate Education in I-O Psychology

Bruce V. Moore had been deeply concerned about the state of graduate education in I-O psychology for many years, and he played a crucial role in facilitating its development, promoting a scientist-practitioner model during his services on APA's Committee on Doctoral Education.

In 1952, he was named to the APA Education and Training Board and chaired its Committee on Doctoral Education (Bernreuter, 1979). There, he contributed to reports and studies assessing the state of psychology education. He analyzed the career trajectories of psychology students, including the outcomes of BA and MA psychology students at Brown and Wayne Universities, APA fellows across divisions, and recent PhDs in psychology (Moore, 1954b). Moore also examined the issues and trends in master's degree programs in psychology, highlighting the balance between theoretical education and professional training, with a particular emphasis on professional training in specific fields, such as I-O psychology. Additionally, his reports on educational facilities and financial assistance (Moore, 1954a) provided valuable insights for students seeking graduate studies in psychology during the 1950s, outlining admission requirements, application processes, and the diversity of programs and financial support.

Moore's commitment to a scientist-practitioner model and his efforts to link I-O psychology with broader societal and professional psychology issues have significantly shaped the educational landscape of I-O psychology, ensuring that practical application remained at the forefront of graduate training.

Conclusion

Bruce V. Moore's enduring influence on I-O Psychology stems from his groundbreaking work and visionary leadership. His efforts in refining psychometric assessments and advancing personnel interview techniques laid a critical foundation for the field. Moore's dedication to applied psychology is exemplified by his leadership role at Penn State and with the APA. His lasting impact is honored at Penn State, where the psychology building stands as a tribute to his legacy, inspiring future generations to continue in his footsteps.

Notes

1 At that time, Psychology fell within the School of Education (Farr & Tesluk, 1997).
2 Thurstone was also one of the world's great psychologists and he made significant contributions to psychometrics, a quantitative side

of psychology. At that time, Thurstone worked as an Associate Professor of Psychology at the University of Chicago (Guilford, 1955).
3 In 1945, the APA and the American Association for Applied Psychology merged into a new APA (Farr & Tesluk, 1997).

References

Bernreuter, R. G. (1979). Obituary: Bruce Victor Moore (1891-1977). *American Psychologist*, *34*(4), 350–350. https://doi.org/10.1037/h0078275

Bingham, W. V., & Moore, B. V. (1931). *How to interview*. Harpers.

Farr, J. L., & Tesluk, P. E. (1997). Bruce V. Moore: First president of Division 14. *Journal of Applied Psychology*, *82*(4), 478–485. https://doi.org/10.1037/0021-9010.82.4.478

Guilford, J. P. (1955). Louis Leon Thurstone. *Psychometrika*, *20*(4), 263–265. https://doi.org/10.1007/BF02289032

Moore, B. V. (1921). Personnel selection of graduate engineers: The differentiation of apprentice engineers for training as salesmen, designers, and executives of production. *Psychological Monographs*, *30*(5), i–85. https://doi.org/10.1037/h0093191

Moore, B. V. (1923). A tested method of using tests for vocational guidance. *School & Society*, *18*, 761–764.

Moore, B. V. (1929). The interview in social industrial research. *Social Forces*, *7*(3), 445–452. https://doi.org/10.2307/2569818

Moore, B. V. (1930). Objective methods in the personal interview in vocational guidance. *Psychological Clinic*, *19*(4), 105–115.

Moore, B. V. (1941a). Analysis of results of tests administered to men in engineering defense training courses. *Journal of Applied Psychology*, *25*(6), 619–635. https://doi.org/10.1037/h0060853

Moore, B. V. (1941b). *Arithmetic reasoning*. Psychological Corporation.

Moore B. V. (1954a). Educational facilities and financial assistance for graduate students in psychology: 1954–1955. *American Psychologist*, *9*(1), 3–20. https://doi.org/10.1037/h0061323

Moore, B. V. (1954b). The master's degree in psychology. *American Psychologist*, *9*(3), 120–122. https://doi.org/10.1037/h0055022

Moore, B. V. (1962). Some beginnings of industrial psychology. In B. v. H. Gilmer (Ed.), *Walter van Dyke Bingham: Memorial program March 23, 1961* (pp. 1–5). Carnegie Institute of Technology. https://doi.org/10.1037/13362-001

Moore, B. V., & Hartmann, G. W. (1931). *Readings in industrial psychology*. Appleton.

Moore, B. V., Lapp, C. J., & Griffin, C. H. (1951). *Engineering and physical science aptitude test, revised manual.* https://psycnet.apa.org/record/1953-07485-000

Vinchur, A. J. (2018). *The early years of industrial and organizational psychology.* Cambridge University Press. https://doi.org/10.1017/9781107588608

Zak, K. N. (2020, April 3). *Dr. Moore's impact part 1 – "Moore" than a small effect.* Highlands Civic Association. https://statecollegehighlands.org/dr-moores-impact-part-1-moore-than-a-small-effect/

Chapter 22

Shigemi Kirihara (1892–1968)

Miki Takasuna

Shigemi Kirihara, also known as Hoken Kirihara, was one of the pioneers of industrial-organizational (I-O) psychology in Japan. During the 1910s, other psychologists' study of work efficiency in Japan developed under the influence of Hugo Münsterberg and Taylorism. Then, in the early 1920s, Kirihara and his colleagues pursued another study trend by carrying out field research in the workplace. This was prior to the beginning of the Hawthorne studies in 1924.

Biographical Overview

Kirihara was born in the Yagi village of Hiroshima in November 10, 1892. After graduating from the Third High School in Kyoto, he studied psychology at Tokyo Imperial University where he graduated in 1919. During his undergraduate years, he became acquainted with Gito Teruoka (1889–1966), a physiologist at Tokyo Imperial University, whose interest in social problems led him to survey the slums of Tokyo. Around the time of Kirihara's graduation, his father, who was the head priest of a Buddhist temple, died. Kirihara took over the position of head priest, which explains the occasional use of his Buddhist name, Hoken Kirihara (since the same Chinese characters were pronounced differently, "Shigemi" Kirihara is used in the present chapter).

When Kirihara finally returned to school to become a graduate student of psychology at Tokyo Imperial University, Teruoka invited him to join a project investigating women workers at a factory in Kurashiki in Okayama Prefecture. Thus, during the summer of 1920, Teruoka and Kirihara along with Tomoyoshi

DOI: 10.4324/9781003403258-22

Ishikawa (1891–1950), a colleague physiologist of Teruoka, carried out field research, which stimulated Kirihara's further interest in industrial psychology. When in 1921 the Kurashiki Institute for Science of Labour was founded in Kurashiki, Teruoka was appointed head of the Institute and both Kirihara and Ishikawa became members.

Kirihara continued working at the Institute, earning a PhD from Tokyo Imperial University in 1931 with the thesis "Psychological Studies on Factory Labor." Kirihara visited various institutes of I-O psychology in Europe and the United States, spending January 1933–February 1934 mainly in Germany. During the trip, he published a short report on the study of cotton spinning techniques in an American journal (Kirihara, 1934). By 1937, the Kurashiki Institute for Science of Labour detached from the Kurashiki Spinning Works and settled as a legally incorporated foundation in Tokyo, where it was founded as the Japan Institute for Science of Labour. After World War II, the Institute was again renamed, this time the Institute for Science of Labour (*Rodo-Kagaku Kenkyujo*), and Kirihara was appointed as its head from 1951 until 1957. In 1961, Kirihara became one of the Institute's directors and began teaching psychology as a professor of Japan Women's University until 1965. Kirihara died May 2, 1968, at the age of 75 due to stomach cancer. Today, the Institute for Science of Labour remains in Tokyo, though it has again been renamed as the Ohara Memorial Institute for Science of Labour. Kirihara was made an honorary member of the Japanese Psychological Association, International Association of Applied Psychology, and Japan Society for Occupational Health (for biographical information, see Mitsui, 1998; Ohizumi, 2003).

Contributions to I-O Psychology

According to Kirihara himself (Kirihara, 1953), the development of I-O psychology in Japan can be divided into four eras; work psychology (ca. 1900–1910s), efficiency psychology (1916–1920s), aptitude psychology (1930–1945), and social psychology (after 1945). Kirihara studied psychology at the end of the first era, when pioneering work on mental fatigue (Haraguchi, 1914) was published. Next, the study of work efficiency became popular in various public agencies (e.g., telephone offices, navy yards, railway factories) as well as private companies (e.g., Kanegafuchi Spinning Company, Gunze, Fukuske Corporation). Investigations were conducted sporadically and characterized as "studies from above," suggesting that measures for improvement were proposed by the researchers who received short-term funding for the studies (Mitsui, 1998, p.139). In contrast, Kirihara, Teruoka, and others began a series of investigations conducted at the Kurashiki Institute for Science of Labour, a small institute settled on the site of the Manju factory of the Kurashiki Spinning Works in cooperation with the company president Magosaburo Ohara (1880–1943). The studies involved observing everyday labors of the young women workers (most of them aged under 16 years old). Consequently, Kirihara and others practically shared room and board with the workers.

Kirihara repeatedly described how he and his colleagues were immediately dismayed observing in person the actual spinning factory during the summer of 1920. The young women worked in two shifts. Even at night, the spinning machines were operated at high temperature and humidity to prevent yarns from splitting and in an environment full of dust and noise. Witnessing the severe conditions, the young researchers urged workplace improvements. In addition, tuberculosis among the spinners was one of the biggest social problems at that time. After three years of studies, the researchers founded the periodical *Rodo Kagaku* (*The Journal of Science of Labour*), in 1924, which continues to be published today. Kirihara published 37 papers in the journal (Mitsui, 1998).

In Kirihara's book, *Industrial Psychology*, one of the earliest of the genre in Japan, he defined industrial psychology as "a practical science that studies human behavior in industry with psychological methods and findings" (Kirihara, 1938, p. 31). His stance was labor-oriented, not management-oriented, a stance that could be seen as his basic attitude against Taylorism or the "efficiency first" principle, which prevailed in Japan during the 1910s.

During the 1920s, application of the intelligence test as an aptitude test started in various fields of Japan, such as in the Japanese Army. Vocational guidance for the younger generation was needed due to the recession around 1930. Accordingly, it was natural for Kirihara to revise the Will-Temperament test in the 1930s, adapted from June Downey's test (Downey, 1923). In fact, Kirihara was going to present his paper on the mental development of Japanese at the Ninth International Congress of Psychology held at Yale University in September, 1929, but he was unable to do so when he postponed his research trip. In parallel with the study on workers, he measured the general capacity or intelligence of people from childhood to adulthood and planned to "offer civil workers and psychotechnicians some reliable data and normal test methods" (Kirihara, 1930, p. 255).

Among his work on I-O psychology were unique contributions to labor sciences such as his book, *Menstruation and Working Capacity* (Kirihara, 1943). From his earliest research in the field in Kurashiki, Kirihara kept investigating the capacity of women spinners by measuring their grasping power, reaction time, work output, and other parameters. This book was a kind of summarization of papers written from his research conducted in the factory. In it, he concluded that suitable steps needed to be taken to reduce women workers' workload or physical work during menstruation and, moreover, the management of women's health needed to be promoted.

It also should be mentioned that during wartime in the late 1930s to 1940s, Kirihara had a crisis of conscience. In 1942, the Japan Institute for Science of Labour became affiliated with Dainippon Sangyo Hokokukai, a wartime organization of Japanese industries. During this time, Kirihara published some books, including those mentioned earlier, which followed nationalistic wartime requirements, such as encouraging people to work for the country and promoting women to work and mobilize. Among others, *Women's Labor* (Kirihara, 1944) took the brunt of criticism. While *Menstruation and Working Capacity* (1943) was scientific in its attitude toward empirical analysis, *Women's Labor* (1944) counteracted this attitude. To summarize, it promoted working women as crucial to winning the war. Essentially, Kirihara suggested to exploit Japanese women's talents, experience, and ability to work without reference to the health or work-life balance of women's lives (Bae, 2000, p. 85). After the war, Kirihara became aware of the criticism toward his writings during wartime. When his pupils visited his home shortly before his death in 1968, Kirihara told them to burn the book immediately if they found it because he had written it contrary to what he intended (Kosugo, 2006).

During the war, support of nationalistic theories happened everywhere, even in the field of psychology, and some psychologists were not immune to the pressure. Yet, despite Kirihara's commitment to labor science during wartime and his being occasionally criticized for it, his achievements should still be positively remembered by field-oriented I-O psychologists.

Conclusion

In the 1910s, before Kirihara earned a BA in psychology, the efficiency movement caught the attention of industrial employers and bureaucrats who were interested in increasing profits and boosting production. Yoichi Ueno (1883–1957), who graduated from Tokyo Imperial University 11 years earlier than Kirihara, was the pioneer and presumably the most important figure in Japanese I-O psychology. These two psychologists did not work together, rather they contrasted in their contributions to I-O psychology. Ueno, who might be called a management consultant rather than a scholar, was remarkably influenced by Taylorism. In 1924, Ueno established the Japan branch of the Taylor Society and later in 1942 founded the Japan School for Efficiency (now Sanno Institute of Management). Kirihara, on the other hand, was interested in how the work environment affected the factory workers. He pursued some labor reforms especially for women, such as maternity protections, and prohibiting night work. In the 1920s when the effect of World War I was over, Japan experienced an age of economic turbulence and turmoil. Kirihara's statement as I-O psychologist, described in his book "the I-O psychology […], grasps the life of the people as a matter of problem, not as a (research) object" (Kirihara, 1938, p. 31) reflected on his earliest days at the Kurashiki Institute for Science of Labour.

References

Bae, B.-G. (2000). *The theory and practice of labor science: The studies and thoughts of Shigemi Kirihara, an industrial psychologist.* Hihyosha (In Japanese).

Downey, J. E. (1923). *The will-temperament and its testing*. World Book.
Haraguchi, T. (1914). *The study of mental work and fatigue*. Hokubunkan (In Japanese).
Kirihara, H. (1930). On the mental development of the Japanese. In J.M. Cattell (Ed.), *Ninth international congress of psychology proceedings* (pp. 255–256). Psychological Review.
Kirihara, H. (1934). Learning to spin. *Personnel Journal*, 13, 82–83.
Kirihara, S. (1938). *Industrial psychology*. Chikura Shobo (In Japanese).
Kirihara, S. (1943). *Menstruation and working capacity*. Chikura Shobo (In Japanese).
Kirihara, S. (1944). *Women's labor*. Toyo Shokan (In Japanese).
Kirihara S. (1953). Industrial psychology in Japan: Retrospect and prospect. In S. Kirihara (Ed.), *Current industrial psychology* (pp.9–18). Kanazawa Shoten (In Japanese).
Kosugo, R. (2006). The historical background of *Women's labor*. In Z. Otagaki & R. Kosugo (Eds.), *The productivity of labor. Part 1: Science of labor by Shigemi Kirihara* (pp.7–10). Institute for Science of Labor (In Japanese).
Mitsui, D. (1998). Formation of field psychology in Japan: Through the work study of Shigemi Kirihara. In Shinri-Kagaku-Kenkyukai (Ed.), *Study of the history of psychology in Japan* (pp.139–176). Hosei Shuppan (In Japanese).
Ohizumi, H. (2003). *The dictionary of Japanese psychologists*. Kress-Shuppan (In Japanese).

Chapter 23

Donald G. Paterson (1892–1961)

Michael J. Zickar

Donald G. Paterson was an important applied psychologist who made lasting contributions to the measurement of individual differences, both for helping organizations select the best employees and to help individuals make sound career decisions. During World War I (WWI), he served on the United States (US) Army team to examine recruits for selection and placement, and after the War he worked at the Scott Company before taking a position at the University of Minnesota as a faculty member. Throughout his long tenure at Minnesota, he shaped a program that was known for its rigorous approach to measurement of individual differences in the service of helping individuals. His career is an important reminder of the interconnection between personnel selection and vocational counseling.

Biographical Overview

Donald Gildersleeve Paterson was born on January 18, 1892, in Columbus, OH, one of five children of his two parents who were both deaf as a result of childhood illnesses. He studied at Olivet College in Michigan where he became interested in the early 20th century progressive reformer Frank Parsons who was a key figure in the early vocational guidance movement (see Paterson, 1976). He transferred to Ohio State University, though, and completed his bachelor's degree as well as a master's degree at Ohio State University working under behaviorist A.P. Weiss as well as noted differential psychologist Rudolf Pinter, an important psychologist who made a career out for working with and developing assessments for the handicapped

DOI: 10.4324/9781003403258-23

and especially the deaf community (see Hollingworth, 1943). Working with Pinter, Paterson helped develop the Pinter–Paterson Performance Test (Pinter & Paterson, 1917), which was a nonverbal intelligence test, a test that eventually served as a precursor to the Army Beta, the nonverbal intelligence test used to assess non-native English-speaking as well as illiterate military recruits during WWI. He took an instructor position at the University of Kansas with the intention of completing a dissertation at the University of Chicago. His plans, though, like so many men of the era were disrupted by the United States' entry into WWI. Paterson enlisted in the army, serving in the US Army Committee on the Psychological Examining of Recruits, working under Robert Yerkes. He rose to the level of Captain and served alongside other notable psychologists including Lewis Terman, Walter Dill Scott, and Richard M. Elliott.

After the War, like many other psychologists who served in the US Army testing efforts, Paterson worked at the Scott Company (named after Walter Dill Scott), one of the first consulting firms devoted to applying psychology to private businesses. In 1921, he took an associate professor faculty position at University of Minnesota, hired by another war colleague Richard M. Elliot, to bring applied psychology to Minnesota. He was quickly promoted to Full Professor in 1923. He finally retired from University of Minnesota in 1960. An interesting fact about Paterson is that he never attained his PhD. His service in the war interrupted his doctoral studies at Ohio State University and at one point, people joked that there was no one in the field of industrial psychology who was competent enough to evaluate him. He did receive an honorary LLD (doctorate in law) from Ohio State University in 1952.

Paterson's formal accomplishments are impressive. He was instrumental in building up the doctoral program in industrial-organizational (I-O) psychology at the University of Minnesota, a PhD program that has been strong throughout the history of the field. Paterson served as major advisor to approximately 300 masters students and 88 doctoral students at the University of Minnesota (Baker, 2006). At the University of Minnesota, he helped establish the University of Minnesota Student Counseling Bureau, its Industrial Relations Center, as well as the important

Minnesota Employment Stabilization Research Institute, an institute that helped understand unemployment during the depths of the Great Depression. He served as the Secretary of the American Psychological Association for six years and was elected President in 1938 of the American Association for Applied Psychology, a predecessor of the Society for Industrial and Organizational Psychology.

In the following section, I will detail some of the contributions of Paterson to the field of industrial psychology. Specifically, I will focus on early work that helped establish the importance of scientific methods applied to personnel selection. In addition, I will detail his work in focusing on using psychological tests for both sides of selection, both companies selecting the best employees and individuals choosing the best occupations.

Summary of Contributions

Establishing the Importance of Rigor and Science in Personnel Selection

In the early 20th century as businesses expanded, they were no longer able to rely on friends and family to fill key positions and turned to a variety of techniques to identify the right person to hire at a particular time. Applied psychologists began to promote the use of their standardized and validated tests as a key hiring tool, especially after WWI, when organizations like the Scott Company made concerted efforts to convince hiring managers to use their tests. There were a variety of other approaches that did not rely on validation and assessment. One particular prominent voice was Dr. Katherine Blackford who advocated a form of character analysis that made distinctions based on physical characteristics such as color of hair as well as shape of face (see Blackford & Newcomb, 1914). Blackford relied on testimonials from satisfied customers to demonstrate the validity of her work and never empirically tested her findings.

Paterson undertook some of the first studies to disprove Blackford's theories. Along with a student Kathleen Ludgate, they asked 94 participants to evaluate 374 individuals who were either blond or brunette. They asked individuals to rate the candidates on 26 traits that Blackford hypothesized to correspond to either blonds or brunettes. They concluded that individuals with blond hair were just as likely to have traits endorsed that Blackford associated with brunettes and vice versa (Paterson & Ludgate, 1922). Paterson went on to conduct other studies disproving Blackford's system and even wrote a book entitled *Physique and Intellect* (Paterson, 1930) that was helpful in disproving theories based on phrenology and physiognomy.

Besides helping establish the importance of scientifically validated approaches to personnel selection, Paterson himself helped develop tests that were important in the history of personnel selection. As mentioned in the overview, Paterson's work in conjunction with his graduate mentor Rudolph Pintner was important in helping understand nonverbal ways to measure cognitive ability, work that eventually inspired the Army Beta test. In addition while at the Scott Company, Paterson worked on a measure of clerical abilities, developing the Scott Company's File Clerk Test, which measured different aspects of traditional clerical jobs (at least from the era), including comparing names and numbers, alphabetizing names, and reading comprehension (see Brewer, 1942). Paterson believed fully in the importance of individual differences and throughout his career, he worked and supported efforts to measure individual differences that were helpful in predicting successful job outcomes.

In addition to developing predictors, Paterson recognized that measuring job performance was important both for validating predictors and for helping companies make sensible promotion decisions. He felt that having well-researched systems was important in that it was crucial that managers made ratings using the same dimensions and questions across employees and he felt that a good rating system could help managers understand the development progress of employees (Paterson, 1923). Consistent with his views on the importance of ratings, while at the Scott Company, he created a new version of the Scott Company's Graphic Rating Scale, which allowed respondents to make fine distinctions on whether performance ranged from satisfactory to unsatisfactory on a variety of dimensions (Paterson, 1922). In addition, he developed innovative ways to compute overall performance ratings based on ratings of individual rating dimensions.

Throughout his career, Paterson believed in the importance of assessing individual differences in a rigorous and scientific approach to help organizations make better personnel decisions. He developed innovative assessments as well as innovative approaches to measure performance. As will discussed in the next section, Paterson also worked on developing assessments and programs that would help individuals make better career decisions.

Advocacy for the Importance of Vocational Counseling

In the early days of industrial psychology, applied psychologists were interested in both using psychological tests to help organizations make better hiring decisions and for individuals to use psychological tests to make better career decisions. It was only in the 1950s and onward when the fields of personnel selection and vocational counseling split apart with specialists focusing on one or the other. Individuals who pursued personnel selection were more likely to identify as I-O psychologists and those focused on vocational counseling were more likely to identify as counseling psychologists. Paterson would have likely lamented this division as he was a strong advocate that industrial psychology should use its tools to both help managers and help workers. Throughout his career, he conducted research in both personnel selection (helping companies) and vocational counseling (helping individuals) (see Erdheim et al., 2007 for more on this division).

Much of this view was formed during the Great Depression when Paterson was instrumental in founding the Minnesota Unemployment Project. The project had three goals: (1) to investigate the underlying factors of employment and unemployment; (2) looking at the effectiveness of vocational assessment and guidance and training in helping the unemployed achieve employment; and (3) setting up a system that could help make public employment offices more effective (see Paterson, 1932). Minnesota was devastated by the Great Depression with over 30,000 workers unemployed in the three big cities of Minnesota that were targeted by the project, Minneapolis, St. Paul, and Duluth. As part of Paterson's program, the unemployed who came for help in seeking jobs were given a vocational interview, a series of vocational interest tests, as well as a complete medical and physical examination. The culmination of this work was perhaps his book published with colleague John Darley *Men, Women, and Jobs: A Study in Human Engineering* (Paterson & Darley, 1936).

Consistent with Paterson's work with the unemployed, Paterson helped develop the student personnel guidance program at the University of Minnesota, a program that assessed individual students and helped guide their choice of major and career choice. The University of Minnesota became a leader in vocational guidance because of seminal work by Paterson and colleagues (see Beck, 1982).

Conclusion

Paterson was an important advocate of rigor in assessment as a way of helping both individual employees prosper and find satisfying careers and to help organizations function better. He bridged the two purposes of selection (employee-focused and organizational-focused) perhaps more than any other applied psychologist before or since. In addition, Paterson was instrumental in shaping the University of Minnesota I-O psychology program, creating the "Minnesota tradition" that combined hard-nosed assessment with a humanistic urge to use our work to help all individuals.

References

Baker, D. B. (2006). An individual difference: The career of Donald G. Paterson. *Portraits of Pioneers in Psychology*, 6, 135. https://doi.org/10.4324/9781315822464

Beck, R.H. (1982). *Beyond pedagogy: A history of the University of Minnesota College of Education*. North Central Publishing.

Blackford, K.M.H., & Newcomb, A. (1914). *The job, the man, the boss*. Doubleday & Page.

Brewer, J.M. (1942). *History of vocational guidance*. Harper. https://doi.org/10.1037/13575-000

Erdheim, J., Zickar, M.J., & Yankelevich, M. (2007). Remembering Donald G. Paterson: Before the separation between industrial–organizational

and vocational psychology. *Journal of Vocational Behavior*, *70*(1), 205–221. https://doi.org/10.1016/j.jvb.2006.09.001
Hollingworth, H.L. (1943). Rudolph Pintner: 1884-1942. *The American Journal of Psychology*, *56*(2), 303–305.
Paterson, D.G. (1922). The Scott Company graphic rating scale. *Journal of Personnel Research, 1*, 361–376.
Paterson, D.G. (1923). The vocational testing movement. *Journal of Personnel Research, 2*, 295–305.
Paterson, D.G. (1930). *Physique and intellect.* The Century.
Paterson, D.G. (1932). The Minnesota unemployment research project. *Personnel Journal, 10*, 318–328. https://doi.org/10.1086/631012
Paterson, D.G. (1976). Reminiscences concerning the development of student personnel work at the University of Minnesota. *Journal of College Student Personnel, 17,* 380–385. (Posthumous publication of a 1958 speech).
Paterson, D.G., & Darley, J.G. (1936). *Men, women, and jobs: A study in human engineering: A review of the studies of the Committee on Individual Diagnosis and Training*. University of Minnesota Press.
Paterson, D.G., & Ludgate, K.E. (1922). Blond and Brunette traits: A quantitative study. *Journal of Personnel Research, 1,* 122–127.
Pinter, R. & Paterson, D.G. (1917). *A scale of performance tests.* Appleton.

Chapter 24

Elsie Oschrin Bregman (1896–1969)

Laura Koppes Bryan

Elsie Oschrin Bregman was an early applied psychologist who had a successful career in applying psychology while working full time in industry and managing her own consulting business from home (Koppes, 1997). While studying for her doctorate, she studied directly with E.L. Thorndike and maintained a partnership with him throughout her career. She also worked with James McKeen Cattell of the Psychological Corporation. Some credit Bregman as the only individual to profit from the Psychological Corporation during the early years as a result of royalties she received from the revisions of the Army Alpha General Intelligence Examinations for use by businesses and educational institutions (Sokal, 1981). Her pioneering work changed how psychologists measured ability and intelligence.

Biographical Overview

Elsie Oschrin was born in Newark, NJ, 1896, to Aaron and Theresa (Goldstein) Oschrin. She received a baccalaureate degree from Barnard College, Columbia University, in 1918 and then married Adolph Bregman, a consulting metallurgical engineer, in 1919; they had two daughters, Judith and Cynthia. She was awarded a PhD in psychology from Columbia University in 1922 where she was a student of E.L. Thorndike, an original researcher of intelligence testing and employee selection (Sokal, 1981). Thorndike proved to be an important influence on Bregman's lifelong work. While enrolled at Columbia University, Bregman took several courses with a noteworthy psychologist of the first generation of American female psychologists, Leta

DOI: 10.4324/9781003403258-24

S. Hollingworth who was married to Harry Hollingworth, a key thinker included in this text. Bregman's (1922a) dissertation was published as Studies in Industrial Psychology.

Bregman, after beginning her career at Guardian Life Insurance Company as a psychologist in 1918, was hired as a psychologist for R.H. Macy and Company from 1919 to 1921 to examine the company's personnel processes, one of several businesses that hired psychologists to examine their personnel processes after World War I (WWI; Sokal, 1981). From 1922 to 1927, she was a research assistant, and from 1931 to 1934, a research associate, at the Institute for Educational Research at Teachers College, Columbia University, where Thorndike was director. From 1924 until 1934, she was the assistant secretary of the Psychological Corporation, which was founded in 1921 by James McKeen Cattell for advancing applications of psychology (Cattell, 1923). From 1927 to 1929, she was Assistant Director of the Child Study Association followed by a fellowship with the National Research Council from 1929–1930. She returned to the Institute of Educational Research and then in 1935, she was a research associate at the Progressive Education Association, which is when she conducted a large-scale educational and vocational test survey with the New York City public schools (Bregman Biography, 1970). Bregman then managed a private consulting practice from her home in New York from 1936 to 1962, an unusual practice but similar to other women psychologists at the time (e.g., Lillian Gilbreth; Koppes, 1997). Elsie Oschrin Bregman died July 26, 1969, in New York City.

Contributions to I-O Psychology

Bregman contributed to I-O psychology in many ways during the early years of the discipline. Based on a previous study of her career (Koppes, 1997), I will outline two areas of her contributions: field research and the applications of measurement and testing in business and educational settings.

Field Research

Bregman's groundbreaking research while working for the R.H. Macy and Company focused on topics such as adjustment of sales and clerical positions, recruitment, selection, and training (Bregman, 1921; Bregman Biography, 1970; Sokal, 1981). For example, she developed the first testing and employee training programs for department store sales. She applied criteria developed by Thorndike in the "Fundamental Theorems in Judging Men" (1918) for selection purposes (Sokal, 1981). At "one of the largest department stores of New York City" (Oschrin, 1918, p. 148), she used the Spearman formula to compute correlations between actual sales ability and performance on 13 tests of retail saleswomen. Colleagues respected her research as one wrote in a letter to Bregman "This appears to be the most important single piece of work done in the department store field so far" (Craig, 1921).

In the introduction of the publication from her dissertation research, Bregman (1922b) espoused the value of field research. She wrote,

> The studies are not laboratory studies. They come out of the midst of a very busy industry. They were in consequence subject to restrictions, exercised not only by the factors of time and cost, but also certain other factors, inherent in the situation of the youngest of the sciences trying to work out its usefulness in an environment traditionally and actually so foreign to it.
>
> The writer believes that notwithstanding their shortcomings the studies have certain significance and usefulness, and in this belief they are presented to the reader in this volume. (p. 4)

In another publication (Bregman, 1922a), she described how the company took the lead in researching tests in the field and highlighted the originality of these studies by stating

> At R.H. Macy and Company the possibilities of this field of work had been brought out to the executives, even before the use of the Army Tests, by some tests I carried out on clerks in the store when I was a student. And so, about three years ago, an almost unprecedented experiment was begun. Almost never before had a psychological laboratory been equipped in an industrial organization, certainly not in a department store,

> and a psychologist commissioned to experiment in his own field of science.
>
> (p. 696)

> The result of this experimental work was the discovery of tests which could be used in the employment of two kinds of workers, salesclerks and clerical workers.
>
> (p. 696)

In addition to advocating for field research, Bregman published her field research in journals such as *Journal of Applied Psychology*, *Psychological Bulletin*, and *Journal of Education Research*.

Measurement and Testing

Much of Bregman's field research provided the basis for her dissertation as well as changed how psychologists measured mental ability and intelligence. She described the pioneering use of psychological tests in industry in the following way:

> At the time when this work was under way almost no research of a similar character had been undertaken. Very little appeared in the literature that bore directly on the problem, and organizations in which psychological tests, adequately evaluated and properly administered, functioned with any degree of importance, were hardly to be found.
>
> (Bregman, 1922a, Foreword)

Bregman is most widely known for the revisions of the Army Alpha General Intelligence Examinations (initially developed for testing the intelligence of Army recruits during WWI) for use by businesses and educational institutions while employed with the Psychological Corporation. Interestingly, the Psychological Corporation did not succeed as anticipated during its early years, and beginning in 1923, Cattell utilized tactics to save the corporation (Sokal, 1981). One such tactic was hiring Bregman as an associate (1924–1925) and later assistant secretary (1925–1934). During this time, she developed and published the

Bregman Revision of the Army Alpha Examinations for General Intelligence Forms A and B (Bregman, 1926, 1935a), which were sold and administered by the Psychological Corporation as a means to generate revenue. Bregman noted

> The examinations are suitable for use with adults and with students at high school and college levels. They are published by the Psychological Corporation, 522 Fifth Avenue, New York N.Y. The blanks are 8 [cents] each, $6.50 for 100. A specimen set costs 25 [cents]. The manuals give grade and age norms, and also a scale for converting scores into percentiles of the general adult population.
>
> (Bregman, n.d., p. 1)

Unfortunately, after royalties and overhead expenses were paid, there was little net income (Sokal, 1981). Bregman received royalties (10% of every sale) throughout her lifetime and is considered to be the only individual to profit from the Psychological Corporation during its early years (Sokal, 1981).

While at the Psychological Corporation, Bregman published books with E.L. Thorndike and others: examples include *Adult Learning* (Thorndike et al., 1928), and *The Prediction of Vocational Success* (Thorndike et al., 1934). Additionally, she handled other activities, such as writing articles requested by Cattell and developing the Bregman Language Completion Scales (Bregman, 1935b). She had a lifelong professional relationship and friendship with Cattell, and from 1942 until her death, she was named a trustee of the James McKeen Cattell Fund, a small foundation that gave grants for applied psychology research. From 1950 until 1963, she was the secretary-treasurer of the fund.

Bregman continued measurement and testing research beyond the department store. She collaborated with Thorndike on a benchmark study they published in 1926 titled *The Measurement of Intelligence* (Thorndike et al., 1926). In 1931 when hired as a psychology consultant in the Department of Nursing Education at Teachers College, Columbia University, Bregman developed a program of vocational tests for nurses, and later published a national survey on the intelligence of nurses (Bregman, 1933). She designed and administered a significant education and vocational test survey for the New York City public schools. Additionally, she developed a record blank for retaining a thorough record of a student's performance as they progressed through primary and secondary grades (Bregman, 1936). This pioneering field research greatly influenced how psychologists measured intelligence, especially for applied purposes, during the early years of I-O psychology.

Recognition

Bregman was highly engaged in professional organizations and was frequently recognized for her contributions by serving in leadership roles. She was a fellow of the American Association for the Advancement of Science and the American Psychological Association. She was vice president (1931), member of the Executive Committee (1925–1937), and chair of the Committee on Constitution and Bylaws (1933) of the Association of Consulting Psychologists (organized in 1930), an organization that supported applied psychology. She was also a member of the American Association for Applied Psychology (organized in 1937) for which she served as chair of the Committee on Membership and was involved with the American Board of Examiners of Professional Psychology as a diplomate in Counseling. Bregman chaired the Legislative Committee (1939) and the Committee on Constitution and Bylaws (1938) of the New York State Association of Applied Psychology. She is included in *American Men of Science* (Cattell & Cattell, 1944) and *Who's Who of American Women* (Who's Who of American Women, 1958–1959)

Conclusion

Elsie Oschrin Bregman was recognized by her contemporaries for leading the way in scientific field research. Her applied research was considered at the forefront of many current research studies on predictors, criteria, predictive validity, and other testing issues. Particularly noteworthy was her pioneering work with measurement and testing in applied settings for business purposes. She was one of few women psychologists who earned a PhD and was actively engaged in the nascent discipline of I-O psychology.

References

Bregman, E.O. (n.d.) *Bregman revision of the Army Alpha examination for general intelligence: Forms A and B* (p. 1). Psychological Corporation.

Bregman, E.O. (1921). A study in industrial psychology – Tests for special abilities. *Journal of Applied Psychology*, *5*, 127–151. https://doi.org/10.1037/h0072210

Bregman, E.O. (1922a). Studies in industrial psychology. *Archives of Psychology*, *9*, 1–60.

Bregman, E.O. (1922b). A scientific plan for sizing up employees. *System*, June, 696–763.

Bregman, E.O. (1926). *Revision of the Army Alpha examination. Form A*. Psychological Corporation.

Bregman, E.O. (1933). *The performance of student nurses on tests of intelligence*. Teachers College, Columbia University.

Bregman, E.O. (1935a). *Revision of the Army Alpha examination. Form B*. Psychological Corporation.

Bregman, E.O. (1935b). *Bregman language completion scales. Forms A and B*. Psychological Corporation.

Bregman, E.O. (1936). *Comprehensive individual history record form and manual: Infancy through high school*. Psychological Corporation.

Bregman Biography. (1970, March 12). *E.O. Bregman collection*. University of Akron, Archives of the History of American Psychology.

Cattell, J.M. (1923). The Psychological Corporation. *Annals of the American Academy of Political and Social Science*, *110*, 165–171. https://doi.org/10.1177/000271622311000117

Cattell, J.M. & Cattell, J. (1944). *American men of science* (7th ed.). Science Press.

Craig, D.R. (1921, October 12). [Letter to E.O. Bregman]. *E.O. Bregman collection*, Box M296, Folder: Correspondence 1936-1922. University of Akron, Archives of the History of American Psychology.

Koppes, L.L.(1997). American female pioneers of industrial and organizational psychology during the early years. *Journal of Applied Psychology*, *82*(4), 500–515. https://doi.org/10.1037//0021-9010.82.4.500

Oschrin, E. (1918). Vocational tests for retail saleswomen. *Journal of Applied Psychology*, 2, 148–155. https://doi.org/10.1037/h0075948

Sokal, M.M. (1981). The origins of The Psychological Corporation. *Journal of the History of the Behavioral Sciences, 17*, 54–67. https://doi.org/10.1002/1520-6696(198101)17:1%3C54::aid-jhbs2300170108%3E3.0.co;2-r

Thorndike, E.L. (1918). Fundamental theorems in judging men. *Journal of Applied Psychology,* 2(1), 67–76. https://doi.org/10.1037/h0074876

Thorndike, E.L., Bregman, E.O., Cobb, M.V., Woodyard, E., & Inst of Educational Research Div of Psychology, Teachers Coll, Columbia U. (1926). *The measurement of intelligence.* Teachers College Bureau of Publications. https://doi.org/10.1037/11240-000

Thorndike, E.L., Bregman, E.O., & Metcalfe, Z.F. (1934). *The prediction of vocational success.* Commonwealth Fund.

Thorndike, E.L., Bregman, E.O., Tilton, J.W., & Woodyard, E. (1928). *Adult learning*. Macmillan.

Who's Who of American Women, Vol. 1, 1st cd. (1958-1959). *Bregman, Elsie Oschrin* (p. 161). Marquis—Who's Who.

Chapter 25

Max Freyd (1896–1951)

Andrew J. Vinchur

Max Freyd is not as well-known as the other industrial-organizational (I-O) psychologists who appear in this volume. As far as I can determine, he received no honors or awards; no articles or book chapters have previously been written about him; he had no cadre of graduate students to carry his legacy; and when he passed away in 1951, no obituaries appeared in professional journals. Yet I believe that Freyd has earned his chapter for the following reasons. First and foremost, his ideas about what was then termed industrial psychology were interesting and prescient: Freyd wrote about how industrial psychologists should approach their discipline and about the nature of applied psychology. He also made contributions to our understanding of employee selection, personality assessment, vocational interests, and other topics. Second, Freyd was involved in some of the foundational events in the history of I-O psychology, among them the first doctoral program in industrial psychology at the Carnegie Institute of Technology (CIT), the Personnel Research Federation, and the *Journal of Personnel Research*. Freyd's career was varied and encompassed academia, consulting, editing, and government service. And finally, Freyd can act as a proxy for the many other accomplished individuals who had solid careers and made substantive contributions to I-O psychology, but who, for whatever reasons, are little remembered today.

Biographical Overview

The Life

Born in Seattle, WA, on June 1896, Freyd received his BA in psychology in 1918 and an MS in psychology and education in

DOI: 10.4324/9781003403258-25

1920, both from the University of Washington. In 1920 he began a fellowship at the CIT in the Bureau of Personnel Research, part of the Division of Applied Psychology, the first doctoral program in industrial psychology. Walter Van Dyke Bingham, the director of the program, would become an important mentor, colleague, and collaborator for Freyd. Freyd (1951) noted that one of Bingham's "finest traits was the personal interest he took in all the students of the Division, and the efforts to which he went in furthering their professional careers" (p. 4). In June 1922, Freyd received his PhD from that institution, one of the first four students in the United States to earn doctoral degrees in industrial psychology.[1] In addition to Bingham, many students and faculty associated with the short-lived (1915 to 1924) CIT program were important in the history of I-O psychology, such as Marion A. Bills, Arthur Kornhauser, Bruce V. Moore, Walter Dill Scott, Edward K. Strong, Jr., and L. L. Thurstone.[2]

Following graduation, Freyd taught as an instructor at the University of Pennsylvania for the 1922–1923 academic year. Associated with that institution was the industrial psychologist Morris Viteles, who was at the beginning stages of his long career at the University of Pennsylvania and who would later engage in an interesting debate with Freyd on the clinical versus the statistical viewpoint in employee selection, described later. From 1923 to 1925 Freyd was employed as a research psychologist at the J. Walter Thompson Company, where he worked with John B. Watson, the noted behaviorist. At the Thompson Company, Freyd conducted research on merchandizing, marketing, and advertising. He then reunited with Bingham at the Personnel Research Federation, an organization founded in 1921 as a clearinghouse for personnel research information that also provided industrial consultants and personnel-related research (Bingham, 1928). While there, Freyd conducted personnel research and was managing editor of the *Personnel Journal* (formerly the *Journal of Personnel Research*) (Vinchur, 2018). In 1928, he took the position of head of the Merchandizing Research Division at the Retail Research Association. Freyd moved to Washington, D.C., in 1936 to become the head of the Personnel Division of the Social Security Board; later he worked for the Civil Service Commission supervising the development of personnel manuals for government service. Poor health forced an early retirement in 1946 (Freyd, 1951). Freyd died in St. Petersburg, FL, in 1951.[3]

The Work

As part of the generation of American industrial psychologists who followed the founders of the field, Max Freyd and his cohort defined the scope of industrial psychology and went about refining the discipline's methodology. By the time Viteles's landmark text *Industrial Psychology* was published in 1932, there was a general understanding of what constituted industrial psychology and what methods were appropriate for research and practice. Freyd's contributions to that understanding include the following: in graduate school at CIT under the supervision of Clarence Yoakum, Freyd and his fellow students Grace Manson, Bruce Moore, and Merrill Ream conducted some of the earliest research on vocational interest inventories (Ferguson, 1962–1965). This research influenced CIT faculty member Edward K. Strong, Jr., who later with his student Karl Cowdery at Stanford University developed his well-known Strong Vocational Interest Blank (Ferguson, n.d.; Strong, 1927). Freyd's (1922) dissertation, later published in *Psychological Monographs*, was an investigation of the use of personality correlates for differentiating individuals, based on interests and abilities, who prefer working with people (e.g., sales jobs) versus those who prefer working with machines (Freyd, 1924). This work was an early example of the use of the contrasted group method of test construction. During his career Freyd published interest inventories, rating scales, an introversion–extroversion inventory, and various tests. As is true for many who worked outside of academia, he conducted and supervised numerous unpublished research studies (Freyd, 1951).[4]

A notable research area for Freyd was employee selection. In the 1920s, the familiar criterion-related validation model for selection was becoming standardized, and Freyd and other researchers such as Link (1919), Kornhauser and Kingsbury (1924), and Burtt (1926) discussed selection methodology and the assumptions that underlie it. Freyd's (1922–1923) approach can be summarized as follows: if possible, first consult with a cost consultant in the organization to determine where a valid selection procedure is most needed. Next, conduct a job analysis and determine the criteria for success. Then, select individuals who are to participate in the validation study. Determine the abilities required for success on the job, and construct or select measuring instruments such as psychological tests, questionnaires, and rating scales. Administer these measures to the sample under carefully controlled conditions. Empirically evaluate the relationship between predictor scores and criteria; Freyd discussed various correlational methods for accomplishing this. Combine predictors for maximum efficiency; Freyd preferred multiple regression for this step. If the scores are predictive of success, compare the new procedure with the old method of selection to determine what today is termed incremental validity. Finally, periodically examine the relationship between predictor and criterion to see if that relationship remains consistent over time.

In 1926, Freyd and Bingham published *Procedures for Employment Psychology: A Manual for Developing Scientific Methods of Vocational Selection* (Bingham & Freyd, 1926). In this volume, Bingham and Freyd expanded on earlier work, discussing topics such as how to determine if a new selection system is needed, the need for a large applicant pool and large sample sizes, the need for reliable and valid criteria, and the importance of managerial cooperation in the process. Viteles (1932) called the book the most complete text describing test construction for vocational selection.

Freyd (1922–1923) was overtly scientific in his approach, for example, referring to applicants as subjects and the whole process of selection as an experiment. A strong advocate for a scientific orientation in selection, in 1925 Freyd engaged in an interesting debate with Morris Viteles in the pages of the *Journal of Applied Psychology*. Viteles (1925) advocated for a more clinical approach to selection, rather than relying on statistical validity. He stated that reliance on a single test score is inadequate and that a "psycho-technician" without extensive training in psychology cannot properly interpret test results. Viteles was, however, in no way arguing for the elimination of the statistical approach, but rather, that the use of valid tests should be in concert with a more worker-centered, clinical approach. He was an admirer of the European approach, which he considered more humane in its emphasis on the well-being and interests of the worker. Over-reliance on statistical methodology, Viteles argued, with its emphasis on the group rather than the individual, fails to adequately take the worker into account.

Freyd (1925), echoing Thorndike (1918), disagreed. If the proper procedures are followed, that is, a careful analysis of the job requirements, proper test construction and criterion selection, and evidence for a strong correlation between the test and criterion, the statistical approach provides verifiable evidence that the test is valid. By providing this empirical evidence for validity, employee selection can have a firm scientific basis. In criticizing the clinical position, Freyd noted problems with substituting judgment for empirical evidence. He saw no reason to assume that the judgments of psychologists would be better than those of managers, discussed the problem of unreliability of judgments, and was concerned with what he saw as an unavoidable bias in the clinical methods. Summarizing his position, Freyd wrote: "The field for psychologists in industry is experimental research. If other fields seem greener they are a mirage" (p. 352).[5]

Consistent with Freyd's advocacy for empirical research and the use of statistically valid procedures in industrial psychology, he questioned the distinction between applied psychology and experimental psychology. Concerned about the appropriation of the applied psychology label by pseudoscientists who promise much more than they can deliver, Freyd (1926) examined applied and general (experimental) psychology from the perspective of method, content, and viewpoint. He noted that the psychological experimental method is just an example of the general scientific method, which is common to all science and therefore the same for applied and general psychology. Regarding content, Freyd described how the laboratory psychologist manipulates single variables in carefully controlled conditions. Results from such studies, he argued, cannot be directly applied to real-world situations, as the context of those settings is too complex. Lab studies can, however, provide a path to follow for further investigations in the field. In both general and applied psychology, the subject matter or content is the same: behavior. Freyd noted that both pure and applied psychologists are interested in providing accurate information to others. While applied psychologists are seen as more economically motivated than experimental psychologists, basic science can have unforeseen future economic value, and applied psychology can reveal general patterns and contribute to a basic understanding of behavior. Freyd concluded that the usual distinctions between general and applied psychology break down under analysis; psychologists study human behavior under all conditions. The real distinction is between psychologists and pseudo-psychologists. Freyd (1926) stated:

> The psychologist is differentiated from all others who use psychology in that he constantly maintains the research attitude, putting every fact to the experimental test, and recommending no application of findings which are not verified for the problem in question.
>
> (p. 314)

The Legacy

Freyd's career was varied, encompassing academia, consulting, journal editing, applied research, and government. He thought and wrote about how industrial psychology could be a true science, and conducted early research on vocational interests, personality characteristics, and other topics that influenced those who followed him. Freyd's work on personnel selection and validation is particularly noteworthy; Guion (1976) found Freyd's (1923–1924) article on the process "marvelously up to date" (p. 783). Was Max Freyd a key thinker in the history of I-O psychology? Freyd did not think so. In 1951, Leonard Ferguson, who was writing a history of the Division of Applied Psychology at CIT, wrote to Freyd and asked him for information about his career. In his reply, Freyd wrote: "… what I am able to give you is brief, which is just as well, since I have always considered myself one of the lesser lights of the C.I.T. group" (1951, p. 1). I disagree. While not as prominent as his sparring partner Viteles or his CIT cohort members Bills, Bingham, Kornhauser, Moore, Scott, Strong, and Thurstone, all who have chapters in this volume, Freyd was a solid contributor to the development of

I-O psychology, and as such, a worthy representative of all the other lesser-known key thinkers whose ideas and research shaped the discipline.

Notes

1 The other three who received PhDs were Bruce Moore (1921), Merrill Ream (1921), and Grace Manson (1923). These were the only doctoral degrees awarded by the CIT Division of Psychology program, which closed in 1924 (Vinchur, 2018). Freyd (1951) recalled that he majored in psychology and personnel administration. However, the Registrar at Carnegie-Mellon University (the successor to CIT) could not locate a degree that included the phrase "personnel administration" (J. Papinchak, personal communication, February 12, 2018).
2 Other influential psychologists associated with the CIT program include Grace Manson, James B. Miner, Merrill Jay Ream, Richard S. Uhrbrock, Guy Montrose Whipple, and Clarence Stone Yoakum (see Ferguson, 1962–1965 for a history of the CIT program).
3 Freyd's very brief obituary in the *St. Petersburg Times* (1951) stated that he was a veteran of World War I, however, I have not been able to confirm that. It also erroneously has him receiving his doctorate from the University of Pittsburgh, rather than CIT and his age at death as 54 (he was 55).
4 Freyd (1951) estimated about 100 unpublished research studies.
5 Viteles continued to advocate for his clinically-oriented position in his 1932 text.

References

Bingham, W. V. (1928). Industrial psychology: Its progress in the United States – Psychology as science, as point of view and as method. *Bulletin of the Taylor Society, 13*, 187–198.

Bingham, W. V., & Freyd, M. (1926). *Procedures in employment psychology: A manual for developing scientific methods of vocational selection*. McGraw-Hill.

Burtt, H. (1926). *Principles of employment psychology*. Harper.

Ferguson, L. W. (n.d.) *New light on the history of industrial psychology*. Unpublished manuscript, (Ferguson Collection), Carnegie Mellon University, Pittsburgh PA.

Ferguson, L. W. (1962–1965). *The heritage of industrial psychology* [14 pamphlets]. Finlay Press.

Freyd, M. (1922–1923). Measurement in vocational selection. *Journal of Personnel Research, 1*, 215–249, 268–284, 377–385.

Freyd, M. (1924). The personalities of the socially and the mechanically inclined. *Psychological Monographs, 23*. https://doi.org/10.1037/h0093204

Freyd, M. (1925). The statistical viewpoint in vocational selection. *Journal of Applied Psychology, 9*, 349–356. https://doi.org/10.1037/h0074663

Freyd, M. (1926). What is applied psychology? *Psychological Review, 33*, 308–324. https://doi.org/10.1037/h0073383

Freyd, M. (1951, March 7). [Letter to Leonard W. Ferguson]. Carnegie Mellon University (Ferguson Collection, Box 4), Pittsburgh, PA.

Guion, R. M. (1976). Recruiting, selection, and job placement. In M. D. Dunnette (Ed.), *Handbook of industrial and organizational psychology* (pp. 777–823). Rand McNally.

Kornhauser, A. W., & Kingsbury, F. A. (1924). *Psychological tests in business*. University of Chicago Press. https://doi.org/10.2307/3901566

Link, H. C. (1919). *Employment psychology: The application of scientific methods to the selection, training, and grading of employees*. Macmillan.

St. Petersburg Times (1951, September 2). Obituaries: Ex-civil service official, Max Freyd, is dead at 54.

Strong, E. K., Jr. (1927). Vocational interest test. *Educational Record, 8*, 107–121.

Thorndike, E. L. (1918). Fundamental theorems in judging men. *Journal of Applied Psychology, 2*, 67–76. https://doi.org/10.1037/h0074876

Vinchur, A. J. (2018). *The early years of industrial and organizational psychology*. Cambridge University Press. https://doi.org/10.1017/9781107588608

Viteles, M. S. (1925). The clinical viewpoint in vocational selection. *Journal of Applied Psychology, 9*, 131–138. https://doi.org/10.1037/h0071305

Viteles, M. S. (1932). *Industrial psychology*. Norton.

Chapter 26

Arthur Kornhauser (1896–1990)

Michael J. Zickar

Arthur Kornhauser was one of the first industrial psychologists who advocated for using the science to better advocate for the lives of workers including strengthening the effectiveness of labor unions. His research career spanned a variety of topics including early work on psychological tests applied for employee selection as well as studying employee attitude surveys. His most ambitious work, and his last published research, involved surveying Detroit autoworkers and their families on their mental health and drawing connections between mental health and working conditions. Throughout his career, Kornhauser collaborated with private industry, labor unions, and social scientists outside of psychology in a broad way to promote his progressive values.

Biographical Overview

Kornhauser was born in 1896 in Steubenville, OH, a working-class community that was centered around the steel industry (it was 33 miles from Pittsburgh). Kornhauser studied psychology and biology as an undergraduate at University of Pittsburgh and then got his MA in 1919 from Carnegie Tech, the first program in the country in industrial psychology; at Carnegie Tech, Kornhauser worked with Walter Van Dyke Bingham. He received his PhD in psychology at the University of Chicago. During World War I (WWI), Kornhauser assisted Colonel Walter Dill Scott in developing trade tests to determine which recruits had specialized skills (e.g., mechanical and electrical) that were needed for military success. After the war, Kornhauser worked with the Scott Company to tailor trade tests for industry.

DOI: 10.4324/9781003403258-26

Kornhauser's first academic appointment was at the University of Chicago, holding a dual appointment with psychology and business, a trend that would become more popular over time though rare at the time. In the early 1940s, he worked at the Bureau of Applied Social Research at Columbia University, working closely with eminent sociologist Paul Lazarsfeld. Finally, in 1947 he was recruited to Wayne University (now called Wayne State University) where he worked in the psychology department. Kornhauser was excited to be located in Detroit where he could work closely with the strong labor unions in the Motor City. Kornhauser retired from Wayne in 1962 and died in 1990 (see Zickar, 2003 for more background of Kornhauser's life).

Summary of Contributions

Based on a previous study of Kornhauser's career (see Zickar, 2003), I outline four areas that Kornhauser made key contributions: early research on psychological testing, employee opinion research, work with labor unions, and mental health of workers.

Early Work on Psychological Testing

Kornhauser's first work on psychological testing was with the United States (US) Army during WWI where he worked with Colonel Walter Dill Scott in developing and evaluating trade tests to determine which recruits had specialized skills that were prized by the military. Given the late entry of the US into the war, and with little formal buildup of the US military forces, there was little time for the military to train recruits in these specialized skills, and so it was important to identify recruits who could perform these tasks without training (see Chapman & Chapman, 1921). Kornhauser's work during the war, like so many other future psychologists, provided him a real interest in the measurement of human aptitudes that could be used to predict organizational effectiveness.

Kornhauser's dissertation at the University of Chicago was entitled *A Statistical Study of Some Methods Used in Judging College Students*; in the dissertation, Kornhauser evaluated the relative ability of various tests in predicting undergraduate success. This work, along with his work during the war, led to an interest in how psychological tests could predict important outcomes in private industry. His work in the area of psychological testing culminated in the 1924 publication of the book *Psychological Tests in Business* which was coauthored with University of Chicago colleague Forrest Kingsbury (Kornhauser & Kingsbury, 1924). At the time, there was very little understanding of the importance of personnel selection, let alone much knowledge on how to pick and use such tests, and this work was an important text in that it was geared to businesspeople and presented a summary of existing research in a way that could be understood without knowledge of psychological concepts.

Employee Opinion Research

The field of employee opinion surveying began in the late 1920s with J. David Houser forming a consulting organization, Houser Associates, that worked with companies such as Sears, Roebuck and Company to assess employees' reactions to different aspects of their employment (see Jacoby, 1988 for an excellent summary of this early research). These surveys provided management important information on what employees liked and disliked, and although some managers used them to improve the workplace, others used them as ways to identify places where employees were likely to unionize. Kornhauser was an early advocate for the use of opinion surveys to be used for a wide variety of purposes, not just providing information that management wanted.

Kornhauser believed that using opinion polling could be useful to help government and communities function better. During World War II, he conducted polling on attitudes toward war and peace among Chicago residents (Kornhauser, 1943) and later he sampled Detroit residents to understand attitudes about various problems Detroit was facing (Kornhauser, 1953). He critiqued management's use of opinion surveys in that he believed management often asked questions in a way that biased employee responses and perhaps more importantly, ignored asked questions that would lead to answers for which management would be uncomfortable.

Although others like Houser deserve credit for pioneering the techniques of employee opinion polling, Kornhauser deserves credit for advocating for using polling and surveys as a way to understand attitudes of a wide range of people and questions. Instead of viewing surveys just as a management tool, Kornhauser advocated for surveys that could help all, as long as they were done correctly. His efforts in Detroit and Chicago provided models for other survey researchers to follow.

Work with Labor Unions

Perhaps Kornhauser's most defining and distinctive contribution to psychology was his lifelong advocacy for the importance of labor unions. Throughout his long career, he criticized the field of industrial psychology as being beholden to management interests and indifferent or even hostile to labor unions. In fact, Kornhauser's work was cited frequently as a rare exception by historian Loren Baritz in his trenchant critique of social science's bias in favor of management (Baritz, 1960). As an example of his critiques, Kornhauser wrote, "I know of no instance in which a study undertaken to improve employee morale has discovered that the company needs a stronger, more vigorous labor union to represent its employees" (1957, p. 199). Kornhauser viewed his role as a university professor as a privileged position that required him to research questions that psychologists employed by industry would not be allowed to study.

Kornhauser worked with labor unions in a variety of ways, including testifying to the US Congressional subcommittee hearing on proposed labor legislation, testifying as an expert witness for unions in a National Labor Review Board hearing, lecturing to unions such as the International Ladies Garment Workers Union, and providing training to members of the American Federation of Labor on how to use applied psychology to improve shop steward performance. In addition, he facilitated interdisciplinary forums that brought a wide variety of social scientists, including political scientists, economists, and sociologists, to discuss research issues along with leadership of various labor organizations. Finally, his research on the mental health of workers that is mentioned in the next section was funded by the United Auto Workers, providing an important collaboration between psychology and labor.

Although there were other industrial psychologists who had explicitly pro-labor perspectives, notably Kornhauser's eventual colleague at Wayne, Ross Stagner, none were as prominent as Kornhauser who was elected President of the Business Division of American Association of Applied Psychology, a predecessor organization to what is now called Society for Industrial and Organizational Psychology.

Mental Health of Workers

While at Wayne University, Kornhauser spent the last years of his career working on a massive research project that investigated the mental health of Detroit-area auto workers, a work that would be published in book form, *Mental Health of the Industrial Worker* (Kornhauser, 1965). In the early days, little attention had been given to understanding the mental health of workers. In fact, Kornhauser wrote in a 1931 book review, "too little emphasis has been placed on objective conditions contributing to [worker] maladjustment" (Kornhauser, 1931, p. 505). The little work that had been done on mental health and work examined how pre-existing work conditions impacted worker performance. Very little research had examined how work might impact worker mental health.

Kornhauser and his graduate student assistants interviewed 400 workers using what we would call now a mixed-methods approach that included traditional Likert-format measures of constructs as varied as positive and negative mental health items (anxiety and self-esteem), job attitudes (e.g., job satisfaction and attitudes toward labor), as well as personal life outcomes (life satisfaction and family satisfaction) as well as open-ended questions that allowed interviewees to explain how they felt in their own language. Kornhauser wanted to make sure that respondents felt comfortable and free to express any opinions and so all interviews were conducted outside of the workplace and the interviews were so comprehensive that they required two separate two-hour sessions.

Kornhauser conducted an extensive series of analyses that showed the connections between mental health and job attitudes as well as life outcomes. In fact, Kornhauser identified what he called the "spill-over" hypothesis, which demonstrated that negative experiences at work could impact family and leisure outcomes. This notion of the spillover hypothesis is one that has been well researched and established, particularly by researchers in the field of occupational health psychology (OHP), a field that did not formally exist during this time but could be argued that Kornhauser's work on mental health of auto workers was an important predecessor. This research project consumed the last years of Kornhauser's professional life and was the last publication of Kornhauser's long and distinguished career (Kornhauser, 1965).

Conclusion

Kornhauser was an important early industrial psychologist who made early contributions to psychological testing, though his work was most distinguished by his lifelong advocacy for an industrial psychology that was devoted to helping workers maintain a sense of dignity and power in the workplace. To those ends, Kornhauser was one of the few industrial psychologists who worked directly with labor unions. In addition, he studied the mental health of United Auto Workers and linked working conditions to mental health. His monumental study published in 1965 can be considered a landmark work in what would later be labeled OHP. Although the individual contributions of his career were impressive, what was perhaps his most lasting contribution was his lifelong advocacy for an industrial psychology that focused on worker well-being.

References

Baritz, L. (1960). *Servants of power*. Wesleyan University Press. https://doi.org/10.1037/11283-000

Chapman, J. C., & Chapman, D. R. (1921). *Trade tests: The scientific measurement of trade proficiency*. H. Holt. https://doi.org/10.1037/10892-000

Jacoby, S. M. (1988). Employee attitude surveys in historical perspective. *Industrial Relations: A Journal of Economy and Society*, 27(1), 74–93. https://doi.org/10.1111/j.1468-232x.1988.tb01047.x

Kornhauser, A. (1931). Review of *The Dissatisfied Worker* by V.E. Fisher and J.V. Hanna. *American Journal of Sociology*, *37*, 504–504. https://doi.org/10.1086/215772

Kornhauser, A. (1943). Chicago surveys concerning the public's beliefs and desires about the war. *Journal of Social Psychology*, *18*, 371–382. https://doi.org/10.1080/00224545.1943.9918791

Kornhauser, A. (1953). *Detroit as the people see it: A survey of attitudes in an industrial city*. Wayne University Press.

Kornhauser, A. (1957). Democratic values and problems of power in American society. In A. Kornhauser (Ed.), *Problems of power in American democracy* (pp. 184–217). Wayne University Press.

Kornhauser, A. (1965). *Mental health of the industrial worker: A Detroit study*. Wiley. https://doi.org/10.2307/3101771

Kornhauser, A., & Kingsbury, F. W. (1924). *Psychological tests in business*. University of Chicago Press. https://doi.org/10.1037/13460-000

Zickar, M. J. (2003). Remembering Arthur Kornhauser: Industrial psychology's advocate for worker well-being. *Journal of Applied Psychology*, *88*(2), 363. https://doi.org/10.1037/0021-9010.88.2.363

Chapter 27

Emilio Mira y López (1896–1964)

Jesús F. Salgado

Emilio Mira y López was the most eminent Spanish psychologist in the first half of the 20th century and one of the most relevant European psychologists of his time. He was one of the founders of the International Association of Psychotechnics (IAP; now called the International Association of Applied Psychology) and participated in all the IAP conferences from 1920 to 1964. He was enormously active internationally. From the 1920s onwards, he was an invited lecturer in many European, American, and South American universities and scientific academies giving over 350 invited speeches. In a survey conducted three years after Mira's death by Annin et al. (1968), he was included among the most important psychologists in the history of psychology from 1660 to 1967.

Biographical Overview

Emilio Mira y López was born on October 24, 1896, in Santiago de Cuba, when Cuba still was part of Spain. His father was Rafael Mira Merino, medical colonel of the Spanish army, stationed in Cuba. In 1898, after the Independence of Cuba, Mira's family returned to Spain, living in La Coruña (Galicia) for five years, and from 1903 in Barcelona (Catalonia). Emilio Mira lived in Barcelona until 1939. He died from a heart attack in Petropolis (Brazil) on February 16, 1964. He married twice and had seven children, three Spaniards and four Brazilians.

Mira graduated in medicine with honors from the University of Barcelona in 1917. He earned a doctoral degree in medicine with honors from the University of Madrid in 1922. The title

DOI: 10.4324/9781003403258-27

of his doctoral thesis was "The Somatic Correlations of Mental Work." He spoke and wrote in Spanish, Catalonian, French, English, German, and Portuguese.

In 1918, via a competitive selection process, he was appointed as physician of the Council of Barcelona and in 1919 he was appointed as chief of the Psychometric Laboratory of the Institute of Guidance and Professional Selection of Barcelona. In 1920, he attended the first International Conference of Psychotechnics in Geneva and, the next year, he organized the 2nd International Conference of Psychotechnics in Barcelona. In 1925, he was appointed as physician of the Psychiatric Service of the Council of Barcelona and, in 1926, Director of the Institute of Professional Guidance of the School of Work of the Municipality of Barcelona. In 1927, Mira was appointed General Director of the Institute of Psychotechnics of Barcelona. In 1930, he organized the 7th International Conference of Psychotechnics in Barcelona. In 1933, he was appointed as the first chair of psychiatry at the University of Barcelona.

Between 1920 and 1963, Mira participated in numerous international psychological conferences. For example, he attended the psychotechnics conferences held in Geneva (1920), Barcelona (1921), Milan (1922), Paris (1926), Utrecht (1927), Barcelona (1930) Moscow (1931), and Prague (1934), Gothenburg (1951), Paris (1953), and Rome (1958). In 1929, by invitation, he attended the meeting of the American Association for the Advancement of Science (AAAS) at Northwestern University, was "summer professor" at Ohio University, and Section President in the 9th International Congress of Psychology (1929) held at Yale University, and he was appointed as the President of the 11th International Congress of Psychology held in Copenhagen (1932). He was a guest attendant at the meeting of the AAAS, together with C. Spearman, W. Köhler, and H. Pieron (1933).

During the Spanish Civil War (1936–1939), he was appointed as lieutenant-colonel and chief of the Psychiatric and Psychological Service of the Spanish Republican Army (1938) until February 1939 when he was exiled in France (Mira 1943). There, Mira was interned in a concentration camp for Spanish refugees until the end of September 1939. When he was released, he moved to Paris where his family lived in very poor conditions. With the help of Charles S. Myers, in October 1939, he was appointed as a research fellow of the Society for Protection of Science and Learning at the Maudsley Hospital in London.

Since he was born in Cuba, he obtained a Cuban passport, and because of the beginning of World War II, his family traveled to Argentina in 1940. Meanwhile, he traveled to the United States (US) where he was invited to lecture at some of the most prestigious US universities, including Princeton, Yale, Washington, Harvard, California-Los Angeles, Houston, Ohio, and New Orleans. When he finished this lecturing tour, he traveled to Argentina to join his family and remained there until 1945, working as a psychiatrist. He visited the US in 1942, to deliver the *Salmon Memorial Lecture* at the New York Medical Academy. In 1947, he was invited by the Brazilian government to fund and direct the Institute of Selection and Guidance (ISG) of the Getulio Vargas Foundation in Rio de Janeiro (Braga da Silva & Rosa, 1997). He remained there until his death in February 1964.

Main Contributions to Industrial, Work, and Organizational (IWO) Psychology

Mira's contributions to IWO psychology began as early as 1919 when he was appointed as chief of the Psychometric Laboratory of the Institute of Professional Guidance and lasted until his death in 1964. Mira contributed to different areas of IWO psychology, including a model of human abilities, occupational analysis and classification, personnel selection, occupational training, the development of ability and personality assessment methods, and to the domain currently known as occupational health psychology (e.g., professional fatigue, occupational stress). He also contributed to psychiatry and vocational guidance (Mira, 1947, 1952–1955). Next is a short summary of some of these contributions.

In the domain of the theory of cognitive abilities, as early as 1922, at the Conference of Psychotechnics held in Milan, Mira proposed a model of intelligence that distinguished three abilities: (1) abstract intelligence, (2) spatial-mechanical intelligence, and (3) verbal intelligence. Mira postulated that the three abilities correlated and that there was a general intelligence factor. In this domain, Mira adopted a personal approach that reconciled Spearman's position (i.e., a single general factor) and Thurstone's position (i.e., several independent factors) when these two theorists were totally at odds. Mira maintained this approach throughout his whole life. In this sense, Mira's model can be considered as a precursor of the subsequent hierarchical models of intelligence of Vernon and Carroll, both of which included these three ability factors. Mira also defined a fourth type of intelligence that he termed "affective intelligence," however, it was not in the cognitive domain but in the affective domain. This affective intelligence strongly resembles the emotional intelligence construct of Salovey and Mayer (1990).

At the same time that Mira proposed his view of cognitive abilities, the German psychologist Otto Lipmann suggested that occupations varied according to their cognitive requirements and proposed a scheme to classify jobs and occupations. According to Lipmann, the difference between occupations was not only the different mental functions they required but also the intensity of those requirements. So, to classify occupations, Lipmann suggested the classification should be based on the nature of the object which the work is done with. Consequently, occupations might be classified in three main categories depending on whether the incumbent action is done on "things," "persons," or "concepts (ideas)." Examples of occupations based on *persons* could be physicians and lawyers, examples of occupations based on *things* could be watchmakers and carpenters, and examples of occupations related to *concepts and ideas* could be mathematicians and philosophers.

Mira extended Lippman's classification by adding the relationship between Lipmann's dimensions and the required cognitive abilities. Combining the Lipmann model of occupations with his model of cognitive abilities, Mira maintained that the occupations mainly characterized by *things* are more related to spatial intelligence, while those occupations mainly characterized by *persons* are more related with verbal intelligence, and those occupations predominantly characterized by *concepts* are more related to abstract intelligence. Therefore, occupations predominantly characterized by one of Lipmann's elements would be more related to one of these three cognitive abilities.

Between 1919 and 1922, Mira did his initial scientific research that focused on the study of the psychophysiological reactions to intellectual fatigue. These studies would permit him to obtain a doctoral degree in medicine at the University of Madrid in 1922. He advanced the findings of those studies in the 1st and 2nd International Conference of Psychotechnics held in Geneva in 1920 and Barcelona in 1921. For example, at the Barcelona Conference he presented his study on the cardiovascular correlations of mental work.

In 1922, he conducted his first Spanish study on the validity of psychological tests for the selection of drivers of the General Bus Company of Barcelona (Mira, 1922–1923). Mira measured (a) the speed perception and comparative judgments of speed and distances, (b) the distribution, intensity, and duration of visual attention, (c) the rapidity and accuracy of visual-motor and audio-motor reactions, and (d) the candidate's emotional characteristics (e.g., self-control). His measures of speed perception and comparative judgments of speed and distances are particularly interesting. Mira constructed an apparatus called a *perceptotaquimeter* that was used in his and other psychotechnical laboratories for almost two decades. Over the next 15 years, Mira perfected this selection method, and it was used not only for selecting bus drivers but also compulsory for the attainment of truck, taxi and car driving licenses in Spain (Chleusebairgue, 1940).

In 1924, he initiated a program for the psychological selection of police officers in Barcelona, and, four years later, under his command, the Institute of Professional Guidance began a program for the selection of airplane pilots (Chleusebaigue, 1940). This program was enlarged during the Spanish Civil War when Mira was commanded to select candidates for the Military School of Aviation (Mira, 1943). For this selection program, he developed a new apparatus named the *axistereomenter*, to measure the accuracy of the kinesthetic perception of space.

During the Spanish Civil War, Mira was responsible for the program for the selection of soldiers and officers for different army units (Mira, 1943). The use of cognitive and psychomotor tests as well as personality questionnaires and interviews formed the basis for the selection decision.

When the Spanish Civil War ended, and he and his family went into exile in France (1939), Great Britain (1939–1940), Argentina (1940–1945), and Brazil (1945–1964), Mira continued his research mainly in the domain of personality. Based on the ideas of Kurt Lewin about the vectorial expression of conative trends, Mira was particularly interested in *Myokinetic Psychodiagnosis* (Mira, 1940; 1958), a method that is based on the "involuntary expressions of the predominant attitude of reaction evaluated as a function of the shiftings observed during blind execution of linear movements in the fundamental directions of space" (Mira, 1940, p. 174) and that avoids faking. Mira made the official presentation of this method on October 12, 1939, at a meeting of the Royal Society of Medicine in London.

Mira was also the main force behind the establishment of scientific personnel selection in Brazil (Braga da Silva & Rosa, 1997). At the Brazilian ISG, Mira did numerous scientific studies. Under his supervision, an extensive program of selection was carried out at the ISG, which included the designing, adapting, validating, and norm development of dozens of tests, and their application to the selection of candidates for more than 40 different occupations of all levels of job complexity.

Development of Assessment Tools

Mira was a prolific developer of psychological tools, including apparatus, psychometric tests, questionnaires, and situational procedures for assessing many psychological characteristics.

In the domain of cognitive abilities, his first tests were the previously mentioned perceptotaquimeter and axistereomenter. Around 1925, Mira adapted to Spanish and modified a previously developed test of Thurstone's for assessing general intelligence, and, subsequently, known as the Test of Intelligence Thurstone-Mira or the Test of Barcelona. This test consists of verbal comparisons, series of numbers, inductive and deductive reasoning questions, synonyms, and some items of general culture. The Thurstone-Mira Test was widely used in Europe and Latin America for about four decades. Mira also developed the EVA Battery for assessing the three aptitudes of his intelligence model. This battery has been widely used in Brazil.

In the domain of personality, he was extremely proud of the conception and development of the Test of Myokinetic Psychodiagnosis (PMK). The Spanish technical manual of the PMK has been translated into English, French, German, Italian, and Portuguese, and hundreds of articles and several doctoral dissertations have examined the characteristics and psychometric properties of this test (Galland de Mira, 1987). He also developed a situational judgment test named the Ethical Discrimination Test for assessing moral behavior in police jobs. In this domain, he also developed several situational tests, such as the blood donation test. In addition, he created several biodata and interview forms, including a fully structured panel selection interview.

Conclusion

In summary, Emilio Mira was the most influential Spanish and Latin-American psychologist of his time who deserves to be rescued from oblivion for his many scientific contributions in numerous psychological domains. His scientific production includes 31 books, over 300 papers and conference contributions, and over 350 invited speeches. Together with his articles in Spanish, Brazilian, and Latin-American journals, he extensively published in top international journals such as *Occupational Psychology* (now *Journal of Occupational and Organizational Psychology*), *L'Année Psychologique*, *Journal of Clinical and Experimental Psychopathology*, *Bulletin de Psychologie*, *Journal of Criminology*, *Lancet*, *British Journal of Medicine*, and the *Proceedings of the Royal Society of Medicine*, among others. Many of the greatest psychologists of his time were his friends. His acquaintances and relatives characterized him as a person full of energy, imaginativeness and innovativeness, a leader with contagious enthusiasm, and a well-organized and hard worker.

References

Annin, E. L., Boring, E. G., & Watson, R. I. (1968). Important psychologists, 1600-1967. *Journal of the History of the Behavioral Sciences,* 4(4), 303–315. https://doi.org/10.1002/1520-6696(196810)4:4<303::aid-jhbs2300040402>3.0.co;2-b

Braga da Silva, J., & Rosa, P. (1997). *Mira y López è a psicología aplicada no Brasil* [*Mira y López and the applied psychology in Brazil*]. Fundación Getulio Vargas.

Chleusebairgue, A. (1940). The selection of drivers in Barcelona. *Occupational Psychology, 14*, 146–161.

Galland de Mira, A. L. (1987). *PMK: Psicodiagnóstico Miocinético* [*PMK: Myokinetic psychodiagnosis*]. Vertor.

Mira, E. (1922–1923). La selecció dels xòfers de la companya general de'autòmnibus. [Selection of drivers for the general company of autobus] *Anals de l'Institut d'Orientació Professional, 3–4*, 60–71.

Mira, E. (1940). Myokinetic psychodiagnosis: New technique of exploring the conative trends of personality. *Proceedings of the Royal Society of Medicine. 33*, 173–194. https://doi.org/10.1177/003591574003300402

Mira, E. (1943). *Psychiatry in war*. Norton.

Mira, E. (1947) *Manual de Orientación Profesional* [*Handbook of vocational guidance*]. Kapelusz.

Mira, E. (1952–1955). *Tratado de psiquiatría* [*Treatise of psychiatry*]. 3 Vols. El Ateneo.

Mira, E. (1958). *Myokinetic psychodiagnosis. Foreword by Gordon Allport.* Logos Press.

Salovey, P., & Mayer, J. D. (1990). Emotional intelligence. *Imagination, Cognition and Personality*, 9(3), 185–211. https://doi.org/10.2190/DUGG-P24E-52WK-6CDG

Chapter 28

Morris Viteles (1898–1996)

David Devonis

Morris Viteles brought a practical Philadelphian approach to industrial and organizational (I-O) psychology. Mentored at the University of Pennsylvania (Penn) by Lightner Witmer and Edwin Twitmyer, he maintained a connection to the University as an instructor and administrator for 45 years and developed his extensive consulting skills and networks with local companies. His salient achievements were gathering and bringing knowledge of European I-O psychology to the early notice of psychologists in the United States (US) and his 1932 text *Industrial Psychology*, which was instrumental in defining the field.

Biographical Overview

Early Life and Education

Morris Viteles represents the nexus between prehistory and modernity in industrial psychology in the US, and to some extent worldwide as well. He was born in Western Russia in 1898, but before six months of age was living in England in Leeds. By 1904, Viteles was living in Philadelphia, PA, which was his home and the center of his professional activities for the rest of his very long life. He described his upbringing as comfortable, though not excessively so: his father, who had been a forestry manager in Russia, was now plying the trades of restaurateur and hotelier as an immigrant American. Though he mentions it directly in neither of his autobiographies, his older brother Harry Viteles became general manager of the Central Bank for Cooperative Institutions in Palestine (New York Times, 1971), and his sister-in-law, Rose

DOI: 10.4324/9781003403258-28

Viteles (nee Rassell), trained as a social worker, became instrumental in and honored for community educational development in Palestine from the 1920s through the founding of Israel (Kadosh, 2024). Precocious and ambitious, Viteles skipped several grades and was awarded a scholarship to the University of Pennsylvania in 1914. Before attending Penn he took classes at the Philadelphia School of Pedagogy, where he encountered a psychology teacher, one 'Melville' who, Viteles noted, though not a great psychologist, nonetheless determined his later psychological career. Viteles was an undergraduate history student: his kindled psychological interest was increased by his parallel study of psychology in courses by his eventual graduate mentors. He was fortunate to encounter an established psychology department at Penn with historical connections to Wundt's peculiarly American disciple, James McKeen Cattell. This connection was personified by Viteles's first mentor, Lightner Witmer, Cattell's first assistant at Penn and a native Philadelphian, and by his second, Edward Burket Twitmyer (PhD Penn, 1902). Twitmyer is usually remembered for describing a conditioned reflex in humans a few years earlier than the popularization of Pavlov's research. Viteles remembered him as a dedicated and masterful teacher who, like Wundt and Cattell, put the laboratory in the forefront of psychology (Irwin, 1943). Viteles' 1921 dissertation was supervised by Witmer: both Witmer and Twitmyer are the dedicatees of Viteles's *Industrial Psychology* (Viteles, 1932).

Through his youth Viteles felt compelled to work while studying to augment his family's income, first as a tutor. In 1918 he tried to enlist in the US Army testing service under R. M. Yerkes but was rejected, and enrolled instead in officer training with the Student Army Training Corps. The war ended and Viteles, now a graduate assistant in the Penn psychology department, became an observer of the activities of the Federal Bureau of Vocational Rehabilitation's Philadelphia office (Viteles, 1967). This activity led to Viteles's organizing a vocational guidance clinic at Penn on the lines of clinical psychology as it had developed under Witmer. Meantime, the Director of the Federal Rehabilitation Bureau had become the Director of Education in the Milwaukee Electric Railway and Light Company and this led Viteles to his first hands-on consulting position in industry there in the summer of 1920. At Milwaukee he developed a test for motormen, the results of which were included in his dissertation and established him as a practical worker in the field. Undecided after graduation as to whether he would pursue a career as an academic or as a consultant in industry, on the strength of his proficiency in French he received an American Field Service Fellowship for study in France in 1922. Beginning with study with Pierre Janet at the College de France, he soon traveled to all of the centers of industrial psychology in France, England, and Germany. His primary contacts in France were Henri Piéron and J.-M. Lahy. In Germany he met and was impressed by the work of Fritz Giese, William Stern, and Otto Lipmann, but perhaps his closest bond was formed with C. S. Myers in England, whom, Viteles said in his 1967 Autobiography, "strongly influenced the position on the role of an experimental and theoretical framework taken in my book *Industrial Psychology* and also in later years—in fact, until the present time" (Viteles, 1967, p. 432).

Academic and Consulting Career

On his return to the US in 1923, he published a summary of what he had observed in Europe (Viteles, 1923) and set about his career as an "academic moonlighter" as he termed himself in his second autobiography (Viteles, 1974). He became a consultant to the Yellow Cab Company in Philadelphia between 1924 and 1927 (and continued to consult with them later in his career), and in 1927 began a decades-long association with the Philadelphia Electric Company. Alongside his university teaching, he was able to work in-house in all the aspects of industrial psychological consulting so that his reportage and ultimately his texts had the ring of realistic truth. During the 1920s he also attended several international conferences on psychology and psychotechnology, and in 1934 he was awarded a Social Science Research Council Fellowship to investigate industrial psychology in the Soviet Union. In 1940 he was promoted to full professor and became a National Research Council (NRC) representative on the Technical Board for the Occupational Research Program of the US Employment Service. This appointment and other activities resulted in Viteles, after the beginning of World War

II (WWII), becoming a central figure in the development of aviation psychology in the service of national defense, and ultimately becoming chair of the NRC Committee on Selection and Training of Civilian Aircraft Pilots (expanded in 1941 to include the US Navy's selection and training and, after the war was in full swing, to investigate all aspects of the interaction of humans and flight and renamed the NRC Committee on Aviation Psychology). His activity in organized scientific research committees was augmented through the war years and afterward by connections to the National Defense Research Committee of the Office of Scientific Research and Development through which Viteles supervised a wide variety of training and personnel assignment programs for the US Navy. After this ten-year period of government consulting, Viteles returned to his previous mix of teaching and consulting with private industry, continuing his association with the Philadelphia Electric Company and also adding the Bell Telephone Company of Pennsylvania to the mix. In 1958, he began serving as President of the International Association of Applied Psychology, and he finished his administrative career as the Dean of the Graduate School of Education at Penn from 1964 until his retirement in 1968.

Accomplishments, Networks, and Character

In the landscape of his life, there are three prominent peaks: he was a synthesizer, a builder of relationships (what we would today call a networker), and a liberal humanist. Regarding his synthesizing, he was not the first to attempt to structure the field of industrial psychology: that distinction goes to those European (and European-transplant) psychologists early in the 20th century—Hugo Münsterberg, C. S. Myers, William Stern, and Otto Lipmann—who first gave substantial form to the field. But in the US at that time he was a necessary and pivotal figure. The publication of his textbook *Industrial Psychology* (Viteles, 1932) coincided with several contemporary movements within American psychology toward systematization, many of which carried this task out through influential textbooks. It defined a major sector of applied psychology comprehensively in a way similar to the way that R. S. Woodworth's and S. S. Stevens's comprehensive surveys of experimental psychology or Kurt Koffka's and Wolfgang Koehler's compendia of Gestalt psychology did theirs. Perhaps Viteles's greatest achievement, through forging connections with the leading industrial psychologists in Europe, was bringing to American attention the vast amount of psychotechnical knowledge that had accumulated in Europe the decades preceding his textbook's publication. Viteles was always intending to revise it, but that task got put off many times, while he expanded its sections on vocational counseling and employee motivation and morale into books (Viteles & Keller, 1938; Viteles, 1953). *Industrial Psychology*'s empirical emphasis combined with its breadth of coverage was a template for the texts in applied psychology which began to appear in the 1940s and contributed to the growth in parity of applied psychology with theoretical psychology in the following decades. It also set a template for comprehensive textbooks in I-O psychology which followed it, providing a "one-stop-shop" for all dimensions of the field.

Viteles is rarely mentioned in recent psychohistoriography. One exception is Shayna Fox Lee's calculation via algorithms of interconnecting patterns of influence among the individuals whose autobiographies were included in the series *A History of Psychology in Autobiography* (Lee, 2014). The earliest of Viteles's two autobiographical contributions is included in Volume V of that series (Viteles, 1967). As Lee observes, the selection process for inclusion in autobiography collections results in a "prosopography of the elite" (Lee p. 77), and Viteles is conspicuous, among the other elite individuals in that volume, as having virtually no interconnections with the others. He appears as the "odd man out." She acknowledges his career as an industrial psychologist, but only as a factor in his relative isolation from centers of activity in psychology in his cohort. Yet Viteles is not without networks. Alongside those connections with the originators of modern European industrial and business psychology which he formed in his 1922 fellowship year, Viteles describes collections of contemporaries to whom he was introduced by S. C. Fernberger at Penn and Walter Van Dyke Bingham. Viteles noted particularly close connections to Elton Mayo, Donald Paterson, and Arthur Kornhauser, all formed during that period. His work with the

NRC and associated committees during WWII and afterward put him in contact with even more psychologists but also with scientists and engineers in related areas. For example, in a 1951 report edited by Paul Fitts on human engineering in the design of air navigation and air traffic control for the Air Navigation and Development Board of the NRC Committee on Aviation Psychology (Fitts, 1951), Viteles is at the head of the Executive Subcommitee, which included, among others, Dean Brimhall and S. S. Stevens. Among those contributing to the several reports in the volume were Alphonse Chapanis, W. R. Garner, and a very young David Bakan, who became one of the originators of the specialty of the history of psychology in the US. One could construct a highly interconnected set of the networks of applied psychology's infrastructure from an analysis of Viteles's published contributions and autobiographical reminscences.

Viteles described himself, from his youth, as liberal, and this orientation displayed itself in several aspects during his career. He was liberal, yes, but also a realist. Partly this was a result of his firm grounding in a strict empiricism, and partly—and perhaps most strongly—was the effect of his exposure to the realities of industrial development and practice in the Soviet Union during 1934–1935. There he experienced not only the contradiction of Soviet use of wage and piecework compulsion to increase production and the ideals of socialism, but also observed the forces that resulted in the purging and execution of Russian scientists at that time. His intimate acquaintance with Isaac Spielrein (1891–1937) and the knowledge of his fate—Spielrein was arrested and executed in a Stalinist purge—reinforced Viteles's dedication to melioristic capitalism and contributed to his disapproval of psychologists' Utopian schemes (Viteles, 1955, 1972). His early training in individual differences, a central feature of his undergraduate courses at Penn in the 1910s, was reflected in substantial chapters in his 1932 text (and its 1934 popular version) on the theories and methods for testing individual differences. His survey of testing of what was then called Negro intelligence (Viteles, 1928) was characterized as "neutral" by contemporaries (e.g., St. Clair Price, 1934), yet it appears clear that Viteles was a contributor to the egalitarian reaction to early excesses in the use and interpretation of intelligence testing. Viteles frequently quoted W. S. Gilbert to soften his criticisms, and his consistent refrain regarding definitive statements about individual differences derived from Gilbert's "The Periwinkle Girl":

> Headstrong youths
> Of decent education
> Determine all important truths
> With strange precipitation.
> The ever-ready victims they
> Of logical illusions
> And in a self-assertive way
> They jump at strange conclusions
> (quoted in Viteles, 1932, pp. 107–108)

Conclusion

Finally, what distinguishes Viteles as a psychologist is his underlying humanism. From the beginning he was concerned that industrial psychology be part of a larger human story. His description of the reading underlying his decision to shift from history to industrial psychology mentions "the novels of such authors as Butler, Wells, Balzac, Tolstoy, Dostoyevski, Maeterlinck, and Rolland" before H. C. Link and H. L. Hollingworth (Viteles, 1967, pp. 422–423): much later in life he prescribed a course in "humanistic education" for executives of the Bell Telephone System (Viteles, 1974, p. 474). His popular version of his *Industrial Psychology*, *The Science of Work* (Viteles, 1934), whose title echoes that of another broadly humanist psychologist's work, Otto Lipmann's *Grundriss der Arbeitswissenchaft* (*Outline of the Science of Work*) (Lipmann, 1926) opens not with a theoretical outline but with a historical account of work from ancient to modern times. He had an immigrant's faith in and optimism about work. *The Science of Work* closes with the statement that "(t}he long record of human society shows work—economic activity—to be at the basis of its development" (Viteles 1934, p. 414): the epigraph on its title page is "Di omnia laboribus vendunt" (The Gods give everything in return for effort). Viteles's career is testament to persistent effort to establish I-O psychology as a science, an academic discipline, and a profession.

References

Fitts, P. M. (Ed.) (1951). *Human engineering for an effective air-navigation and traffic-control system.* National Research Council. https://apps.dtic.mil/sti/pdfs/ADB815893.pdf

Irwin, F. W. (1943). Obituary: Edwin Burket Twitmyer, 1873-1943. The *American Journal of Psychology, 56*, 451–453.

Kadosh, S. (2024). Rose Viteles. *Shalvi/Hyman Encyclopedia of Jewish Women.* 31 December 1999. *Jewish Women's Archive* (online archive). Accessed March 25, 2024, at http://jwa.org/encyclopedia/article/viteles-ros

Lee, S. F. (2014). *Networking Western psychology's elite: A digital analysis of "A History of Psychology in Autobiography".* MA Thesis, York University (Toronto, Canada). Available online at https://core.ac.uk/download/pdf/77104398.pdf

Lipmann, O. (1926). *Grundriss der Arbeitswissenschaft und Ergebnisse der arbeitswissenschaftliche Statistik.* Verlag Gustav Fischer.

New York Times (March 3, 1971). Harry Viteles, 77, in Co-op movement. (Obituary). *New York Times* (online newspaper). Accessed March 25, 2024 at www.nytimes.com/1971/03/03/archives/harry-vitele-77-in-coop-movement.html

St. Clair Price. J. (1934). Negro-white differences in general intelligence. *Journal of Negro Education, 3(3)*, 424–452. https://doi.org/10.2307/2292382

Viteles, M. S. (1923). Psychology in business—in England, France, and Germany. *Annals of the American Academy of Political and Social Science, 110*, 207–220. https://doi.org/10.1177/000271622311000123

Viteles, M. S. (1928). The mental status of the Negro. *Annals of the American Academy of Political and Social Science, 140*, 166–177. https://doi.org/10.1177/000271622814000122

Viteles, M. S. (1932). *Industrial psychology.* W. W. Norton.

Viteles, M. S. (1934). *The science of work.* W. W. Norton.

Viteles, M. S. (1953). *Motivation and morale in industry.* W. W. Norton.

Viteles, M. S. (1955). The new Utopia. *Science, 122*, 1167–1171. https://doi.org/10.1126/science.122.3181.1167

Viteles, M. S. (1967). Autobiography. In E. G. Boring & G. Lindzey (Eds.). *A history of psychology in autobiography* (Vol. V; pp. 415–449). Appleton-Century-Crofts. https://doi.org/10.1002/1520-6696(196907)5:3<296::aid-jhbs2300050319>3.0.co;2-p

Viteles, M. S. (1972). Psychology today: Fact and foible. *American Psychologist, 27(7)*, 601–607. https://doi.org/10.1037/h0033260

Viteles, M. S. (1974). Industrial psychology: Reminiscences of an academic moonlighter. In T. S. Krawiec (Ed.), *The psychologists, Vol II* (Chapter 11, pp. 440–500). Oxford University Press.
Viteles, M. S., & Keller, F. J. (1938). *Vocational guidance throughout the world.* W. W. Norton.

Chapter 29

Chen Li (陈立) (1902–2004)

Yeh Hsueh

This chapter offers a brief biographic account of Chen Li, the founding father of Chinese industrial-organizational (I-O) psychology. In the early 1930s, he trained in experimental psychology and industrial psychology in London, United Kingdom. Back in China, his 1935 monograph on industrial psychology established him as a trail blazer there. He made significant contributions by tackling industrial and management problems. However, from 1937 to 1976, Chen's career faded in and out of brutal wars, industrial demise, political turmoil, and oppressive ideologies. He resumed his active role in I-O psychology after 1977 and remained a paramount figure until his death in 2004. Chen's life epitomized the field of Chinese psychology in the 20th century.

Pioneer of Chinese I-O Psychology

Chen Li (1902–2004) stands as a legend in modern Chinese psychology, notably acclaimed as the founding father of Chinese industrial psychology. He authored the first Chinese book on industrial psychology in 1935, marking the initiation of the field in China. Over a remarkable span of 70 years, Chen remained a trailblazer in I-O psychology. However, he most actively developed China's I-O psychology only during two periods, 1935–1937 and 1977-the mid-1990s (Yang, 2011), altogether fewer than 20 years. Of the two nearly comprehensive collections of his writings (Chen, 1992a, 2001a), only about 20% of his 186 published items focus on I-O psychology. Despite this, as the longest-living Chinese psychologist, Chen's influence transcended I-O psychology. His impact on Chinese modern psychology and

DOI: 10.4324/9781003403258-29

scientific thought is well acknowledged across various fields, including child psychology, educational psychology, general psychology, philosophy of science, scientific methodology, and higher education management.

Chen's life spanned the entire 20th century of China, marked by historical events such as the anti-Japanese war, civil wars, and the Cultural Revolution. He endured numerous hardships, political discriminations, and absurd accusations, which curtailed his career as an I-O psychologist by over 40 years. However, his life epitomizes Chinese modern psychology in the century. It shows his unwavering pursuit of psychological science aligned with a deep-rooted Chinese perspective on the role of psychology in improving human living within society. These themes stand out in examining Chen Li's life and work. Much like his diverse contributions to psychological science, Chen's work in I-O psychology belonged to his time and place.

Becoming a Social Activist and a Psychologist (1919–1932)

In his brief autobiography, Chen describes his youthful passion for science and societal change, a passion that was nurtured and affirmed by the May 4th movement in 1919 in which he participated as a middle schooler. In 1924, he received a penalty for being late to register at the college in Shanghai because of his interest in the Chinese Communist Party delayed his trip. This incident marked one of several early attempts by Chen to connect with the newly formed party (Chen, 2001b).

In the summer of 1930, at the age of 28, Chen secured a study-abroad scholarship from the Hubei provincial government. He took the trans-Siberia railway to go to London and there he found guidance from Sir Percy Nunn (1870–1944), the Dean of the College of Education at University College London (UCL). Nunn recommended Chen to study psychology under Charles Spearman (1863–1945), who, in turn, encouraged him to enroll in the psychology PhD program.

By 1932, Spearman retired, and Chen continued his studies under John Carl Flügel (1884–1955) at UCL, who was known for bridging academic psychology and psychoanalysis in Britain.

Chen successfully met all requirements, including learning French and German, spending a term at Cambridge University, and having his dissertation examined by Sir Cyril Burt (1883–1971), John Flügel, and Stanley J. F. Philpott, who specialized in mental efficiency as measured by intelligence tests.

Entering I-O Psychology (1933–1934)

With a PhD in hand, Chen initially sought a postdoc in psychoanalysis but faced obstacles due to the required multi-year commitment. Subsequently, he eyed a trainee program at the National Institute of Industrial Psychology, yet the high tuition was forbidding. Fortunately, Charles Samuel Myers (1873–1946), the institute director, who knew Chen from his Cambridge days, offered training on the condition that he would neither receive a certificate because the training was unpaid for, nor seek employment later in England because the immigration law during the severe economic recession restricted foreigners from acquiring jobs.

The six-month training involved readings, site visits, factory work, and a practicum in the last month. Afterward, Chen moved to Humboldt University in Berlin in November 1933 to study with Wolfgang Köhler (1887–1967), tasked with researching personal preference for vocal frequency. However, in October 1934, Köhler advised Chen to return to China due to Nazi persecution of Jews, leading Köhler, who was not himself Jewish, to resign in 1935 and emigrate to the United States.

In four years in Europe, Chen "brushed shoulders … with some of the most significant pioneers of psychology in the West" (Blowers, 1998, p. 315). These unique experiences significantly influenced Chen's later perspectives in I-O psychology and his experimental approach in psychology.

Founding Chinese I-O Psychology (1935–1937)

Back in China, Chen Li embarked on a groundbreaking journey, splitting his time between Tsinghua University and Academia Sinica. In the spring of 1935, he completed *Essentials of Industrial Psychology* (Chen, 1935), the first Chinese book on I-O psychology, with effective illustrations, covering such topics as environmental factors, fatigue, efficiency, accidents, organization, and incentives. Although citing mainly Western industrial research, Chen warned his readers that China's industrialization must avoid the Western pitfalls of pursuing efficiency at the cost of humanity, "People's lifetime happiness is the priority" (p. 8). This advice appeared often even in his I-O writings 50 years later.

In this book, he wove in Chinese workers' needs and experiences as he addressed accidents caused by traditional attire and emphasized the role families play when discussing factory incentives. Notably, he cited the new landmark interview program at Hawthorne led by Elton Mayo who applied Piaget's theory and method (Hsueh, 2002, 2004; Trahair, 1984). Chen's book was not just an introduction to I-O psychology; it was a strategic manifesto, outlining his ambition to propel China's industrial psychology forward.

The year 1936 saw Chen fully engaged in industrial psychology research. In the spring, he conducted experimental research at Academia Sinica, creating China's first fatigue lab and devising a method to measure rickshaw pullers' fatigue through their oxygen consumption levels. In the meantime, he visited many factories in the Changjiang (Yangtze River) delta to survey their management. However, his suggestions for management improvement were met with skepticism. The local board of factories complained, "These are all foreign experiences. We cannot apply them in our domestic factories" (Chen, 2001b, p. 414). Undeterred, these responses fueled his focus on unraveling distinctly Chinese industrial challenges.

Later in 1936 at Tsinghua University, Chen delved into a major rolling stock factory in Beijing. He met the challenges the factory presented in producing, maintaining, and organizing rolling stock equipment. Colonial powers, such as Belgium, Britain, Germany, Japan, Russia, dominated the factory operation as if it were an international locomotive expo, making the factory overwhelmingly difficult to manage. His field research used the strategy from his book to organize materials and tools and found that if an efficient management plan was adopted, "The saving would be astronomical at that time," recalled Chen (2001b, p. 415).

In the spring of 1937, Chen continued designing new industrial research. Returning to the Changjiang delta region, he developed a worker selection instrument by crafting an analogical test that simulated real-world scenarios, steering away from the then commonplace analytical skill tests. Concurrently, he published *A Study of Indoor Meteorology of a Factory* (1992b/1937), drawing from data collected a year earlier in a textile factory. The pioneering investigation demonstrated his pursuit of a dialectical approach. The study explored the dynamic interactions of environmental conditions like indoor temperature, its distribution, air streams, and humidity.

Psychologist at Large Amid Wars (1937–1948)

However, the promising research trajectory was abruptly disrupted on July 7, 1937, when war broke out with Japan. Along with many faculty members and students, Chen relocated to the southwestern provinces, where he engaged in teaching university students from various parts of China. His research halted. In 1939, Chen was hired by Zhejiang University in exile to teach psychology and statistics in the Department of Education (Yao, 2006), marking the beginning of his 64-year affiliation with the University. His inaugural lecture was on Engels' dialectical materialism, which was "awakening and inspiring" (Zhu, 2006, p. 47). Among wartime challenges, a psychological lab for teaching was a low priority for the university. Chen (2001c/1946) lamented, "Obtaining lab space was always the most problematic... Nevertheless, we psychology instructors believed that psychology without experiments would lose its scientific spirit" (p. 442). The absence of access to lab space or factories meant little research. Instead, Chen immersed himself in teaching psychology, education reform, and popularizing science. During the wartime between 1938 and 1949, he authored 29 newspaper articles promoting education and science, including industrial psychology, but few studies. While many students remembered him as a highly sought-after teacher, research collaboration was limited (Editing Team, 2006).

The tumultuous wartime hindered China's emerging industrialization and curtailed Chen's research endeavor in industry, forcing him to direct his research attention toward educational and child psychology. A notable discovery he made during this time was that the general factor of intelligence ("g") undergoes changes between nine and 19 years of age. This groundbreaking finding challenged Spearman's claim that the "g" factor remains stable during this developmental period (Chen & Chow, 1948).

Struggling to Remain a Psychologist (1949–1977)

After China's political system changed to the socialist in 1949, Chen actively engaged in Zhejiang University's transition, shouldering significant administrative responsibilities and spearheading extensive education reform. Meanwhile, he took charge of the provincial division of the China Association for Science and Technology, an organization he co-initiated in 1945 with the dual purpose of disseminating scientific knowledge and facilitating the political transition to New China. Subsequently, his Department of Education was relocated to Zhejiang Normal College, where he served as its head for two years before its integration with Hangzhou University, where he assumed the role of vice president. The demands of administrative roles greatly reduced his research across the board. Documented in the records shows his intense involvement in the incessant political movements before 1966. Empirical research in industrial psychology during this period was sporadic, with only one study published (Chen & Zhu, 1959). Regardless of the chaotic distractions, he was planning on big research projects, persuading colleagues that China's psychological science required "a campaign-like maneuver, not unorganized assaults on isolated psychological issues" (Chen, 2001b, p. 419).

Months before the eruption of the Cultural Revolution in 1966, Chen and Wang's (1965a, b, c) experimental studies on children's perceptions of colors and shapes received a vicious attack from a propaganda writer (Ge, 1965) in the newspaper, *Guangming Daily*. The writer accused Chen of referencing works from Western bourgeois psychologists and pursuing bourgeois experimental aesthetics. Chen (1965) immediately published a rebuttal to counter this science-illiterate jabbering. Although his courage to defend psychological science was quietly admired by many, the already struggling field of psychology was drowned to death as the Cultural Revolution swept across China. Reflecting on this incident many years later, Chen (2001b) lamented, "[This incident] destroyed my entire research plan... Since then, I have never conducted any experimental studies; never worked in the lab to do systematic research. I ended up writing mostly odds-and-ends articles" (p. 422).

Embracing a New Era of I-O Psychology (1977–2004)

The Cultural Revolution ended in 1976, with the return of psychology the next year. Two years later, the China Society of Psychology officially approved the first master's program in industrial psychology, with Chen at the helm. In 1980, he assumed the presidency of Hangzhou University but noted, "Industrial management in our country remains in a most primitive state" (Chen, 1992c/1979, p. 425). It is worth noting that, despite being the founder of China's industrial psychology, Chen spent 40 years in the education department until 1980 when a psychology department was finally established at Hangzhou University. There, in 1987, he awarded China's first PhD in industrial psychology.

As China's psychology underwent rehabilitation, Chen found himself on a tight schedule, revitalizing and promoting I-O psychology education amid administrative and professional responsibilities. He joined the Communist Party in 1979 and became a spokesperson and liaison for his colleagues on the international stage for the next 15 years. Suddenly, at the age of 75, the world of psychology opened up to him anew. He embraced this opportunity with youthful vigor, avidly reading, discussing, and disseminating new psychological knowledge. His work also involved revisiting and elaborating on his early ideas, such as experimental methods, a dialectical approach to scientific research, a systematic campaign for tackling psychological issues, and, most significantly, educating psychology students. He advised graduate students in I-O psychology from age 77 until 100.

Conclusion

At the age of 99, Chen Li (2001b) reflects, "my whole life has been anything but having a plan as I tend to go with the flow. With many external influences impacting and obstructing my paths, having a plan does not mean that anything will come to fruition" (p. 379). These words bear testimony to his journey as the preeminent industrial psychologist of China's 20th century. It was a lived experience, both unique and common, through which he survived and thrived, not without regrets and high hopes.

References

Blowers, G. H. (1998). Chen Li: China's elder psychologist. *History of Psychology*, *1*(4), 315–310.

Chen, L. (1935). 《工业心理学概观》 [*Essentials of industrial psychology*]. 上海商务印书馆.

Chen, L. (1965, Dec 3). 对心理学中实验法的估价问题 [Assessment of the experiment method in psychology]. 《光明日报》 1965年12月3日，第4版.

Chen, L. (1992a). 《陈立心理科学论著选》 [*The selected works of Chen Li in psychological science*]. 杭州大学出版社

Chen, L. (1992b). 一个工厂中的室内气象研究 [A study of indoor meteorology in a factory]. In L. Chen (Ed.), *The selected works of Chen Li in psychological science* (vol. 2 ; pp. 363–375). Zhejiang University Press. (Original work published 1937.)

Chen, L. (1992c). 科学管理与劳动心理学 [Scientific management and labor psychology]. In L. Chen (Ed.), *The selected works of Chen Li in psychological science* (vol. 2; pp. 425–432). Zhejiang University Press. (Original work published 1979.)

Chen, L. (2001a). 《陈立心理科学论著选》（续编）[*The selected works of Chen Li in psychological science* (vol. 2)]. 浙江大学出版社.

Chen, L. (2001b). 我从事心理学研究的回顾 [My career in conducting psychological research in retrospect]. 《陈立心理科学论著选》(续篇), 397–441.

Chen, L. (2001c). 抗战期间的浙大心里实验室 [Zhejiang University psychology lab during the eight years of anti-Japanese war.] In L. Chen (Ed.), *The selected works of Chen Li in psychological science* (vol. 2; pp. 442–446). Zhejiang University Press. (Original work published 1946).

Chen, L., & Wang, A. (1965a). 儿童色、形抽象发展的跟踪研究 [The development of colors and form abstraction in children]. 《心理学报》 *9*(2), 154–162.

Chen, L., & Wang, A. (1965b). 儿童色、形抽象发展的研究 [The development of colors and form abstraction in children: A follow-up study]. 《心理学报》 *9*(2), 163–164.

Chen, L., & Wang, A. (1965c). 色、形爱好的差异 [Differences in preferences for color and form]. 《心理学报》 *9*(3), 265–269.
Chen, L., & Zhu, Z. (1959). 细纱工培训中的几个心理学问题 [A few psychological issues in the training of spinning frame operators]. 《心理学报》 *3*(1), 44–52.
Chen, T-Y. L., & Chow, H-H (1948). A factor study of a test battery at different educational levels. *Pedagogical Seminary & Journal of Genetic Psychology, 73*, 187–199.
Editing Team (2006). 《陈立先生纪念文集》 [*In memory of Chen Li xiansheng*]. 浙江大学出版 社.
Ge, M. (1965, Oct 8). 这是研究心理学的科学方法和正确方向吗？[Does this study demonstrate a scientific method and a correct direction in psychological research?]. 《光明日报》 1965年10月8日，第4版.
Hsueh, Y. (2002). The Hawthorne experiments and the introduction of Jean Piaget in American industrial psychology, 1929-1932. *History of Psychology*, *5*(2), 163–189.
Hsueh, Y. (2004). "He sees the development of children's concepts upon a background of sociology": Jean Piaget's honorary degree at Harvard University in 1936. *History of Psychology, 7*(1), 20–44.
Trahair, R. (1984). *The humanist temper: The life and work of Elton Mayo*. Transaction.
Yang, S. (2011). 陈立与20世纪中国工业心理学 [Chen Li and Chinese industrial psychology in the 20th century].《心理学报》 *43*(11), 1341–1354.
Yao, W. (2006). 陈老师在贵州遵义 [*Professor Chen in Zuinyi, Guizhou Province*] (pp. 99–101). 《陈立先生纪念文集》浙江大学出版社.
Zhu, Z. (2006). 深切悼念陈立先生 [*Remember Chen Li xiansheng*] (pp. 47–48). 《陈立先生纪 念文集》浙江大学出版社.

Chapter 30

Rensis Likert (1903–1981)

Thomas A. Stetz

Rensis Likert (pronounced "Lick-urt" not "Like-urt") made significant contributions to industrial-organizational (I-O) pychology. While most readers are likely familiar with the measurement technique named after him, the Likert Scale, much fewer know of his other contributions. He was influential in the development of intensive open-ended interview study techniques, under his supervision advances in probability sampling procedures were made, he participated in the initiation of human resource accounting (HRA), and he made contributions to organizational management and theory. In addition, to these methodological contributions, he led several influential organizations that helped advance the fields of psychology and survey research.

Biographical Overview

Rensis Likert was born in Cheyenne, WY, in 1903. As a child, he and his family moved to several states because of his father George Herbert Likert's job as an engineer with the Union Pacific Railroad. His mother, Cornelia Adrianna Likert, was a former schoolteacher. After graduating from high school, he began his undergraduate studies at the University of Michigan in civil engineering in 1922. Likert studied engineering for three years, but upon meeting Robert Angell, a young sociology professor, Likert switched majors. He received his bachelor's degree in sociology in 1926 (Kish, 1982).

Likert then began his graduate studies at Union Theological Seminary in New York City. The seminary was across the street from Columbia University, and it was common for students

DOI: 10.4324/9781003403258-30

to take courses at Columbia. When several of his friends (Theodore Newcomb, Ernest Hilgard, and Carl Rogers) transferred to Columbia, Likert likewise transferred after his first year (Pachella, 2010). While in graduate school, Likert married Jane Gibson whom he had met at the University of Michigan. She was a lifelong source of support and was at times his collaborator in professional endeavors (Kish, 1982).

Development of the Likert Scale

At Columbia, Likert studied under Gardner Murphy, who served as his dissertation committee chairperson. He completed his PhD in 1932 with his dissertation researching the psychometric measurement of attitudes. From this work, the famed "Likert Scale" was developed. Likert published his dissertation in a 1932 article titled "A Technique for the Measurement of Attitudes" in the *Archives of Psychology*. A follow-up article, which further explored the method, was published in 1934 in the *Journal of Social Psychology* and was titled "A Simple and Reliable Method of Scoring the Thurstone Attitude Scales" (Edmondson, 2005; Likert et al., 1934).

At the time, Thurstone's method of equal-appearing intervals was the principal method of developing scales and measuring attitudes. Likert's dissertation sought to overcome statistical assumptions required by the method and the "laborious" development process (Likert, 1932, p. 6). Thurstone's method involved generating many potential scale items and then having judges rate each item on how favorable or unfavorable the item was to the concept or construct. In Likert's (1932) and Likert et al.'s 1934) articles, he used preexisting scales measuring a variety of constructs. He made modifications where required and asked respondents to indicate if they strongly agreed, agreed, were undecided, disagreed, or strongly disagreed with each statement. He explored different scoring strategies with the simplest being the assignment of the values of 1–5 to the response (strongly agree-strongly disagree) alternatives. Likert found that this simple scoring strategy correlated highly with the Thurstone approach indicating that they were "measuring essentially the same thing" (Likert et al., 1934, p. 689).

Early Career and Governmental Work

After completing his graduate studies, Likert spent a brief period in the Psychology Department at New York University. He then accepted a position as Director of Research for the Life Insurance Association in Hartford, Connecticut, and he held that position from 1935 to 1938. During his time there he instituted a series of large-scale studies on the effectiveness of distinctive styles of supervision, resulting in three volumes of *Morale and Agency Management* which he coauthored (cited in Kish, 1990). This was an early example of Likert's interest in the effects of leadership and management within an organizational context which would more fully appear later in his career.

Likert's next position ushered in a highly productive and influential period of his life. Henry Wallace, the Secretary of Agriculture, and a pioneering statistician, invited Likert to establish a new organizational unit to assess farmers' experiences and reactions to the department's programs. Likert formed and headed the Division of Program Surveys from 1939 to 1946. Under his leadership, the organization made significant methodological contributions to survey research. First, the division established standardized interview protocols, and required field agents to follow them without deviation. Previously interviewers were free to ask whatever questions they desired. Second, Likert and his team broke from the established interviewing method of asking direct, objective questions. They used a technique called funneling where they began with broad nondirective open-ended questions and then narrowed the focus to more specific questions assessing the desired attitudes. This approach allowed researchers to understand the broader context and provided rich descriptive data. Third, the division utilized efficient multistage probability sampling methods for households and individuals. This allowed the division to use smaller samples while improving accuracy (Seashore & Katz, 1982).

During World War II (WWII), the Office of War Information and other agencies called upon Likert's division to measure the public's attitudes and behavior, expanding its work beyond the agricultural area, and raising its prominence and influence. One example of this work was a study examining the buying and redemption of war bonds. Another example was the Strategic Bombing Surveys which used innovative sampling strategies and interviewing techniques to assess how bombing raids affected the German and Japanese civilian populations' attitudes and behavior. For this work, Likert received the Medal of Freedom in 1946 (Kish, 1982).

University of Michigan and the Institute for Social Research

After WWII many of the researchers in the Division of Program Surveys returned to university positions. A small group believing in the potential of survey and social research remained with the government. They were interested, though, in continuing to investigate social issues with interdisciplinary large scale (survey) research in a university setting. Several of Likert's friends and professional associates were at his alma mater, the University of Michigan, and they expressed interest in establishing such a research center. The university's administration, however, was "friendly but skeptical" (Cannell & Kahn, 1984, p. 1257) and concerned about the financial obligations that the university could incur. After these concerns were addressed, the Survey Research Center (SRC) was established in 1946 and became a self-supporting research institute under the umbrella of the University of Michigan with its funding coming from grants and contracts.

Likert and Angus Campbell (who had worked with Likert at the Division of Program Surveys) led the SRC through its early developmental years assembling a team of highly skilled researchers many of whom became well-known researchers in their own right. In 1949, the SRC merged with the Research Center for Group Dynamics from the Massachusetts Institute of Technology. The resulting new organization was named the Institute for Social Research (ISR), and Likert was named the first Director of the ISR, a position he held until his retirement in 1970. During this time under Likert's vision, leadership, and management the ISR grew significantly and became the nation's leading academic laboratory for social science research (Cannell & Kahn, 1984).

Likert also held leadership positions at the American Statistical Association, serving as the Vice President (1953–1955) and President (1959). Despite all of Likert's administrative responsibilities he continued to pursue his own scholarly activities. During this time, he authored two books, *New Patterns of Management* (Likert, 1961) and *The Human Organization* (Likert, 1967). Likert was also an early proponent of HRA believing that "all forms of human resources are ignored in a firm's accounting reports" (Likert & Bowers, 1969, p. 588) and that human resources are not just purely costs, but assets as well. In conjunction with accounting professor Lee Brummet and other colleagues at the University of Michigan, Likert initiated at the ISR longitudinal studies designed to examine how managerial behavior, organizational structure, as well as other individual-level variables commonly studied in I-O psychology influence productivity and financial performance.

"Retirement"

After Likert retired from the ISR in 1970 he moved to Hawaii and established yet another organization. He wished to put into practice his ideas about organizations and management and created Rensis Likert and Associates with offices in Ann Arbor and Honolulu. In addition, during this time he coauthored *New Ways of Managing Conflict* (Likert & Likert, 1976) with his wife, Jane Gibson Likert. It was also during this time that Likert developed and presented his systems of management (Likert, 1979). He identified four styles of management: Exploitative authoritative, benevolent authoritative, consultative, and participative. Exploitative authoritative is a task-oriented style of management where leadership makes all decisions and communicates downward to subordinates who are not involved in decision-making. Employees lack power and leaders use threats and fear to control employees. In the Benevolent Authoritative style, decision-making still rests with leadership, but rewards, not fear, are used to motivate employee performance. Communication is in both directions upward and downward, but the upward flow to leaders is geared toward their interests and expectations. In the consultative style, leaders seek input from lower levels during decision making. Employees are motivated by rewards and their involvement and participation in the process. Communication flows well in both directions. In the participative style, leadership actively encourages and seeks employee input into decisions. Leadership and employees actively support each other, trust each other, and jointly pursue goals.

Likert remained active in research and consulting until his death in 1981 while visiting Ann Arbor.

Summary of Contributions

Likert is most widely known for his contribution to survey measurement, namely the "Likert Scale" which simplified scale and survey development and greatly increasing the ability to study complex human attitudes, experiences, and opinions. This alone would warrant his inclusion as a key thinker in I-O psychology. However, his contributions to I-O psychology and survey research are much broader. He established and led several influential organizations. Under his leadership they made substantial contributions in a variety of areas. For example, standardized interview protocols and the development of intensive open-ended interview study techniques were pioneered, and innovative probability sampling techniques were developed. In addition, Likert participated in the initiation of HRA. Finally, he made significant contributions to organizational management and theory.

Likert had a talent for assembling groups of highly skilled researchers and facilitating their work. His leadership was characterized by "enthusiasm and optimism" for the good that social research could achieve, and this set the tone for the rest of the organization, he was a "continuing source of new research ideas," and he put into practice his ideas surrounding participative management (Cannell & Kahn, 1984, p. 1257). While much of his time was spent supporting the work of others, he still found time to publish over 100 articles, multiple books, and make his own methodological and theoretical contributions to I-O psychology (Kish, 1982).

References

Cannell, C. F., & Kahn, R. L. (1984). Some factors in the origins and development of the Institute for Social Research, the University of

Michigan. *American Psychologist, 39*(11), 1256–1266. https://doi.org/10.1037/0003-066X.39.11.1256

Edmondson, D. (2005, May). Likert scales: A history. In *Proceedings of the conference on historical analysis and research in marketing* (Vol. 12, pp. 127–133). https://ojs.library.carleton.ca/index.php/pcharm/article/view/1613/1456

Kish, L. (1982). Rensis Likert 1903–1981. *American Statistician, 36*(2), 124–125. https://doi.org/10.1080/00031305.1982.10482804

Kish, L. (1990). Rensis Likert. *Choices: The Magazine of Food, Farm and Resource Issues*, 5(4), 36–38.

Likert, R. (1932). A technique for the measurement of attitudes. *Archives of Psychology, 22*(140), 5–55.

Likert, R. (1961). *New patterns of management*. McGraw-Hill.

Likert, R. (1967). *The human organization: Its management and values*. McGraw-Hill.

Likert, R. (1979). From production-and employee-centeredness to systems 1-4. *Journal of Management, 5*(2), 147–156. https://doi.org/10.1177/014920637900500

Likert, R., & Bowers, D. G. (1969). Organizational theory and human resource accounting. *American Psychologist, 24*(6), 585–592. https://doi.org/10.1037/h0028020

Likert, R., & Likert, J. G. (1976). *New ways of managing conflict*. McGraw-Hill.

Likert, R., Roslow, S., & Murphy, G. (1934). A simple and reliable method of scoring the Thurstone attitude scales. *Journal of Social Psychology, 5*(2), 228–238. https://doi.org/10.1080/00224545.1934.9919450

Pachella, R. G. (2010). *Creating the modern Michigan Psychology Department: The chairmanship of Donald Marquis, 1945–1957*. https://prod.lsa.umich.edu/content/dam/psychassets/psychdocuments/History/Pachella%20Department%20History.pdf

Seashore, S. E., & Katz, D. (1982). Obituary: Rensis Likert (1903–1981). *American Psychologist, 37*(7), 851–853. https://doi.org/10.1037/0003-066X.37.7.851

Chapter 31

John Clemans Flanagan (1906–1996)

Michael J. Zickar and Samuel T. McAbee

John Clemans Flanagan was a pioneering psychologist who made contributions to aviation psychology, education, personnel selection, measurement of job performance, and the study of aging. He led the United States (US) Army Air Corps' aviation selection program during World War II (WWII) and after the war, he used that work to help private airlines develop selection systems. He pioneered the critical incident technique (CIT), a cornerstone for selection, and headed Project TALENT, which provided data that helped many researchers in educational and psychological fields. Finally, he was an important researcher in the study of retirement and the aging workforce. In addition to his scholarly work, he founded the American Institutes for Research (AIR), an important private-sector research hub that worked closely with public and private industry.

Biographical Overview

John C. Flanagan was born in Armour, SD, on January 7, 1906, and his family moved to the state of Washington at the age of three where he spent the rest of his childhood. He began his undergraduate studies in electrical engineering and physics at the University of Washington, where he also quarterbacked for the Huskies football team. He completed his degree in education with minors in math and physics. After graduating, Flanagan worked as a high school mathematics teacher and football coach for several years and then pursued a PhD in mental measurement at Harvard, working under Truman Lee Kelley, who was an Edward Thorndike student and an early expert on measurement and statistics, particularly in the realm of education.

DOI: 10.4324/9781003403258-31

Upon completing his dissertation, Flanagan took a job at the American Council on Education's (ACE) Cooperative Test Service, where he worked on a large-scale achievement test, foreshadowing his eventual work on Project TALENT. While working at ACE, he worked on a project that involved interviewing Air Force pilots. In 1941, as the US was on the brink of entering WWII, he joined the US Army Air Corps (the predecessor to the US Air Force, which was created in 1947) as a commissioned officer at the rank of Major, and he was later promoted to the rank of Colonel. During the war, Flanagan created and directed the Aviation Psychology Program, which designed and implemented a selection system for the Air Corps.

In 1946, Flanagan accepted a position as a professor of psychology at the University of Pittsburgh. There, Flanagan founded the nonprofit research institute AIR, tapping colleagues from the Air Corps. AIR worked with public and private organizations to carry on much of the personnel work started in the Air Force. While at AIR, he conducted multiple studies aimed at understanding working conditions and experiences for older adults. His biggest contribution was Project TALENT, a nationwide longitudinal study of 440,000 high school students that was modeled on his work at ACE. Project TALENT assessed participants on many measures and provided important insights into many different areas of education and psychology (see American Psychological Association [APA], 1977; Clemans, 1997; Cucina & Bowling, 2016; Hans & Hamilton, 2023 for additional biographical details). In 1976, he was awarded the APA Distinguished Professional Contribution Award, one of the organization's highest honors (APA, 1977).

Description of the Contributions

Air Force Selection

When Flanagan was commissioned as an officer in the Air Force, there were only 51,000 service members in the Air Corps, a number vastly inadequate to the number that would be needed to fight in WWII (by the end of the war, there would be almost 2.3 million Air Corps members). The Air Corps wanted a system designed to help select individuals who would be successful in the wide range of jobs that the Air Corps had (e.g., pilot, navigator, mechanic). Given that many of these jobs required technical skills that were not readily available in the general population, it was clear that the selection program needed to be paired with an extensive training program. Flanagan formed a large team of up to 150 psychologists and 1,500 assistants at its peak. A key part of the selection battery was that there were *multiple hurdles*, an innovation that would later be standard in many selection programs. Recruits had to pass an initial screening test and then if they passed that they completed an intensive 20-test placement battery that included assessments ranging from temperament, proficiency, and aptitude. To validate the assessment, Flanagan showed that the battery was positively correlated with successful completion of pilot training and negatively correlated with aircraft accidents (see Flanagan, 1946; Flanagan, 1948). One of the unique contributions of the efforts was that Flanagan convinced the Air Corps to allow participants who failed the selection battery to participate in pilot training to better establish the validity of the test by having less restricted variance. Most selection efforts that establish concurrent validity rely on a restricted sample that includes people who were only selected on the initial battery. Flanagan showed that an unrestricted sample resulted in even higher validity. For his war work, Flanagan was awarded the Legion of Merit in 1946.

Critical Incident Technique

One of the key methodological contributions that Flanagan made during this time was the CIT. This work began during the war and continued afterwards under the aegis of AIR (as well as the University of Pittsburgh where Flanagan was hired as an Assistant Professor). Flanagan used the CIT to identify what he labeled "any observable human activity that is sufficiently complete in itself to permit inferences and predictions to be made about the person performing the act" (Flanagan, 1954, p. 327). In a series of projects that involved identifying critical requirements for Air Corps officers, commercial pilots, and US Navy research personnel, Flanagan developed a five-step process to identify these critical incidents.

The CIT has been viewed as a foundation of personnel psychology and is used as an essential component for job analysis, performance evaluation, and test development. As a testament to its importance, the original work has been cited over 16,000 times according to Google Scholar at the date of writing this entry. Cucina and Bowling (2016) labeled this work as his most lasting impact in I-O psychology, whereas Dunnette and Borman (1979) labeled the work as one of "the most important personnel selection milestones of the past 60 years" (p. 478).

Project TALENT

While at AIR, Flanagan and his colleagues wanted to study ways to identify talents among US high school students and created an ambitious project that has had enormous impact in the realms of education, psychological measurement, and vocational interests. In Project TALENT, which was funded by the US Department of Education, around 450,000 students from over 1,300 high schools across the US were measured on a variety of academic skills (e.g., vocabulary, abstract reasoning, quantitative reasoning), personality traits, and vocational interests, as well as performance in various activities such as athletics, the arts, and future career intentions (see Flanagan, 1979a). Students were followed up with additional surveys upon graduation 1, 5, and 11 years later, and even more recent data collections continue to this day. The massive data sets were made available to researchers around the country and resulted in a large number of publications and insights about the nature of education in the US.

From the over 350 publications that relied on the datasets, insights included the nature of change in average student performance over time, as well as research that showed that when students career choices were consistent with interests and abilities that they resulted in maximum satisfaction, to insights about the importance of spatial ability in the success of PhDs in science (see Cucina & Bowling, 2016 for an excellent summary). One finding that bothered Flanagan was that students needed greater alignment between instruction and career planning. To rectify this, Flanagan created Project PLAN (Program for Learning in Accordance with Needs), which involved using computer technology to tailor educational programs to individual students. The program was limited, though, by the lack of widespread computing capabilities during the late 1960s and early 1970s.

Quality of Life Especially among Aging Americans

In 1971, the AIR board of directors reviewed the organization's past 25 years of research and accomplishments and decided to direct efforts to improve the quality of life for Americans across the lifespan. In an ambitious project, researchers collected more than 6,500 critical incidents related to the quality of life from almost 3,000 individuals, making sure to sample across ages, races, and backgrounds throughout the country. Based on this, researchers coded the critical incidents into 15 quality-of-life components that fit into five categories: physical and material well-being; relations with other people; social, community, and civic activities; personal development and fulfillment; and recreation. Survey items were then written to assess these areas and were then administered to a nationally representative sample of Americans. Researchers then examined how individuals differed across age groups and found interesting findings such as the importance of learning increased over time and was higher for 70 year olds than 30 year olds, whereas the importance of participation in active recreation seemed to not change over age (see Flanagan, 1978 for an overview of the project).

In a follow-up effort, Flanagan (1979b) used nationally representative samples of 1,000 50 year olds and 1,000 70 year olds and administered the indicators of the 15 dimensions identified in the previous efforts. He found that self-reported overall quality of life was significantly related to nearly each of the dimensions though the magnitude of the correlations changed based on age and sex. Material comfort was the highest correlate for each age and sex group, though the importance of work and health depended on the age group.

These research efforts were important in that they helped researchers try to quantify the subjective notion of quality of life and spurred research into better understanding the experiences of older Americans. In terms of industrial-organizational (I-O) psychology, its efforts to better understand the importance of work to the lives of older Americans was important and presaged much work on aging in the workplace.

Conclusion

John Flanagan had an impressive range of contributions to I-O psychology that shared many features. First, *his work was ambitious and large scale*. Whether in the Air Corps selection project, Project TALENT, or the Quality of Life work, Flanagan believed in the importance of measuring a vast number of constructs, aptitudes, interests, attitudes, and behaviors. In addition, he felt it important to capture the range of Americans' experiences and worked hard to have nationally representative samples so that his findings would be relevant for different racial, sex, and age groups. Second, he was a *master in organization and realized the importance of team science*, much earlier before the term was coined. In a short time, he built a big team of psychologists working together in Air Corps selection and then after the war, he founded AIR, an organization that continues to conduct important research. Finally, Flanagan *had a deep respect for psychological and educational measurement* and his creation of the CIT is an important contribution that is foundational to educational and social science measurement.

References

American Psychological Association. (1977). Distinguished professional contribution award for 1976. *American Psychologist*, *32*, 72–87. https://doi.org/10.1037/h0078484

Clemans, W. V. (1997). John Clemans Flanagan (1906-1996). *American Psychologist*, *52*, 1375–1376. https://doi.org/10.1037//0003-066x.52.12.1375

Cucina, J. M., & Bowling, N. A. (2016). John C. Flanagan's contributions within and beyond I-O psychology. *Industrial-Organizational Psychologist*, *53*(3), www.siop.org/Research-Publications/TIP/TIP-Back-Issues/2016/January/ArtMID/20278/ArticleID/832/History-Corner-John-C-Flanagans-Contributions-Within-and-Beyond-I-O-Psychology

Dunnette, M. D., & Borman, W. C. (1979). Personnel selection and classification systems. *Annual Review of Psychology*, *30*(1), 477–525. https://doi.org/10.1146/annurev.ps.30.020179.002401

Flanagan, J. C. (1946). The experimental evaluation of a selection procedure. *Educational and Psychological Measurement, 6*, 445–466. https://doi.org/10.1177/001316444600600403

Flanagan, J. C. (1948). Contributions of research in the armed forces to personnel psychology. *Personnel Psychology, 1*, 53–62. https://doi.org/10.1111/j.1744-6570.1948.tb01293.x

Flanagan, J. C. (1954). The critical incident technique. *Psychological Bulletin*, *51*(4), 327–358. https://doi.org/10.1037/h0061470

Flanagan, J. C. (1978). A research approach to improving our quality of life. *American Psychologist*, *33*(2), 138–147. https://doi.org/10.1037//0003-066x.33.2.138

Flanagan, J. C. (1979a). Findings from Project TALENT. *The Educational Forum, 43*, 489–490. https://doi.org/10.1080/00131727909336131

Flanagan, J. C. (1979b). *Identifying opportunities for improving the quality of life of older age groups*. American Institutes for Research.

Hans, R., & Hamilton, A. D. (2023). Profiles in military psychology: John C. Flanagan. *Military Psychologists, 38*, 33–35.

Chapter 32

Abraham Maslow (1908–1970)

Samuel T. McAbee and Michael J. Zickar

Abraham H. Maslow is one of the most recognizable names in psychological science history. He was one of the founders of the "Third Force" of humanistic psychology, providing an alternative to the entrenched behaviorist and psychoanalytic paradigms of the times. Throughout his career, Maslow contributed to such topics as the study of dominance and sexuality in animal and human behavior and human motivation. He is most well-known for his works in the areas of self-actualization and for his taxonomy of human needs, which have had a profound influence in the training and practice of management.

Biographical Overview

Abraham H. Maslow was born on April 1, 1908, in New York City, the eldest child in a family of seven children, one of whom died in infancy (Coon, 2006; Hoffman, 1988). Maslow recalled his childhood as an unhappy one, where his father was unavailable and his mother cruel. Growing up in New York, Maslow faced a great degree of anti-Semitism in school. His refuge came from members of his extended family, including a close friendship with his cousin, Will Maslow, with whom he attended Boys High School in Manhattan. At age 14, Maslow met his first cousin, Bertha Goodman, a recent emigre from Russia. The two of them developed a close relationship and would eventually marry in December of 1928.

Maslow had a winding educational trajectory. He first attended college at the City College of New York (CCNY), then he transferred to Cornell University for one semester in the spring of 1927. After this brief time apart, Maslow grew homesick for his

DOI: 10.4324/9781003403258-32

wife, Bertha, and moved back to New York City. In the fall of 1928, he transferred to the University of Wisconsin, where he earned his baccalaureate degree. He continued his graduate education at the University of Wisconsin, studying under primatologist Henry Harlow. Maslow conducted his doctoral dissertation on sexual behavior and dominance in nonhuman primates, completing his doctorate entitled *The Role of Social Dominance in Social Behavior of Primates* in 1934.

After completing his doctoral studies, Maslow struggled to find a postdoctoral position, a result of anti-Semitic sentiment at the time (DeCarvalho, 1991). In 1935, Maslow was offered a fellowship under Edward L. Thorndike at Columbia University, where he enjoyed relative freedom in his research pursuits. At Columbia, Maslow extended his research on the study of sexuality and dominance motives into human subjects, primarily women, pioneering the field of sexology (Coon, 2006).

In 1937, Maslow accepted his first academic position at Brooklyn College, where he continued until 1951 (DeCarvalho, 1991). There, he quickly began to socialize with several well-respected social science researchers at the time out of the New School for Social Research, including scholars such as Alfred Adler, Ruth Benedict, and Max Wertheimer. In much of his early work, he focused on the abnormal side of human functioning, even publishing a textbook on the topic. In 1938, he was inspired by his colleague cultural anthropologist Ruth Benedict to visit the Blackfoot Native American Indian Tribe in Alberta Canada, an experience that he sought out to better understand his own cultural biases (Hoffman, 1988). This experience influenced him to question many assumptions about his own work and psychology in general. Frustrated with the pessimism that he viewed as inherent in Freudian psychoanalytic theory, as well as with the deterministic worldview of Behaviorism, Maslow transitioned to focusing on the positive side of human functioning, developing the humanistic psychology work that would define his career.

In 1951, Maslow was offered a position as head of the department of psychology at the recently established Brandeis University where he continued to conduct research and publish on topics related to human thriving, concentrating on topics such as peak experiences and belonging. To promote this new humanistic psychology, Maslow co-founded with Anthony Sutich the *Journal of Humanistic Psychology*, which published its first volume in 1961. Maslow was elected and served as President of the American Psychological Association in 1968. In 1969, he accepted a fellowship with Laughlin Foundation in Menlo Park, California (DeCarvalho, 1991). Maslow died of a massive heart attack on June 8, 1970.

Summary of Contributions to Organizational Psychology

Although Maslow's contributions to psychology are vast, in this review we focus on several contributions that are most relevant to industrial-organizational (I-O) psychology: the Hierarchy of Needs as well as his concept of Eupsychian Management.

Hierarchy of Needs

As outlined in the biographical summary, Maslow's early career covered many different research directions, such as focusing on negative aspects of psychology including deprivation in humans and animals, as well as abnormal psychology. In 1943, he was asked to give a lecture on motivation and eventually published an article in *Psychological Review* entitled "A Theory of Human Motivation" (Maslow, 1943). In proposing what he called a "positive theory of motivation," Maslow cited the functionalists, specifically Dewey, the Gestalt psychologists Wertheimer and Goldstein, and the psychodynamic psychologists Freud and Adler. Maslow proposed that there was a hierarchy of needs such that "the appearance of one need usually rests on the prior satisfaction of another, more pre-potent need" (Maslow, 1943, p. 370). These needs, in order, were physiological (e.g., hunger and thirst), safety needs, love and social belonging needs, esteem needs, and then self-actualization. Although self-actualization is associated with Maslow, the concept was first coined by Gestalt psychologist Kurt Goldstein (see Goldstein 1995; Whitehead, 2017). Goldstein originally purposed self-actualization as a biological urge that applied to all organisms, a general process of individuation. Maslow, however, used the term in "a much more specific and limited fashion" (Maslow, 1943, p. 382), and he defined the concept in his theory as "the desire to become more and more what one is, to become everything that one is capable of becoming" (Maslow, 1943, p. 382). This latter concept of self-actualization would be the inspiration for much of Maslow's subsequent work.

Maslow wrote expansively on his hierarchy of needs and expanded the work into general theories of motivation, most extensively in the book *Motivation and Personality* (Maslow, 1954, later updated in a second edition). In addition, he explored many of the implications of self-actualization in works that became bedrocks of humanistic psychology such as *The Farther Reaches of Human Nature* (Maslow, 1971).

Given the popularity of Maslow's Hierarchy of Needs, key tenets were empirically tested by psychological researchers. The basic assumption that lower-order needs needed to be met before higher-order needs were important was not supported by data (see Alderfer, 1969). Maslow himself argued that higher needs become "of secondary importance" in the place of unfulfilled lower needs, suggesting a less rigid position than many ascribed to him (see Maslow, 1943, pp. 373–374). Despite this lack of empirical support of a key concept, the theory is a classic presented in nearly all Introduction to Psychology textbooks, and it continues to inspire new research. In addition, management researchers and thinkers such as Douglas McGregor began incorporating Maslow's theory into their own works, promoting the notion that managers should encourage their employees to develop their higher-order needs (see Bridgman et al, 2019). Maslow's theory, along with the encouragement of others like McGregor, inspired organizations to develop motivation programs based on the hierarchy of needs. For example, Texas Instruments created a job redesign based on the hierarchy of needs that included participatory management and personality assessment linked to employees' perceptions of their unmet needs (see Lussier, 2019).

One important theory inspired by Maslow's theory was psychologist Frederick Herzberg's two-factor model of work motivation, the Motivator-Hygiene Theory (Herzberg et al., 1959). In Herzberg's theory, hygiene factors, such as workplace conditions, are predictive of job dissatisfaction whereas motivator factors, such as the intrinsic nature of the work itself, are predictors of job satisfaction. In general, research testing specific assumptions of Herzberg's model, just as research testing Maslow's model, has been critical (see Ewen et al., 1966), though the idea itself continues to inspire managers and researchers.

Eupsychian Management

Later in Maslow's career, he turned his attention directly to issues of organizations and work motivation. In the Summer of 1962, Maslow spent time at Non-Linear Systems (NLS), Inc., an electronics company in Del Mar, California. He was invited by the company's founder, Andy Kay, who was inspired by Maslow's work on motivation and prided himself on building a company run by democratic principles. Maslow was given a generous stipend and no job description except to walk around, observe, and interview workers, and talk with Kay once a week (see Hoffman, 1988). He was energized by what he saw at NLS and was motivated to read works by management writers Peter Drucker and Douglas McGregor, both whose work was mentioned by Kay and other NLS leaders as inspirational. At the end of the Summer, Kay offered Maslow a full-time permanent position at NLS though Maslow turned him down to return to academia.

His journal of observations from that time was published in a book *Eupsychian Management* (1965). In 1998, the book was published again with contributions from others with the more appealing title, *Maslow on Management* (Maslow et al., 1998). Eupsychia was an imaginary utopian society that Maslow hypothesized was full of self-actualized individuals and so in the book, Maslow hypothesized what it would be like to manage employees who were enlightened, motivated, and creative. The book was free-flowing and was described in the forward by management scholar Warren Bennis as "a sketch-pad for his [Maslow's] unfinished, and possibly, most creative work" (Bennis in Maslow, 1965, p. vii). Maslow's writings ranged from how to encourage employees to engage in self-actualizing work, the need to adapt management practices in diverse ways to different individuals, and the importance of creativity in the workplace. Although Maslow thought that psychotherapy was helpful in promoting self-actualization, he realized that it was impractical for all of society to engage therapists. He viewed the workplace as the one arena in life that, if designed and managed well, held the most potential for promoting individual self-actualization. One disappointment is that Maslow passed away just five years after the publication of the book, not giving him enough time to write more systematically on the ideas that he brainstormed in this influential book. Fortunately, though, subsequent researchers and management thinkers have been inspired by the ideas in this book (e.g., Regan, 2023).

Conclusion

Maslow was a towering figure in 20th-century American psychology, an individual who made important contributions to a wide range of areas. In this chapter, we have focused on his contributions germane to I-O psychology and management theory. His work on motivation, and particularly his theory of the hierarchy of needs, inspired researchers and practitioners to develop programs that addressed higher-level needs such as esteem and self-actualization. His work in industry that culminated in the publication of *Euspychian Management* continues to inspire management thinkers.

References

Alderfer, C. P. (1969). An empirical test of a new theory of human needs. *Organizational Behavior and Human Performance*, *4*(2), 142–175. https://doi.org/10.1016/0030-5073(69)90004-X

Bridgman, T., Cummings, S., & Ballard, J. (2019). Who built Maslow's pyramid? A history of the creation of management studies' most famous symbol and its implications for management education. *Academy of Management Learning & Education*, *18*(1), 81–98. https://doi.org/10.5465/amle.2017.0351

Coon, D. J. (2006). Abraham H. Maslow: Reconnaissance for eupsychia. In D. A. Dewsbury, L. T. Benjamin, Jr., & M. Wertheimer (Eds.), *Portraits of pioneers in psychology* (vol. 6; pp. 255–271). American Psychological Association.

DeVarvalho, R. J. (1991). Abraham H. Maslow (1908–1970): An intellectual biography. *Thought: Fordham University Quarterly*, *66*(1), 32–50. https://doi.org/10.5840/thought199166141

Ewen, R. B., Smith, P. C., & Hulin, C. L. (1966). An empirical test of the Herzberg two-factor theory. *Journal of Applied Psychology, 50*(6), 544–550. https://doi.org/10.1037/h0024042

Goldstein, K. (1995). *The organism: A holistic approach to biology derived from pathological data in man.* Zone Books. (Original work published 1934)

Herzberg, F., Mausner, B., & Snyderman, B. B. (1959). *The motivation to work.* Wiley.

Hoffman, E. (1988). *The right to be human: A biography of Abraham Maslow.* Jeremy P. Tarcher.

Lussier, K. (2019). Of Maslow, motives, and managers: The hierarchy of needs in American business, 1960–1985. *Journal of the History of the Behavioral Sciences, 55*(4), 319–341. https://doi.org/10.1002/jhbs.21992

Maslow, A. H. (1943). A theory of human motivation. *Psychological Review, 50,* 370–396.

Maslow, A. H. (1954). *Motivation and personality.* Harper & Row.

Maslow, A. H. (1965). *Eupsychian management: A journal.* R.D. Irwin.

Maslow, A. H. (1971). *The farther reaches of human nature.* Viking Press.

Maslow, A. H., Stephens, D., & Heil, G. (1998). *Maslow on management.* Wiley.

Regan, J. R. (2023). Eupsychian management in the age of the knowledge worker. *Journal of Humanistic Psychology, 63*(4), 502–514. https://doi.org/10.1177/0022167821110129

Whitehead, P. M. (2017). Goldstein's self-actualization: A biosemiotic view. *Humanistic Psychologist, 45*(1), 71–83. https://doi.org/10.1037/hum0000047

Chapter 33

Patricia Cain Smith (1917–2007)

William K. Balzer and Jeffrey M. Stanton

Patricia Cain Smith left a rich legacy in the science and practice of industrial and organizational (I-O) psychology. Pat[1] maintained a broad range of interests and made trailblazing contributions to industrial monotony, behaviorally anchored rating scales (BARS), and job satisfaction that shaped best practices in I-O psychology. Pat's pioneering work as a consultant and academic broke down longstanding biases against women professionals. Along with Lillian Gilbreth, Mary Parker Follett, Marion Bills, Mary Tenopyr, and others, Pat opened the door for generations of women entering the field of I-O psychology.

Biographical Overview

Early Life

Pat was born October 28, 1917, in Minneapolis, MN, but her family moved frequently because of her father's changing jobs and fortune, eventually settling in his hometown of Falls City, NE (Smith, 1988). As an only child, Pat learned to adapt to the perennial stress of being the new student in her class. Pat enjoyed activities that accelerated her reading and arithmetic skills. She discussed books with her mother and played card games with her father while making mental calculations to compute gambling odds. Pat realized that her parents were coaching her for a career outside the home: she received no instruction in cooking, cleaning, or sewing. Her parents instilled care for others, finishing tasks to completion, respect for accuracy and facts, and the merit of trying new ideas.

DOI: 10.4324/9781003403258-33

Pat adored her warm and caring father. Sadly, a series of failed business ventures contributed to his suicide when she was just 15 years old. His death propelled Pat from adolescence into adulthood. Her upbringing had provided a strong foundation for pursuing higher education and a career. At every stage, Pat exhibited academic excellence, a keen interest in numbers and people, the values of hard work and accountability, and an uncanny ability to seize opportunities (Balzer & Sandman, 2017).

Post-Secondary Education

Pat entered the University of Nebraska in 1935 to study mathematics and psychology. J. P. Guilford, her mentor and a pioneer in psychometrics and experimental psychology, directed her honors thesis on gender differences in color preferences. This project provided her first "joy of insight" when the data told an orderly and compelling story. Guilford's mentorship remained important throughout Pat's life.

After graduating in 1939, Pat studied at Northwestern University and Bryn Mawr where she worked with Harry Helson on color perception. Realizing that her interests did not lie in the laboratory, Pat transferred to Cornell University and studied industrial psychology under the guidance of T. A. "Art" Ryan. Her studies with Ryan strengthened insights gleaned at Nebraska: verbal reports could be reliable if the right questions are asked; situational and individual factors influenced behavior; and, meticulous measurement was critical for validity. Ryan's interest in fatigue influenced Pat's choice of industrial monotony for her dissertation: a field study of garment factory workers. In 1942, Pat completed her PhD and married fellow graduate student Olin "Olie" W. Smith. The start of United States (US) involvement in World War II (WWII) thrust Olie into military life while Pat began searching for work in industry (Smith, 1988).

Early Career

Pat had amassed excellent academic credentials, skills, and recommendations, but she underestimated the extent of gender bias against women as professionals. From hundreds of job applications, she received just three expressions of interest and accepted the only offer, an 18-month internship with Aetna Life. Her supervisor, Marion Bills, a woman I-O psychologist and company officer, taught her personnel techniques and, importantly, how to be a successful professional woman in an historically male domain (Smith, 1988).

Pat was subsequently hired by Kurt Salmon and Associates (KSA), a firm founded in 1935 and expanding to serve the garment industry. Pat led the firm's new personnel section where she quickly learned the ropes of consulting. She documented financial benefits resulting from enlightened personnel practices and learned to persuasively sell ideas that improved the lives of employees *and* the company's finances.

Her client list at KSA expanded rapidly. Pat supervised the creation of nearly 100 new personnel departments; in one year, she flew over 100,000 miles, commenting that First Lady Eleanor Roosevelt was the only woman to fly further (Smith, 1988, p. 143). Pat's success brought increasing executive duties, and Pat regretted the loss of opportunities to work directly with employees. Following Olie's demobilization and honorable discharge in 1946, they returned to Cornell University so that Olie could complete his PhD. The challenges of air travel from Ithaca's tiny airport led Pat to leave her full-time role with KSA. During this period, she experimented – very briefly – with being a part-time homemaker.

Later Career

Finding domestic life unfulfilling, Pat began part-time teaching at Ithaca College and Wells College. After accepting a summer appointment at Cornell University to teach psychology to returning veterans, Pat continued teaching through the academic year. With guidance from a colleague on "publish or perish" expectations, Pat ramped up her writing and initiated the remarkable series of contributions described below. Starting with her appointment as an assistant professor in 1949, Pat's achievements marked several firsts for women faculty at Cornell: she was the first to obtain tenure in the endowed schools at Cornell, the first to be accepted as a member of the graduate faculty, and the first to be promoted to full professor in 1963.

After 18 years at Cornell, however, Pat and Olie were ready for a change. In 1966 they joined Bob Guion in the new I-O psychology PhD program at Bowling Green State University (BGSU). Pat's academic and consulting career continued to flourish. Pat retired from BGSU in 1980 for health reasons and was granted emerita status. In this role, Pat maintained a research group that included doctoral students and fellow I-O psychology faculty members. She also consulted until shortly before passing away in 2007.

Major Contributions to I-O Psychology

Industrial Monotony

Pat's dissertation was published in the *Journal of Applied Psychology* in 1953 with the title, "The Curve of Output as a Criterion of Boredom." This article was cited by early publications on goal setting theory, psychological theorizing on the concept of boredom, and studies of financial incentives and work performance. The article's conclusion set the tone for Pat's subsequent career:

> There can be little quarrel with the claim of the British investigators that, other factors being equal, workers tend to slow down, talk, become restless and variable in their production when bored. In most industrial situations, however, one cannot assume that all other factors are equal, and many of these factors may heavily outweigh the influence of interest or boredom in producing changes in working behavior.
>
> (Smith, 1953, p. 74)

Pat was never afraid to follow the data wherever it might lead, regardless of whether the findings contradicted current orthodoxy. Following a second article on industrial monotony it became evident that her curiosity had blossomed into a broader interest in work motivation and job satisfaction.

Behaviorally Anchored Rating Scales

Over the following decade, Pat expanded her topical horizons while also partnering with Olie on research funded by the US

Office of Naval Research. They conducted basic research on perception and coauthored publications in prominent journals (Smith & Smith, 1957, 1961) and conferences.

During this period Pat maintained an active program of research on employment. She coauthored an industrial psychology textbook with Art Ryan, and published multiple journal articles on topics related to employee motivation. Her work on BARS (Smith & Kendall, 1963), however, set the course for the rest of her career. This original BARS article, now cited nearly 1,500 times, caused a major shift in the measurement of employment-related constructs and led to the creation of hundreds of new measures.

The Job Descriptive Index

Undoubtedly, the work for which Pat is best known is the Job Descriptive Index (JDI) and its family of measures (Smith, Kendall, & Hulin, 1969). In his review of this 186-page book, Campbell (1970) noted that, "The chapter on validation is a clear and lucid presentation of three principal lines of evidence. To sum up, this is a very important book" (p. 541). The book spawned more than 800 research studies that used the JDI, based on searching for works in the PsycNet application offered by the American Psychological Association. This is almost certainly an undercount, as a Google Scholar search identifies 14,300 citations related to "JDI job satisfaction."

Part of the broad appeal of the JDI arose from the inclusion of national norms in the original book, as well as ongoing efforts to update those norms and provide supplemental validation evidence. In the three decades following Smith et al. (1969), Pat's research group published dozens of papers, including additional measures – most notably the Job-in-General scale, the Intent-to-Quit Scale, and the Stress-in-General scale – as well as many studies arising from her consulting work.

Hidden in Smith et al. (1969) there is a reference to the promise of a follow-up volume (see Campbell, 1970). It took Pat and her colleagues more than 20 years to fulfill this promise with the publication of Cranny et al. (1992), an edited volume with a contributor list that reads like a "Who's Who" of 20th-century I-O psychology. Pat concludes her introductory chapter with a statement encapsulating much of the thinking from her long and lively career:

> ...If [managers] hope to maintain their organizations, they want their employees to be cooperative, constructive, and open to innovations. It then makes economic sense – while conforming to humanitarian values – to consider whether trust and happiness can be improved by administrative action and, if so, how.
>
> (p. 17)

Pat's final publication, Russell et al. (2004), resulted from a collaboration exemplifying her love for research, numbers, and people. Here's a replay of a scene just before the article was sent out for review: A crew of young, enthusiastic PhD students gathered around a conference room table, discussing detailed correlation matrices with Pat and her faculty colleagues and weaving the result into an abridged version of an old friend, the Job-in-General scale. Pat will be remembered for her skill in promoting I-O psychology to industry leaders, her self-effacing sense of humor, her passion for clarity in thinking and writing, and her contagious enthusiasm for discovery.

Conclusion

Patricia Cain Smith epitomized – and helped define – the scientist-practitioner model during her impactful career in industry, consulting, and academia. She brought both intellectual curiosity and methodological rigor to her work. She evolved a highly influential model of job satisfaction and related job attitudes, creating and updating psychometrically sound measures (including national norms) for more than 50 years. As a practitioner, Pat listened to management and employees and used data to identify the workplace problems that needed to be addressed – and then addressed them. She believed in the dignity of employees and advocated for their right to satisfying and fulfilling work. In parallel, she demonstrated to managers how treating employees well could contribute positively to the bottom line. Pat overcame barriers facing professional women through the quality and quantity of her accomplishments and her optimistic disposition. As her obituary in the *American Psychologist* concluded,

> Pat is remembered for her sense of humor, her passion for clarity in thinking and writing, and her contagious enthusiasm for discovery and the achievement of true understanding. She has left a lasting legacy that has made the world, and especially the world of work, a better place.
>
> (Balzer et al., 2008, p. 198)

Note

1 We the authors were friends and colleagues of hers, so we will refer to her by her preferred nickname, Pat, throughout this chapter.

References

Balzer, W. K., Locke, E. A., & Zedeck, S. (2008). Obituary: Patricia Cain Smith (1917 – 2007). *American Psychologist*, *63*(3), 198. https://doi.org/10.1037/0003-066x.63.3.198

Balzer, W. K., & Sandman, B. A. (2017). Smith, Patricia C.: Second recipient, SIOP Distinguished Scientific Contributions Award. In S. G. Rogelberg (Ed.), *Sage encyclopedia of industrial and organizational psychology* (2nd ed.; pp. 1447–1449). Sage Publications. https://doi.org/10.4135/9781483386874.n496

Campbell, J. P. (1970). The way it should be done [Review of the book *The measurement of satisfaction in work and retirement,* by P. C. Smith, L. M. Kendall & C. L. Hulin]. *Contemporary Psychology, 15*(9), 540–542. https://doi.org/10.1037/013853

Cranny, C. J., Smith, P. C., & Stone, E. F. (1992). *Job satisfaction: How people feel about their jobs and how it affects their performance.* Lexington Books.

Russell, S. S., Spitzmüller, C., Lin, L. F., Stanton, J. M., Smith, P. C., & Ironson, G. H. (2004). Shorter can also be better: The abridged Job in General scale. *Educational and Psychological Measurement, 64*(5), 878–893. https://doi.org/10.1177/0013164404264841

Smith, O. W., & Smith, P. C. (1957). Interaction of the effects of cues involved in judgments of curvature. *American Journal of Psychology, 70*(3), 361–375. https://doi.org/10.2307/1419572

Smith, P. C. (1953). The curve of output as a criterion of boredom. *Journal of Applied Psychology*, *37*(2), 69–74. https://doi.org/10.1037/h0062997

Smith, P. C. (1988). Patricia Cain Smith. In Agnes N. O'Connell, Nancy Felipe Russo (Eds.), *Models of achievement: Reflections of eminent women in psychology*, 2, pp. 137–151. Columbia University Press.

Smith, P. C., & Kendall, L. M. (1963). Retranslation of expectations: An approach to the construction of unambiguous anchors for rating scales. *Journal of Applied Psychology, 47*(2), 149–155. https://doi.org/10.1037/h0047060

Smith, P. C., Kendall, L. M., & Hulin, C. L. (1969). *The measurement of satisfaction in work and retirement*. Rand McNally.

Smith, P. C., & Smith, O. W. (1961). Veridical perceptions of cylindricality: A problem of depth discrimination and object identification. *Journal of Experimental Psychology, 62*, 145–152. https://doi.org/10.1037/h0042383

Chapter 34

Douglas W. Bray (1918–2006)

Rosemary Hays-Thomas

"A legend in the field of the psychology of management" was written in tribute to Doug Bray after his death in 2006 (Lowman, 2008, p. 185). Rodney Lowman was writing an obituary for *The Psychologist-Manager Journal* published by the Society of Psychologists in Management (SPIM), an organization founded by Bray and others. Another obituary written for the *American Psychologist* by Bray's colleague William C. Byham describes his "dynamic personality...charismatic, verbally adroit, and perennially witty ... (with) a commanding presence, intimidating to some...a visionary" (2007, p. 141).

Lowman (2008) identified three life themes in Bray's professional accomplishments: leadership in developing the Assessment Center (AC) as a tool for research, leadership development, and selection; extension of AC methodology beyond AT&T and application of research to management by the consulting firm he co-founded (Development Dimensions, Inc., now Development Dimensions International, DDI); and engagement with and leadership of professional organizations (e.g., American Psychological Association [APA], American Board of Professional Psychology [ABPP], Society of Industrial and Organizational Psychology [SIOP]). Bray developed the AC methodology while conducting research at AT&T, then applied this and other science-based methods at AT&T and in consulting work with DDI, clearly following the scientist-practitioner model that is highly valued in industrial-organizational (I-O) psychology.

DOI: 10.4324/9781003403258-34

Biographical Overview

Biographical information reviewed here appears in sources acknowledging various awards (American Psychological Foundation [APF], 1991; "Awards," 1980) and in obituaries published in the *American Psychologist* (Byham, 2007) and *The Industrial-Organizational Psychologist* ("Obituaries," 2006). As President of SIOP, Bray himself provided the most detailed account of his life in the autobiography prepared for SIOP's history archives (Bray, n.d.).

Early Life and Education

Douglas Bray was born in Springfield, MA, on November 7, 1918, and his early years coincided with the Great Depression. His parents were supportive of their only child's formal education despite having completed the fifth and eigth grades, respectively. His mother, Lena B. Bray, worked in a department store before Bray was born. She is reported to have visited the library while pregnant, "hoping this prenatal environment would help produce a bright child" (APF, 1991, p. 780). His father, Marvin J. Bray, lost employment as purchasing agent with the Fisk Rubber Company during the Depression. Subsequently he found work in sales, during which time he learned of scholarship funding at American International College that enabled his son to earn the baccalaureate degree in sociology in 1940. Bray was awarded a graduate assistantship in psychology at Clark University, where he earned the MA degree in 1941 in abnormal psychology.

Drafted into the Army during World War II (WWII), Bray joined the aviation psychology program in the Army Air Corps, which conducted behavioral evaluations of training outcomes. This experience led to Bray's developing interest in applied psychology. After the War, he enrolled in social psychology at Yale University, completing the doctorate in 1948 with a minor in industrial psychology. During these early years Bray worked with several influential psychologists who later became well-known in early social and industrial psychology: Stuart Cook in the Army Air Corps, Leonard Doob and Carl Hovland at Yale, and Eli Ginzberg at Columbia.

Private Life

Bray was married briefly to his first wife, Rita Delarm. With his marriage to Lois Jacobi, Bray became stepfather to Gerald L. Bray and father to Christopher J. Bray. Upon retirement in 1983, Bray married his longtime research partner at AT&T, Ann Howard (Byham, 2007; Lowman, 2008). He remained active in psychology after retirement, with writing and editing, participating in professional organizations, and helping to promote DDI. Douglas Bray died in 2006 after a period of declining health due to vascular dementia and various physical conditions (Lowman, 2008).

Employment

After completing his degree, Bray accepted employment as a research associate in the study of education at Princeton University. Two years later he moved to Columbia University, joining Eli Ginzberg in the Conservation of Human Resources project from 1950 to 1955. Dwight Eisenhower was then President of Columbia University and influenced the initiation of a study of the War's "ineffective soldiers." This work is described in a book published by Ginzberg and Bray, *The Uneducated* (1953). Bray published a subsequent volume on human resources topics, *Issues in the Study of Talent* (1954). Professional recognition followed.

Carl Hovland, then consultant to AT&T, introduced Bray to executives at the company. This led to his acceptance of employment to conduct a longitudinal study of careers of managers in the Bell System (a large group of telecommunication companies that dominated the industry for over 100 years until its breakup in 1983). This landmark work developed the ACs for which Bray is best known. Based on techniques for selecting spies by the Office of Strategic Services (OSS) during WWII, this procedure became widely used for selection and training of managers at AT&T and elsewhere (Byham, 2007). ACs include a battery of individual tests and interactive experiences over the course of multiple days, during which time personal attributes and interpersonal behaviors are scored by professional assessors and used to develop summary evaluations of participants. Although earlier ACs were used by Harvard personality researchers and the OSS (Bray, 1982), Bray was responsible for developing the first *management* AC used initially for research purposes and later extended to selection and training. Within I-O psychology, he is thought of as the "Father of the Assessment Center."

The initial study (Bray, 1964; Bray et al., 1974) was conceived as developmental research into careers of Bell System managers (then all males). Outcome data (e.g., repeated appraisals, job level, and salary) were collected 8 and 20 years later and confidentially held to prevent criterion contamination. This was followed by the use of ACs in selection and training. Subsequent research with more diverse participants is described in Howard and Bray (1988).

While at AT&T, Bray helped William Byham develop an AC for J. C. Penney. Later, when Byham decided to found a consulting company to provide ACs for client organizations, he invited Bray to partner with him in DDI. Bray worked out an agreement with AT&T management to work with DDI in his free time, barring conflicts of interest (Byham, 2007). Bray remained with AT&T until his retirement in 1983.

Professional Contributions

Within the field of psychology, Bray contributed to all of the major relevant professional organizations of his day. He was a member of the Council of Representatives of the New York State Psychological Association's Division of Personnel Psychology and later became its President. In 1971–1972 Bray served as President of SIOP (then Division 14 of APA). He was also a founding member of SPIM, now the Society of Psychologists in Leadership.

Bray chaired APA's Task Force on the Practice of Psychology in Industry and served on the Board of Trustees of the Association for the Advancement of Psychology. He also participated in the 1970 Vail Conference on Levels and Patterns of Professional Training in Psychology; its final report recommends applying AC methodology to evaluation of psychology graduates. Bray served on and chaired the Committee on Scientific and Professional

Ethics and Conduct, contributed to the Membership Committee, and was a member of APA's Council of Representatives. He was also a member of the Board of Directors for the National Academy of Professional Psychology (Awards for Distinguished Professional Contributions, 1980). ABPP requested his help in developing an AC for judging competence of clinical psychology practitioners seeking the diplomate credential. Bray himself earned diplomate status and later served as Vice President of ABPP. He was also a member of the taskforce that developed *Guidelines and Ethical Considerations for Assessment Center Operations*, which became the major standard for the conduct of ACs (Rupp, 2006).

Outside of I-O psychology, Bray maintained a strong interest in Duke Ellington's jazz. In 1959, he helped found the organization later known as the Duke Ellington Society in New York as a way of maintaining Ellington's musical legacy and served as its President for four years. Bray produced and served as Master of Ceremonies for the group's first three concerts and conducted interviews with band members that became part of the Ellington archives (Byham, 2007; Lowman, 2008). Bray's own life story as prepared for the SIOP history archives evidences this interest: "This title and subsequent section headings are the names of Duke Ellington compositions. His music has been a most important part of my life" (Bray, n.d., p. 1).

Awards

The psychology community recognized the significance of Bray's work with many awards. These include SIOP's first Distinguished Professional Contributions Award (1977) and APA's award for Distinguished Professional Contributions to Applied Psychology as a Professional Practice in 1980 (Byham, 2007). In 1986, he was the first recipient of SPIM's Distinguished Psychologist in Management Award (Lowman, 2008). ABPP recognized him in 1988 with the Distinguished Service and Outstanding Contribution Award, and APF presented him the Gold Medal Award for life achievement in the application of psychology (APF, 1991; Lowman, 2008). His AC work was also recognized in 2000 by the Lifetime Achievement in AC Methodology Award

(Awards for Distinguished Professional Contributions, 1980; Lowman, 2008).

Conclusion

Douglas Bray had great impact on those who knew him professionally. Byham (2007) called him "a natural leader," a "dynamic personality...charismatic, verbally adroit, and perennially witty (with a) commanding presence... visionary...(using) rigorous methodology" (p. 141). Lowman (2008) saw him as "a leader (and) a pioneer" (p. 187), impatient with details but persistent in completing projects. He displayed "intelligence, competitiveness, goal-directedness, wit, focus on the big picture, and a willingness to clearly be the one in charge...empathic and generally supportive of others" (p. 188). Bray was also seen as diplomatic yet competitive, a good listener and negotiator with a "lack of pomposity" (p. 191) despite his professional stature.

Bray's (n.d.) autobiography summarized his life with a Duke Ellington title, "Something to Live For." In a 1982 award address, written around the time of his retirement and marriage to Ann Howard, Bray mused about studying non-employment roles, such as spouse: "Assessment has been used extensively to study achievement. Surely love demands some attention" (p. 189).

References

American Psychological Foundation. (1991). Douglas W. Bray: Recipient of the Gold Medal Award for life achievement in the application of psychology. *American Psychologist*, *46*(7), 780–782. https://doi.org/10.1037/0003-066X.46.7.780

Awards for Distinguished Professional Contributions: 1980. (1981). *American Psychologist*, *36*(1), 52–66. https://doi.org/10.1037/h0078020

Bray, D. W. (n.d.) *Douglas W. Bray: SIOP President 1971-1972. Reminiscing in tempo*. Retrieved from www.siop.org/Portals/84/docs/Presidents/Bray_Douglas_W.pdf

Bray, D. W. (1954). *Issues in the study of talent*. King's Crown Press.

Bray, D. W. (1964). The management progress study. *American Psychologist*, *19*(6), 419–420. doi: 10.1037/h0039579

Bray, D. W. (1982). The assessment center and the study of lives. *American Psychologist, 37*(2), 180–189. https://doi.org/10.1037/0003-066X.37.2.180

Bray, D. W., Campbell, R. J., & Grant, D. L. (1974). *Formative years in business: A long-term AT&T study of managerial lives.* Wiley.

Byham, W. (2007). Douglas W. Bray (1918-2006). *American Psychologist, 62*(2), 140–141. doi: 10.1037/0003-066X.62.2.140

Ginzberg, E., & Bray, D. W. (1953). *The uneducated.* Columbia University Press. doi: https://doi.org/10.7312/ginz94296

Howard, A., & Bray, D. (1988). *Managerial lives in transition: Advancing age and changing times.* Guilford.

Lowman, R. L. (2008). Douglas W. Bray (1918-2006): Career and personal "life themes." *Psychologist-Manager Journal, 11*, 185–199. doi: 10.1080/10887150801967720

"Obituaries." Douglas W. Bray (1918--2006). (2006). *Industrial-Organizational Psychologist, 44*(1), 173–175.

Rupp, D. E. (2006). Douglas W. Bray, PhD: A dedication. *Psychologist-Manager Journal, 9*(2) 67–69. doi: 10.1027/s15503461tpmj0902_1

Chapter 35

Mary L. Tenopyr (1929–2005)

Jerard F. Kehoe

Mary L Tenopyr spent over 50 years from 1951 to 2005 working and leading in the field of industrial-organizational (I-O) psychology. Her primary contributions helped to ensure that the various sources of guidance for this employment-oriented profession including federal employment guidelines, standards of professional practice, and principles for research and use of employment procedures all were based on the same underlying foundation of predictive validity as the primary basis for evaluating the effectiveness and fairness of selection procedures. In addition, Tenopyr provided an exemplary model of professional leadership for women in I-O psychology.

Biographical Overview

Mary Tenopyr was born in 1929 and grew up in rural Ohio during the Great Depression in very humble and constraining circumstances. At age 2, her parents sent her to live on an isolated family farm with her maternal grandparents and a maiden aunt, never to live with her parents again. The farm had no modern conveniences except electricity but no plumbing, no telephone, and only woodstove cooking. When she occasionally went to visit her parents, she was referred to as "company." She nevertheless persevered through a range of obstacles including social naiveté, blatant sexism, and scarce financial resources, and was highly successful in high school. Although not the class valedictorian, she was the homecoming queen, which she had aspired to most of all (Tenopyr, 1979). After graduating from Ohio University with a bachelor's degree in psychology, she quickly followed

DOI: 10.4324/9781003403258-35

that with a master's degree in psychology while still 21 in 1951. Tenopyr's early interest in behavioral assessment was more fully shaped after taking a post-master's degree job as a psychometrist in the test bureau at Ohio University. Her success in her master's program fostered a strong interest in gaining a PhD to pursue a profession in psychology in spite of discouragement from her professors and male classmates (Tenopyr, 1979). The explicit sexism embedded in this early discouragement and subsequent related obstacles fueled Tenopyr's professional accomplishments for the next 54 years...the rest of her life.

Ironically, the sexism that discouraged Tenopyr also shaped her professional direction. One memorable early example occurred in 1955. At that point Tenopyr had worked for three years in the Air Force developing job knowledge tests. She had just moved to California and was intending to apply for a statistician position at North American Aviation, later Rockwell International. When she showed up to submit her application, she didn't even get past the receptionist who informed her that they "want a man for that job" and refused to give her an application. Recognizing her deep disappointment, apparently, he asked what she had done in her previous job. When she described the job knowledge tests that she had developed for the Air Force, he suggested she apply for a different position, heading up the employment testing function, for which he said "they may take a woman" (Tenopyr, 1979). She got that job and remained in that role for 14 years, during which in 1966 she earned a PhD in psychological measurement with J.P. Guilford and William Michael at the University of Southern California. Shortly after earning her PhD Tenopyr began to serve in California state public policy roles including as Vice Chair of the Research Committee in the Technology Advisory Committee on Testing within the state's Fair Employment Practice Commission. At the same time, she also served as an advisor regarding testing to the United States (US) Office of Federal Contract Compliance. Having gotten a taste of public policy regarding employment fairness, she left Rockwell International in 1970 for Washington, D.C. (Tenopyr, 1979; Tippins, 2006; Tippins et al., 2006).

Professional Career

Over the next two years, her professional direction took shape. She took the position of Program Director, US Civil Service Commission, and established a network of federal employment professionals and policy makers, and learned the infrastructure of federal employment law and policy from the inside. Notably, The Civil Rights Act of 1968 had only recently been enacted and the process of establishing new enforcement guidelines was just getting underway. This process required "only" 10 years during which Tenopyr became a highly influential expert. If Tenopyr's network and policy expertise were honed while at the US Civil Service Commission, she established a national platform in 1972 when she accepted a position with AT&T responsible for leading its non-management employment strategy and practices.

Guidelines and Standards

Beginning in the early 1970s Tenopyr established herself as a central actor in the national, multi-faceted effort to establish federal guidelines and professional standards and practices relating to employment practices. The national climate for fairness in social policy and systems including employment was rapidly evolving. The Civil Rights Act of 1968 required new uniform guidelines governing the legal accountability employers had for fair, non-discriminatory employment practices. The profession of I-O psychology was maturing and emerging with its own identity, taking the name the Society for Industrial and Organizational Psychology (SIOP) in 1982 and adopting established documented principles for guiding professional employment practices, the first edition of which was published in 1975. Tenopyr was squarely in the middle of it all. And not just in the middle but leading in many cases (Jim Sharf, personal communication, May 23, 2023).

At the time she joined AT&T, she was serving on the Division 14, later SIOP, committee to develop the first documented *Principles for the Validation and Use of Personnel Selection Procedures* (Society for Industrial and Organizational Psychology, 2018). Because the initial *Principles* preceded the 1978 *Uniform Guidelines on Employee Selection Procedures*

(US Equal Employment Opportunity Commission et al., 1978), a second edition of the *Principles* was soon needed. Tenopyr co-chaired with William Owens the development of the second edition of the *Principles* published in 1979. (Notably, she also served on the committees to develop the third and fourth editions.) Over a period of more than three decades Tenopyr was the common voice in the development of four versions of the *Principles*. During this same time period she served on a Business Roundtable committee, the Ad Hoc Industry Group on Employment Selection Guidelines, and the Equal Employment Advisory Council to provide professional and technical guidance to the lawyers for the Department of Justice, Department of Labor, and the Office of Personnel Management to help ensure that the subsequent *1978 Guidelines* was consistent with professional standards and principles (Jim Sharf, personal communication, May 23, 2023; Tenopyr, 1979). In addition to her formal role on the Equal Employment Advisory Council she was a constant source of advice and counsel to Robert Guion who served in a formal role on behalf of Division 14 advising the development of the *Guidelines* (Jim Sharf, personal communication, May 23, 2023). Similarly, in the early 1980s Tenopyr served as a Division 14 representative on the American Psychological Association's (APA) Council of Representatives during which she strongly influenced the developments of APA's 1985 *Standards for Educational and Psychological Testing* (American Educational Research Association et al., 2014). Her work there helped to ensure that the *1985 Standards* section on Employment Testing was consistent with what she and others had accomplished in the 1978 *Guidelines* and the 1979 Division 14 *Principles*.

As a reflection of the importance of these efforts and an acknowledgement of her accomplishments on behalf of her profession, Tenopyr was elected President of Division 14 (also now known as SIOP) in 1979.

Selection Procedure Predictive Validity

Tenopyr's primary professional and legal policy accomplishment through this decade, by my own assessment, was that she and other peers helped to establish selection procedure predictive validity as the common thread underlying professional standards, practice principles, and legal guidelines relating to efficacy and fairness in employment. In particular, the *Guidelines*, *Principles*, and *Standards* all embrace three core elements: (1) the merit of a selection procedure is captured by evidence of its predictive validity, which can take variety of forms; (2) the user of a selection procedure has a responsibility to establish a validity rationale for its use; and (3) the fairness of a selection procedure is the extent to which it is equally predictively valid for all relevant groups. Certainly, there are professional, technical, and legal nuances to each of these elements as well as significant disagreements among different stakeholders. This is especially the case with respect to the definition of fairness where, for example, some view selection fairness as equality of selection outcomes or proportionality between selection outcomes and work outcomes. While Tenopyr was, herself, frequently faced with sex-based unfairness that impacted her outcomes, nevertheless, she and others worked to produce legal and professional governance documents about selection procedure fairness that were aligned around a shared definition of fairness in terms of the validity of the selection procedure itself and not in terms of outcomes influenced by other factors.

Recognition

As an indication of the professional importance of these accomplishments, as well as her broader impact in a variety of professional I-O psychology leadership roles, Tenopyr received many professional awards and distinctions. A short list includes member of the National Academy of Sciences, president of APA Divisions 5 and 14, SIOP's Distinguished Professional Contributions and Distinguished Service Contributions awards, Board Trustee of the New Jersey Psychological Association, Board Director of the American Society for Personnel Administration, member of the Army Science Board, Fellow of the APA and SIOP, Fellow of the Association for Psychological Science (Tippins, 2006), and, being listed as a noteworthy psychologist in *Marquis Who's Who* (Prabook, 2006).

Conclusion

For Tenopyr, an equally significant measure of her impact on I-O psychology is the growth over her career of the representation of women in SIOP. Perhaps more than any other, the participation and success of women in I-O psychology was Tenopyr's singular over-arching professional mission. A 1967 survey of APA Division 14 – one year after Tenopyr's PhD – showed 3% of the respondents to be women. In contrast, a 2018 survey of SIOP members showed approximately half of the respondents to be women (Jimenez, 2018). While such a dramatic increase over this 51-year period cannot be attributed to any one individual, Tenopyr was undoubtedly one of the most visible examples of a successful woman in I-O psychology. Mission accomplished. Indeed, in 2018 APA's Psych Learning Curve posted a blog titled "4 Innovative Women Who Were Pioneers of Industrial-Organizational Psychology" (Jimenez, 2018). Of this short list, Lillian Gilbreth (1915 PhD), Franziska Baumgarten (1917 PhD), Marion Bills (1917 PhD), and Mary Tenopyr (1966 PhD). Tenopyr is the only "modern" era woman listed. Clearly, Tenopyr's success in her I-O field helped to show the way for the many women who have now followed her.

References

American Educational Research Association, American Psychological Association, & National Council on Measurement in Education. (2014). *Standards for educational and psychological testing*. American Psychological Association.

Jimenez, W. P. (2018). 4 Innovative women who were pioneers of industrial-organizational psychology. *Psych Learning Curve, December 10*, 1–8. https://psychlearningcurve.org/4innovative-women-who-were-pioneers-of-industrial-organizational-psychology/

Prabook. (2006). *Mary Louise Welsh Tenopyr: Psychologist*. https://prabook.com/web/mary_louise_welsh.tenopyr/1698291

Society for Industrial and Organizational Psychology. (2018). *Principles for the validation and use of personnel selection procedures*. doi: 10.1017/iop.2018.195

Tenopyr, M. L. (1979). *Mary L. Tenopyr: SIOP President 1979-1980*. SIOP.ORG/Portals/84/docs/Presidents/Tenopyr_Mary_L.pdf

Tippins, N. (2006). Mary L. Tenopyr (1929–2005). *American Psychologist, 61*(9), 1023. https://doi.org/10.1037/0003-066X.61.9.1023

Tippins, N. T., Reesman, A. E., Kehoe, J. F., Erwin, F., & Thayer, P. (2006). In Memoriam: Mary L. Tenopyr (1919 (sic) – 2005). *APS Observer*, Nov. 1.

US Equal Employment Opportunity Commission, Civil Service Commission, Department of Labor, Department of Justice. (1978). Uniform guidelines on employee selection procedures. *Federal Register, 43*, 38290–38315.

Chapter 36

Fred E. Fiedler (1922–2017)

Kathie L. Pelletier and Janet L. Kottke

Fred E. Fiedler is considered the father of leadership contingency theory. His early observations of patient-therapist relationships and performance of high school basketball teams inspired the development of the Least Preferred Coworker (LPC) contingency theory. Fiedler's tenacity in responding to measurement and practical application critiques was evident through his continued testing of the model and later addition of cognitive resources theory (CRT). His key contributions to industrial-organizational (I-O) psychology include his contingency model, which was the catalyst for additional research in this area. He was a proponent of inductive model-building and cross-disciplinary research, and he also influenced the field to continue studying the leader–situation interaction.

Biographical Overview

Fred, the only child of Victor and Hilda Fiedler, was born in Vienna, Austria, on July 13, 1922. Although Fiedler professed to be a poor student in elementary school, he passed the examination to enter the Realgymnasium, a secondary school that emphasizes the sciences in preparing students for college. There, Fiedler did poorly, failing multiple subjects. After three years, his parents pulled him from school to go into the family business providing fabrics for tailors and other commercial uses (ILA, 2010).

Three months after the Nazi invasion of Austria, Fiedler, at age 16, left on his own for the United States (US). He stayed with distant relatives in South Bend, IN, graduating from high school in 1940. Between high school and college, Fiedler – by his account – held more than 20 jobs, including furrier, assistant

DOI: 10.4324/9781003403258-36

junkyard superintendent, bottling plant employee, auto parts salesman, and hot dog seller (Hooijberg & Choi, 1999; ILA, 2010).

Fiedler entered the University of Chicago in 1942 but was quickly drafted by the US military. The Army assigned him to military civil affairs both stateside and in Europe where he served as an interpreter, communications chief, and military police officer. Of note, while in the military, he took an industrial psychology correspondence course from the University of Chicago. Industrial psychology had been an expressed interest in high school but his counselor had discouraged him from pursuing it because of his poor grades (Hooijberg & Choi, 1999).

Once his military service was completed in 1945, he returned to the University of Chicago, finishing his undergraduate degree in two years. He applied immediately to its PhD program. Because the university did not offer an industrial psychology degree, he began a clinical program, completing a master's degree under the direction of Carl Rogers. His dissertation emanated from his Veterans Administration traineeship to identify criteria for psychotherapeutic effectiveness. Despite opportunities that awaited him from the traineeship and a much-lauded dissertation, Fiedler felt clinical psychology was not the best fit for him. When Lee Cronbach invited him to the University of Illinois-Champaign-Urbana for a Naval Research contract on leadership, Fiedler leapt at the opportunity. Upon completion of the Naval contract, Fiedler was invited to join the psychology department, where he initiated and ran the Group Effectiveness Research Laboratory (GERL). The GERL secured many government contracts, which supported research on leadership, group performance, and cross-cultural training. When he moved to the University of Washington in 1969, Fiedler started the Organizational Research Group, which served as an incubator for much of his subsequent research and theorizing. He also held visiting posts in Belgium, England, and the Netherlands, while consulting widely with private industry and public agencies in the US (Hooijberg & Choi, 1999). Fiedler retired from the University of Washington in 1993 but continued to publish into the early 2000s. He died on June 8, 2017, leaving a legacy of inductive theory building and earning fond tributes from his many devoted former students, collaborators, and colleagues who attested to his integrity, persistence, sense of humor, and intellectual curiosity (Mitchell, 2018).

Contributions to I-O Psychology

Early Leadership Study

Fiedler's work was undertaken as the field of leadership study in the 1950s had shifted from examining traits to analyzing specific behaviors of leaders (e.g., task vs. relationship orientation resulting from the Ohio State and Michigan studies). Whereas some of Fielder's model echoes elements of these behavioral studies (Fleishman & Harris, 1962; Kahn & Katz, 1952), his early leadership study was inspired by his work in assessing therapeutic effectiveness as a function of the similarity of the therapist to the client. For that research, he developed the Assumed Similarity between Opposites (ASo) measure, using the Q-technique. As Fiedler's research focus moved from the clinical (therapist-patient) to the organizational setting (leader-members), he changed his scale from a Q-technique to a semantic differential. As mixed results using the ASo accumulated among a wide variety of groups (e.g., bomber crews, basketball teams), Fiedler observed that there were relational and situational factors that enhanced or diminished the leader's effectiveness; consequently, his contingency model was born. Ultimately, Fiedler extracted from the ASo the LPC scale, which was described, along with his early leadership research, in his 1967 seminal book, *A Theory of Leader Effectiveness*. In this book, Fiedler detailed how certain personality attributes and interaction styles affect group performance, marking the formal exposition of LPC theory.

LPC Contingency Model

LPC differed from other contingency research conducted during the 1960s and 1970s in that the theory was one of the first to consider the importance of leader-member relationships and how leaders viewed their constituents. The guiding principle was that leader perceptions of followers were important to how a leader would interact with his or her workgroup and influence group performance. Further, the model describes how the situation moderates the association between the leader's view of a least preferred worker and how that view influences group performance. Unlike others who focused on the development of a leader to adapt to the needs of the situation, Fiedler argued that to achieve desired outcomes, the organization needed to place leaders in the situation that best aligned with their LPC classification, which will be discussed below.

The LPC model and its namesake construct rests heavily on and was initially measured by an 18-item scale (the number of items on the scale has ranged from 16 to 22; Ayman et al., 1995). The leader is asked to think about the coworker with whom the leader least prefers working while responding to a set of bipolar adjectives (e.g., friendly–unfriendly, efficient–inefficient). The leader's ratings across all items are summed; if the leader describes a coworker in unfavorable terms, the leader is classified as being a low LPC leader (task orientation). Conversely, favorable or positive ratings denote a high LPC leader classification (relationship orientation). This score is considered to be dispositional and fairly stable (Miner, 2005).

According to Fiedler (1967), low LPC leaders would be motivated primarily by successful completion of tasks; high LPC leaders would be more oriented toward and satisfied by building strong interpersonal relationships with their teams. Additionally, Fiedler identified three situational variables: leader-member relationship, position power, and task structure. *Leader–member relationships* considered "good" are established when subordinates are loyal to the leader, are amiable toward one another, and cooperative. *Position power* is considered strong if the leader is seen as having legitimate, reward, and coercive forms of power and the authority to appraise followers' performance. In short, members accept the leader's directions and are willing to comply with their demands. *Task structure* is characterized as either structured or unstructured, with "structured" denoted by the extent of formalization of the task. In classifying situational favorableness, Fiedler believed leader–member relations were the most important factor, followed by task structure. Position power was least important (Miner, 2005).

Fiedler then operationalized the favorableness of the situation facing a leader by dichotomizing each of the three variables – leader–member relationships, position power, and task structure – into high (i.e., good, strong) and low values (poor, weak). This process resulted in eight cells, or octants, which provide every possible combination of high and low values of the three variables. In Fiedler's scheme, Octant 1 provides the most favorable situation (good leader-member relationships, highly structured task, and strong position power), whereas Octant 8 is the least favorable to the leader (poor leader-member relationships, unstructured task, and weak position power). Low LPC leaders are projected to have the most influence in these highly favorable and unfavorable situations whereas high LPC leaders are most likely to exert influence in the moderately favorable situations. An example of a moderately favorable situation is one in which the task is unstructured, position power is weak but the leader–member relationships are good. Thus, group performance will be contingent upon the appropriate match of leadership style (high/low LPC) to the favorableness of the situation for the leader (i.e., the degree to which the situation provides a leader with influence over members). Research has found support for most of the classifications (Schriesheim et al., 1994).

In the final iteration of model building during the late 1970s and 1980s, Fiedler and his students proposed intelligence and experience (i.e., CRT) as additional predictors of leader effectiveness. Fiedler and Garcia's (1987) book, *New Approaches to Effective Leadership: Cognitive Resources and Organizational Performance,* was an attempt to address these qualities in his contingency model. CRT is based on several assumptions: first, effective decisions and action plans are more likely to be made by competent and intelligent leaders than decisions by leaders lacking these qualities. Second, directive leadership will be the primary behavioral form in communicating plans and decisions. Taken together, intelligence and directiveness will result in improved group performance because the leader possesses the needed knowledge and is able to communicate it to the group. Stress will moderate the relationship: in the low-stress condition, intelligent leaders will effectively direct groups toward high performance, whereas in high-stress conditions, experienced leaders will be more effective. CRT was based on 15 years of research accumulated by Fiedler and his students, yet he encouraged researchers to provide empirical support through additional research on this theory. A subsequent meta-analysis has supported Fiedler's assertions that intelligence would be related to leader effectiveness under low-stress situations ($\rho = .32$) but not in high-stress ones ($\rho = -.04$; Judge et al., 2004).

Critique of LPC and Fiedler's Response

Despite support from meta-analyses (Schriesheim et al., 1994; Strube & Garcia, 1981), LPC theory has been comprehensively criticized for conceptual weaknesses. Two primary themes emerge: the meaning of the LPC measure and practical implications of the model (Miner, 2005; Schreisheim et al., 1994). First, the interpretation of the LPC has transfigured over the years. Initially seen as a marker of leader distance from subordinates, and then as evidence of the leader's relationship versus task focus, in its latest iteration, it has been proffered as the leader's cognitive complexity in appraising the situation at hand. In part, this evolution is due to Fiedler's responsiveness to criticism and to additional work conducted by himself and others. Nonetheless, that the meaning seems not to be straightforward complicates the interpretation of conflicting research outcomes (Schreisheim et al., 1994).

With regard to the second theme, although conceptually attractive to place leaders with specific characteristics as determined by their LPC classification into the situations that are best suited for those leader characteristics, it is not often practical to do so. Leaders within organizations are typically assigned to departments or divisions that may undergo changes in structure of tasks required or the type of position power granted the leader. *Leader Match*, a self-paced program, is available to train leaders to become aware of their LPC motivations and how they can reshape a situation more to their style (Fiedler & Mahar, 1979). Yet, changing a situation to align with a leader's LPC score may be counterproductive (e.g., restructuring a task to be unstructured may lead to lower effectiveness) or even unethical (altering leader-member relationships to be unfavorable).

Major Contributions to Leadership, and by Extension, I-O Psychology

A notable contribution of Fiedler's LPC contingency model was a break from the "one best" leader approach that, in turn, led to other streams of leadership research. Despite criticisms of the LPC contingency model, Fielder's work serves as a testament to inductive model-building, extensive research with highly diverse samples, and group-based, "hard" performance criteria of leadership effectiveness. Critics and adherents alike have been motivated by the contingency model to disprove or improve it. Fielder, along with his students, continued working on the model – adding the cognitive resource component two decades after the model's first formal explication in 1967. Further, work on the contingency model, which began with insights into the therapist-patient relationship, demonstrates the value of cross disciplinary work, rather than retreating to comfortable research "silos." Most critically, Fiedler's work pushed the leadership field beyond the leader-centric approach so prevalent in the early years of leadership study.

Awards and Distinctions

Fiedler earned numerous scientific research awards from professional associations. Among them are the American Psychological Society's James McKeen Cattell Award for intellectual contributions to applied research, the Award for Distinguished Scientific Contributions to Industrial and Organizational Psychology from the Society for Industrial and Organizational Psychology, and a Lifetime Achievement Award from the International Leadership Association.

Conclusion

Fiedler's contingency theory has inspired numerous researchers to test new approaches to leadership. Although aspects of his theory have been critiqued, Fiedler reflected on these concerns and countered by conducting yet more research to accommodate those criticisms, and then updating his theory as necessary. His theory is still being researched to this day in an effort to fill in gaps and provide further explanation of his model; however, its popularity in the field appears to be declining as more contemporary theories emerge.

References

Ayman, R., Chemers, M. M., & Fiedler, F. (1995). The contingency model of leadership effectiveness: Its levels of analysis. *Leadership Quarterly*, *6*(2), 147–167. http://dx.doi.org/10.1016/1048-9843(95)90032-2

Fiedler, F. E. (1967). *A theory of leadership effectiveness*. McGraw-Hill.

Fiedler, F. E., & Garcia, J. E. (1987). *New approaches to effective leadership: Cognitive resources and organizational performance*. Wiley.

Fiedler, F. E., & Mahar, L. (1979). The effectiveness of contingency model training: A review of the validation of Leader Match. *Personnel Psychology*, *32*(1), 45–62. https://doi.org/10.1111/j.1744-6570.1979.tb00468.x

Fleishman, E. A., & Harris, E. F. (1962). Patterns of leadership behavior related to employee grievances and turnover. *Personnel Psychology*, *15*, 43–56. http://dx.doi.org/10.1111/j.1744-6570.1962.tb01845.x

Hooijberg, R., & Choi, J. (1999). From Austria to the United States and from evaluating therapists to developing cognitive resources theory: An interview with Fred Fiedler. *Leadership Quarterly*, *10*(4), 653–665. http://dx.doi.org/10.1016/s1048-9843(99)00035-1

International Leadership Association's (ILA) Leadership Legacy Program. (2010, October 28). *Oral history with Fred Fiedler*. https://tobiascenter.iu.edu/research/oral-history/audio-transcripts/fiedler-fred.html

Judge, T. A., Ilies, R., & Colbert, A. E. (2004). Intelligence and leadership: A quantitative review and test of theoretical propositions. *Journal of Applied Psychology*, *89*(3), 542–552. http://dx.doi.org/10.1037/0021-9010.89.3.542

Kahn, R. L., & Katz, D. (1952). *Leadership practices in relation to productivity and morale* (pp. 612–628). Institute for Social Research, University of Michigan.

Miner, J. B. (2005). *Organizational behavior: Essential theories of motivation and leadership. one* (Vol. 1). M. E. Sharpe.

Mitchell, T. (2018). Fred Edward Fiedler (1922–2017). *American Psychologist*, *73*(2), 199. http://dx.doi.org/10.1037/amp0000198

Schriesheim, C. A., Tepper, B. J., & Tetrault, L. A. (1994). Least preferred co-worker score, situational control, and leadership effectiveness: A meta-analysis of contingency model performance predictions.

Journal of Applied Psychology, *79*(4), 561–573. http://dx.doi.org/10.1037//0021-9010.79.4.561

Strube, M. J., & Garcia, J. E. (1981). A meta-analytic investigation of Fiedler's contingency model of leadership effectiveness. *Psychological Bulletin*, *90*(2), 307–321. http://dx.doi.org/10.1037//0033-2909.90.2.307

Chapter 37

Robert M. Guion (1924–2012)

Scott Highhouse

One would be hard-pressed to identify a psychologist who had a greater impact on the development of modern personnel selection than did Robert (Bob) Guion. Guion authored the foundational text *Personnel Testing* first published in 1965. He was principal author of the 1974 *Standards for Educational and Psychological Tests* and co-chair for two editions of the *Principles for the Validation and Use of Personnel Selection Procedures*, both given considerable deference by the courts in employment litigation. Guion founded the doctoral program in industrial psychology (now industrial-organizational; I-O) at Bowling Green State University (BGSU) and served as President of both the American Psychological Association (APA) Division 14 (I-O Psychology; now the Society for Industrial and Organizational Psychology [SIOP]) and Division 5 (Evaluation Measurement and Statistics) during a period when psychologists and employers were wrestling with the implications of Title VII of the Civil Rights Act for workplace hiring and promotion in the United States (US).

Biographical Overview

Guion was born on September 14, 1924, in Indianapolis, IN.[1] His father worked in sales, and his mother was a candymaker. He grew up in Fort Wayne and graduated from South Side High School where he was active in the school newspaper, band, and drama club. He served in the Army during World War II and was stationed in Italy. His favorite post involved personnel work, preparing discharge papers. This was the first time he ever heard of industrial psychology as an area of study.

DOI: 10.4324/9781003403258-37

Guion received his bachelor's degree from the University of Iowa in 1948 and he received a doctorate in industrial psychology from Purdue University in 1952. His doctoral mentor was C. H. Lawshe. Guion was recruited by Bowling Green State University (Ohio) whose dean was keen to start a master's program modeled after the industrial psychology doctoral program at Purdue. As a young married professor, Guion sold shoes at a department store in downtown Bowling Green to supplement his academic income.

In addition to personnel selection, Guion had early interest in motivation, especially achievement motivation. The predominate measure during this period was the Thematic Apperception Test (TAT). Attempting to measure achievement motivation, as well as Maslow's needs using TAT-type pictures were hindered by the fact that he could find no reliable way to score the responses. This was an early lesson for Guion on the importance of competent measurement in all areas of industrial psychology. Aside from research on work meaning, published with Frank Landy (Guion & Landy, 1972; Landy & Guion, 1970), Guion engaged in little empirical research.

Contribution to Employment Law

Guion sang in the First United Methodist choir and credits his Methodist upbringing as influencing his belief that, as an I-O psychologist, he needed to be concerned with problems of fairness and equality in employment. Speaking to a personnel assessment professional group in northern California, Guion mentioned the possibility of differential prediction. A member of the audience, editor of the journal *Industrial Relations*, invited him to write an article on this idea. When Guion returned from his 1963–1964 visiting professorship at the University of California-Berkeley, he produced the article "Employment Tests and Discriminatory Hiring." In the article, Guion (1966) distinguished prediction from description, and argued that "Unfair discrimination exists when persons with equal probabilities of success on the job have unequal probabilities of being hired for the job" (p. 26). He further argued that a test is illegally discriminatory only when a specified group exhibits inferior performance on the test, but not on the job for which the test is used as a predictor. Anne Cleary expanded on Guion's definition of unfair discrimination with her development of a regression approach now known as the "Cleary model" of test bias (Cleary, 1968).

Guion's Bowling Green colleague, Richard Shore, left academia to join the US Department of Labor. One of his first tasks was to draft an order for the Office of Federal Contract Compliance Programs (OFCCP) concerning the use of employment tests. Shore invited Guion to Washington to work on the testing order which was completed in 1968. Guion remained involved as part of an Advisory Committee to OFCCP, which had a hand in developing the Equal Employment Opportunity Commission Guidelines in 1970. At the same time, Guion was a member of APA's Committee on Psychological Tests charged with revising the *Standards* (APA, American Educational Research Association [AERA] and National Council on Measurement in Education [NCME]) in 1966. Guion was listed as the principal author of the revised *Standards* (APA, AERA, and NCME) in 1974, which he described as constituting a full-time job. With Mary Tenopyr, Guion authored the APA Division 14 (now SIOP) *Principles* in 1975. Tenopyr and Guion were both opposed to including content validity in the document. They felt that its inclusion represented a poor understanding of psychometric theory (Guion, 1977). They were overruled by the larger committee.

Philosophy

Guion was deeply committed to social justice and the eradication of unfair barriers to opportunity. He recognized, however, that tests and standardized assessments were an important part of responding to unequal opportunity. That is, educational and employment opportunities could be filled using random selection, preferential treatment, or even quotas. Historically the merit principle, Guion argued, was a cornerstone of the progressive, liberal ideology. At the time of Guion's writing (Guion, 1980a), and some might argue today, the principle of merit had become a symbol of elitism and oppression. According to Guion:

> If it is concluded from reasonable debate that social policy should prefer a different basis for awarding opportunities,

> that the measurement of individual differences is inherently undemocratic, then testing in general, without regard to validity, bias, and other technical issues, should be condemned. If it is concluded, however, that opportunities are to go to those who are in some individual sense 'deserving' of them, then the issue is a technical one of how best to identify those who are deserving.
>
> (p. 3)

Guion viewed his mission as to improve the latter. According to Guion (1965) the waste of human resources should pain the professional conscience of the academic psychologist.

Validity was a major focus of Guion's writing in subsequent years. He was particularly disturbed by what he called the "Holy Trinity" of validity (Guion, 1980b). Guion was referring to the oft-repeated idea that there were three types of validity: criterion-related, content, and construct. He believed that validity should be thought of as evaluating the intended inferences drawn from measures (Guion, 2011). He further distinguished *descriptive* inferences from *relational* inferences. Descriptive inferences collapsed the earlier ideas of construct and content validity, and relational inferences referred to job-relatedness or usefulness. Guion's distinction has contemporary relevance in the age of artificial intelligence for performance prediction, which focuses merely on relational inferences.

The Person

Guion spent his entire career (1952–1985) as a faculty member at BGSU. He guided 21 doctoral dissertations: Frank Landy, Russell Johannesson, Thomas Standing, David Jones, Glenn Ball, Elizabeth Summers, Michael White, John Arnold, Eileen O'Keefe, Ellen Papper, Darryl Lang, Karen Budzeika, Rick Hackett, Susan Stang, Michael Brannick, Anthony Edwards, Joan Brannick, Kelly Jo Brookhouse, Paul Cook, Wade Gibson, and Philip Ikomi. Guion was chair of the department from 1966 to 1971. He was named University Distinguished Professor, the highest honor given to faculty.

Joe Cranny, a long-time friend and colleague, humorously described Bob as "old even when he was young." He was rarely seen without a suit and tie. Many students and colleagues found Guion intimidating and curmudgeonly but also warm with an endearing smile. Former student and lifelong friend, Frank Landy, teased that Guion's writing was often scolding (Guion, 2011). No one could argue that his writing was dull or lackluster.

In retirement, Bob was quite active at gardening, candy making, and glass blowing. His glass pieces were often on display during the Black Swamp Arts Festival in Bowling Green. Guion developed a habit of swimming each morning, which began when he was at a meeting in Colorado in his 40s. He could often be seen in the university recreation center well into his 80s. He was an active volunteer for the Wheeled Meals program, where he once served as director. As a scholar, Guion continued to be recognized well into his later years. The Association for Psychological Science named him James McKeen Cattell Fellow for Distinguished Contributions to Psychological Science. He was especially proud to receive the Stephen E. Bemis Memorial Award that is jointly sponsored by many of the nation's major human resources associations. He was most recently named Scientific Honoree of the Foundation for the Advancement of Behavioral and Brain Sciences.

Conclusion

Guion's pioneering work in personnel selection, contributions to employment law, and dedication to social justice have left an indelible mark on the field. Guion's commitment to rigorous and fair measurement standards has shaped the practices and policies that govern employment testing today. His career at BGSU and his influence on students and colleagues reflect his enduring impact. Even in retirement, Guion remained active in his community and continued to be honored for his contributions to psychological science. His life and work exemplify a deep commitment to improving workplace fairness and effectiveness through scientific rigor and ethical practice.

Note

1 Much of the biographical content is from a combination of personal communication, obituaries, and Guion's SIOP presidential statement.

References

Cleary, T. A. (1968). Test bias: Prediction of grades of Negro and white students in integrated colleges. *Journal of Educational Measurement*, *5*(2), 115–124. https://doi.org/10.1111/j.1745-3984.1968.tb00613.x

Guion, R. M. (1965). Industrial psychology as an academic discipline. *American Psychologist*, *20*(10), 815.https://doi.org/10.1037/h0020934

Guion, R. M. (1966). Employment tests and discriminatory hiring. *Industrial Relations*, *5*(2). https://doi.org/10.1111/j.1468-232x.1966.tb00449.x

Guion, R. M. (1977). Content validity—The source of my discontent. *Applied Psychological Measurement*, *1*(1), 1–10. https://doi.org/10.1177/014662167700100103

Guion, R. M. (1980a, May 14). [Letter to Editor, The Monitor]. Bowling Green State University Archives (Guion Papers, Box 1, Correspondence 1980–1989). Bowling Green, Ohio.

Guion, R. M. (1980b). On Trinitarian doctrines of validity. *Professional Psychology*, *11*(3), 385. https://doi.org/10.1037/0735-7028.11.3.385

Guion, R. M. (2011). *Assessment, measurement, and prediction for personnel decisions*. Routledge. https://doi.org/10.4324/9780203836767

Guion, R. M., & Landy, F. J. (1972). The meaning of work and the motivation to work. *Organizational Behavior and Human Performance*, 7(2), 308–339. https://doi.org/10.1016/0030-5073(72)90020-7

Landy, F. J., & Guion, R. M. (1970). Development of scales for the measurement of work motivation. *Organizational Behavior and Human Performance,* *5*(1), 93–103. https://doi.org/10.1016/0030-5073(70)90007-3

Chapter 38

Bernard M. Bass (1925–2007)

Wayne F. Cascio

Bernard M. Bass was a world-class scholar whom the Society for Industrial and Organizational Psychology (SIOP) describes as having invented organizational psychology. His contributions to a broad range of academic areas include leadership, group dynamics, social psychology, survey feedback, psychometrics, and participative management. The one area where his passion and persistence led him to focus during his entire career, however, was leadership, more specifically, transformational leadership. He was a co-founding editor of *The Leadership Quarterly* journal. In fewer than 20 years, that journal became the top academic publication outlet in the world focusing on the science of leadership.

Biographical Overview

Bernard M. Bass, distinguished Professor Emeritus in the School of Management at Binghamton University, was born on June 11, 1925, in the Bronx, New York, and died in Binghamton, New York, on October 11, 2007, at the age of 82. He attended City College of New York, beginning in 1941 as a chemistry major. Following military service in the United States Army Air Force, he enrolled at The Ohio State University (OSU) to complete his master's and doctorate in industrial psychology, tasks that he accomplished in four years.

At OSU, Cal Shartle and Ralph Stogdill became Bass's initial mentors in the field of industrial psychology and ultimately in his work on leadership. Bass's earliest work on leadership was in the development of what has been referred to as the "leaderless

DOI: 10.4324/9781003403258-38

group discussion." In 1954, he published an article summarizing his work on that topic in *Psychological Bulletin* (Bass, 1954). Using this group dynamic process allows one to examine which individuals emerge as leaders in groups when a formal leadership position is not indicated.

During his career, Bass served on the faculties of Louisiana State University, the University of California Berkeley, the University of Pittsburgh, the University of Rochester, and Binghamton University. At Louisiana State University, Bass became a full professor at the age of 31. At the University of Rochester, Bass established the Management Research Center (MRC) to conduct research in individual, small group, and organizational psychology, with special emphasis on the study of managerial behavior in organizations. MRC researchers included, among others, Gerald Barrett (Deputy Director), Ralph Alexander, Edward Deci, Enzo Valenzi, Zur Shapira, Edward O'Connor, and Wayne Cascio. Many of them conducted transnational studies of managerial behavior in standardized organizational simulations in conjunction with the International Research Groups on Management (IRGOM), which Bass founded. MRC maintained a database collected at training centers in more than 35 countries and provided cooperating agencies with assistance in experimental design, statistical analysis, and data collection (Avolio, 2008; Cascio, 1973; Research.com, n.d.; Wikipedia, 2023).

Scholarship

Bass's research and writing include more than 400 scholarly articles and 31 books, of which he wrote 21 and edited 10. Of all his work, Bass will be remembered for one area where his passion and persistence led him to focus during his entire career: leadership.

Leadership

In the late 1970s, Bass read and reviewed *Leadership* by James MacGregor Burns (1978), in which Burns introduced the concept of transformational leadership. Bass put these ideas together with his experience of meeting someone who had worked for a leader who had motivated him to "perform beyond expectations." That led Bass to begin his work on transformational leadership. He was interested in how a leader influences followers. Followers look to a leader because of their charisma, and because they trust the leader. The leader transforms the followers by having these qualities. Bass wanted to understand how a leader can generate this charisma and trust.

He argued that a leader must be a role model but must also challenge the existing order. He saw revolutionary leaders do this and formed a morally neutral approach, unlike Burns's more moralistic vision of leadership. In addition to the more transactional leadership roles of getting tasks done, and focusing the team on shared goals, Bass saw the transformational role of a leader as one that would appeal to people's higher-order needs.

Bass's model of transformational leadership includes four roles for the transformational leader (Clayton, 2016):

1. Inspirational motivation – The leader is a visionary who makes people feel like a part of something big, worthwhile, energizing, and concerned with purpose and meaning.
2. Individualized attention – The leader focuses on people, celebrates diversity, and builds relationships. Each member of the team feels that the leader knows me, respects me, is interested in me, and helps me.
3. Intellectual stimulation – The leader stretches followers to learn, grow, and perform to exceptional levels. The leader values intellect, encourages imagination, and challenges old ways while emphasizing strategic thinking and constructive challenges.
4. Idealized influence – The leader is a role model who inspires respect and a desire to follow through the leader's personal integrity. Leaders set and display high ethical standards, walking the talk, being honest, open, fair, and principled, and living up to strong values.

By identifying these four roles of a transformational leader, Bass provided a powerful behavioral prescription that spawned considerable research among academics as well as practical implications for developing leaders everywhere.

In 1987, while at Binghamton University, Bass established the Center for Leadership Studies, which had as its overall mission advancing the science and practice of leadership. Over time, the Center's main focus in terms of research was on transformational leadership. During the same period in which the Center was being launched, Bass became the founding editor, along with Bob House and Henry Tosi, of *The Leadership Quarterly* journal. In fewer than 20 years, the journal became the top academic publication outlet in the world focusing on the science of leadership.

The fourth edition of his *Bass Handbook of Leadership: Theory, Research, and Managerial Applications* (Bass & Bass, 2008), which he finished shortly before he died in 2007, is widely regarded as the most authoritative resource on leadership (Clayton, 2016). When he retired from Binghamton University, he was the most cited leadership scholar in the world (Yammarino, 2018). Bass's awards included the Society for Industrial and Organizational Psychology's Distinguished Scientific Contributions Award (1994), the Society of Psychologists in Management's Distinguished Practice in Psychology Award (1997), the Academy of Management's Eminent Leadership Scholar Award (2006), and the Lifetime Achievement Award from the International Leadership Association's Leadership Legacy Program (2008). In 2018, the Center for Leadership Studies that Bass helped to establish in 1987 was renamed in honor of him and his wife, Ruth. They were married for 62 years.

Productivity

Bass's statistics on Google Scholar (2023) reflect his broad influence on the fields of industrial and organizational psychology, organizational behavior, and management. His work has been cited more than 209,000 times, his h-index is 101, meaning that 101 of his publications have been cited at least 101 times, and his i10 index (the number of publications with at least 10 citations) is 280. Five of his most highly cited publications include:

	Cited By	*Year Published*
Transformational leadership B. M. Bass & R. E. Riggio	35,816	2006

	Cited By	Year Published
Leadership and performance beyond expectations		
B. M. Bass	35,085	1985
Bass & Stogdill's handbook of leadership (3rd. ed)		
B. M. Bass	28,804	1990
Transformational leadership development: Manual for the multifactor leadership questionnaire		
B. M. Bass & B. J. Avolio.	16,041	1990
Improving organizational effectiveness through transformational leadership		
B. M. Bass & B. J. Avolio	11,226	1994

Conclusion

Bass worked closely with Bruce Avolio over two decades to refine and advance the study of transformational leadership. In his October 2008 article on Bass and his life, published in the *American Psychologist*, Avolio noted:

> As I look at the field of organizational behavior, leadership, and human resource management, there is hardly a niche in which Bass did not have an impact. Over his long career, Bass mentored many people who have and will continue to carry on his good work.
>
> (p. 620)

I am one of those lucky people.

References

Avolio, B. J. (2008). Bernard (Bernie) M. Bass (1925-2007). *American Psychologist, 63*(7), 620. https://doi.org/10.1037/0003-066x.63.7.620

Bass, B. M. (1954). The leaderless group discussion. *Psychological Bulletin, 51,* 465–492. https://doi.org/10.1037/h0056881

Bass, B. M. (1985). *Leadership and performance beyond expectations.* Free Press. https://doi.org/10.1002/hrm.3930250310

Bass, B. M. (1990). *Bass and Stogdill's handbook of leadership: Theory, research, and managerial applications* (3rd ed.). Free Press.

Bass, B. M. & Avolio, B. J. (1990). *Transformational leadership development: Manual for the multifactor leadership questionnaire.* Consulting Psychologists Press.

Bass, B. M. & Avolio, B. J. (Eds.). (1994). *Improving organizational effectiveness through transformational leadership.* Sage.

Bass, B.M., & Bass, R. (2008). *The Bass handbook of leadership: Theory, research, & managerial applications.* Free Press.

Bass, B. M., & Riggio, R. E. (2006). *Transformational leadership* (2nd ed.). Lawrence Erlbaum Associates Publishers. https://doi.org/10.4324/9781410617095

Burns, J. M. (1978). *Leadership.* Harper Collins.

Cascio, W. F. (1973, April 30). Functional specialization, culture, and preference for participative management. Technical Report No. 58, Management Research Center, University of Rochester. Retrieved from file:///Users/waynecascio/Downloads/Cascio_ParticipativeManage58%20(2).pdf

Clayton, M. (2016, May 24). *Bernard Bass: Transformational Leadership.* www.pocketbook.co.uk/blog/2016/05/24/bernard-bass-transformational-leadership/

Google Scholar. (2023). Bernard M. Bass. Retrieved from https://scholar.google.co.th/citations?user=mr77kVoAAAAJ&hl

Research.com. (n.d.). Bernard M. Bass. Retrieved from https://research.com/u/bernard-m-bass

Wikipedia. (2023). Bernard M. Bass. Retrieved from https://en.wikipedia.org/w/index.php?title=Bernard_Bass&oldid=1151575143 on July 23, 2023.

Yammarino, F., quoted in Nguyen, M-L. (2018, Oct. 2). Center for Leadership Studies named in honor of Bernard and Ruth Bass. www.binghamton.edu/news/story/1367/center-for-leadership-studies-named-in-honor-of-bernard-and-ruth-bass

Chapter 39

Marvin Dunnette (1926–2007)

Leaetta Hough

Affectionately known as Big M, Marvin Dunnette's legacy is one of influence through his seminal publications and mentorship of others. His contributions were intellectual, iconoclastic, scholarly, empirical – always testing his ideas in the real world and publishing the results. He shaped the science and practice of psychology as it applied to the world of work.

Biographical Overview

Formative and Later Years

Born September 30, 1926, in Austin, MN, to Rodney and Mildred (Notestine) Dunnette. Marv was the firstborn of two sons. Their father had successfully argued a case at the Minnesota Supreme Court in favor of pay equity for his future wife. It was a talented family. Marv was active in high school; he ran track, played intramural basketball, acted in plays, and played clarinet in the marching band. After graduation in 1944, he enlisted in the Marines. After basic training, his buddies shipped to Iwo Jima, and Marv, after passing a color test with "poor score" (his suggestion to the medical doctor after failing the test), was enrolled in officer training and sent to the University of California Berkeley. At war's end, he returned to Minnesota where he completed an interest inventory and received the following advice:

> An analysis of your measured interest profile indicates that you would be likely to prefer an occupation involving one or more of the following interest factors: Computational Scientific and Literary. An analysis of your abilities indicates that you have

DOI: 10.4324/9781003403258-39

> excellent mathematical skills; excellent chemistry concepts, and excellent mechanical aptitudes and comprehension…you should be able to do superior college level work.

Recommended occupations were Chemist – Organic; Chemist – Physical; Electrical Engineer; Chemical Engineer, and High School Teacher. In 1948, Marv graduated from the University of Minnesota with a degree in chemical engineering with high honors.

Marv worked for about a year as a chemist but found the work unfulfilling and his boss, who consulted an Ouija board, uninspiring. He entered law school intending to join his father's law practice. In need of money (by then he had married his high school sweetheart Jean Bentrude), he found a job counseling engineering students on probation. The job required him to take a vocational/occupational psychology class taught by Donald G. Paterson. He loved the Law but was more entranced by the substance of the psychology course and the charisma and intellect of Paterson.

He persuaded Paterson to admit him to graduate school in psychology and to be his advisor; he graduated with a PhD in 1954. Marv's doctoral dissertation was the development of the Minnesota Engineering Analogies Test, which was published and marketed by (at the time) the Psychological Corporation. More than 50 years later, he was still receiving royalties. He took a two-year internship at Minnesota's Industrial Relations Center where, in addition to conducting research, he honed his writing skills after Dale Yoder said, "Dunnette, you can't write worth a damn" (Dunnette, 1990). He then took a job at 3M Company as Manager of Employee Relations Research where for five years he conducted research and published widely. Between 1952 and 1961, he and his co-authors published over 50 articles, chapters, and reviews, which made it relatively easy for him to transition back to the University of Minnesota as a tenured Associate Professor of Psychology. During the next five or six years, he and his co-authors published another 65 articles, chapters, and books, and he was elected President of Society for Industrial and Organizational Psychology (SIOP; then Division 14 of the American Psychological Association).

Marv shared his personal life with his three daughters, Alex, Peggy, and Sheri, and his second wife, Leaetta Hough. During his lifetime he also knew and loved three grandchildren – Pauline, Rosalie, and Hunter. Two other grandchildren, Chloe and Sylvan, were born after his death.

Marv retired in 1998 and died September 18, 2007. Even though suffering from severe Alzheimer's disease, he had up until the last year of his life islands of insight even for the thorniest of issues.

Iconic Thinker and Influencer

A young Gary Latham first met Marv in his University office, looked around, noted dozens of PhD dissertations on the shelves, and exclaimed: "Wow, this is a Who's Who of I-O Psychology" (Latham, 2024). Yes, they were. All 62 of Marv's doctoral students were exceptionally well-mentored, trained, and accomplished. Marv's reaction: "Being there – all I needed to do" (Dunnette, 1990).

This exchange captures the essence of Marv's approach to his passion for mentoring eager minds toward excellence beyond their imagination, all while creating his own scientific and intellectual contributions to further the development of a fledgling profession, industrial-organizational psychology (I-O), into one of the most respected scientist-practitioner disciplines in the world.

Marv was one of the pillars of what for many years was known as the Minnesota Tradition in applied psychology – data-driven research that had practical as well as theoretical significance. Under his leadership, the I-O psychology program at the University of Minnesota became, in the latter half of the 20th century, one of the most prestigious schools for I-O Psychology in the world, a legacy that continues into the 21st century.

He played many key roles in transforming I-O psychology from its dustbowl empiricist and technological origins into its present status as a model of science and practice. He is known for his emphasis on individual differences, focus on practical significance, ability to synthesize empirical literature, development of I-O psychologists, and thought leadership. Throughout his working life, he blended science and practice, mentorship and entrepreneurship, research and consulting, academia and industry, always publishing. He helped his students and colleagues, indeed the entire field, to think about issues in different and testable ways. He founded two much lauded organizations, the for-profit, Personnel Decisions International, and the non-profit, Personnel Decisions Research Institute. Both were known for their leading-edge and award-winning applications of science to the human capital assets of the world of work.

He authored some of the most significant publications in the field of I-O psychology in the 20th century. His 1966 book, *Personnel Selection and Placement*, was published in five languages, remained in print without revision for 20 years, and was regarded by many as the bible of personnel selection (1966a). Two of his publications are citation classics. Over the years, 29 of his articles and parts of his books were reprinted in 86 books of readings, 1 article was reprinted in 18 different books. The topics and applications were wide ranging, e.g., motivation, morale, job satisfaction, interpersonal perception and empathy, brainstorming, managerial effectiveness, statistics, psychometrics, non-linear prediction models, scoring algorithms, response distortion, criterion specification and measurement, performance appraisal, survey research methods, improved selection models and measurement methods, predictors of drug involvement and abuse, individual difference measurement (cognitive abilities, personality, interests, attitudes) using a variety of measurement methods (e.g., employment interview, assessment centers, individual assessment, narrative descriptions, biographical, self-report, situational judgment), and so on. Perhaps his most important publication, marking the transformation of I-O psychology into its present status, was his conceptualization and editorship of the 1976 *Handbook of Industrial and Organizational Psychology* (1976a). It was succeeded by the four-volume sequel in the 1990s which he co-edited with Hough (Dunnette & Hough, 1990).

Marv was revered for his creative thinking and research, clarity of writing, iconoclastic critiques (such as "Fads, Fashions, and Folderol in Psychology" (1966b) and "Mishmash, Mush, and Milestones" (1976b), awesome mentorship, remarkable humanity, and sense of humor. Marv has been referred to by some as the "father of I-O psychology." He would have denied that instead pointing to his mentor and life-long friend, Donald G. Paterson.

Mentor

Marv was exceptionally proud of his contributions to the lives of his students. He was a man who truly made a difference in the field of I-O psychology and the lives of the people that he touched, many of whom were not his students, lifting them up, nominating them for awards (sometimes unbeknownst to them until years later), and writing hundreds of letters of recommendation. Their gratitude was expressed many times during his life, individually and jointly.

One such event was a special 1999 SIOP conference event entitled "Marvin Dunnette, Master Creative Technician: Research Mentor, Monitor, and Motivator" during which attendees described their experiences and respect for Marv. Their comments provided a window into his character and insights into his mentoring style and influence on them. A few years later, a set of letters written to Marv from dozens of admirers in anticipation of his 80th birthday provides more insights.

Several themes emerge:

- Marv set standards of excellence for himself and others – very, very high standards.
- He modeled the behavior that was expected.
- He required, no he demanded, clarity in writing, and his feedback was direct, which could be brutally honest but supportive at the same time. He provided rewrites of whole sections. Many mentees (former students and others) recited anecdotes of receiving more feedback than the length of their original paper.
- Many said he was "there for me, always." One colleague summed up that insight into effective mentoring as: "Be there, fully there."
- A particularly poignant metaphor: "I don't think Marv ever used the phrase 'we're all in the same boat'. Marv has always been in his own boat; he will always stay in his own boat. I've had several occasions during my life where 'Marv being in his

boat' is sailing right alongside me, always right there, within arm's reach if I needed to reach out" (McKenna, 1999, p. 33).

- Another characteristic of his listening was that he cared. Despite the many demands for his time, he was never too busy to listen carefully and thoughtfully.
- Several referred to him as a father to them, even those who were not his students.
- A significant part of the "Be Fully There" theme was listening with an open mind, a sort of non-judgmental presence. Descriptions of conversations with Marv about seemingly intractable problems was that the person left the conversation with a new or different perspective on the issue. His mind was flexible, creative, and unconventional. He was interested and curious about almost everything.
- His work ethic was legendary, and nothing was beneath him including the most routine of tasks. He carefully attended to the smallest of details. He loved analyzing data, making his own tables, and ensuring they were correct.
- His zest for life, fun, and adventure was also legendary. Marv and those around him had fun, lots of fun and good comradery.
- Another constant in the testimonials was the heartfelt gratitude for the opportunities and support that he gave others, not just his students.
- Frank Schmidt was not one of Marv's students. A quotation from Frank's (2005) birthday letter to Marv provides a good example of Marv's support and influence:

> Perhaps the thing I remember most about Marv is his support for the research finding and conclusions of my work with Jack Hunter during the 70s, 80s, and 90s. For almost 30 years he was the most important ally we had in I/O. I believe he could do this because he is unusually open to new (and even radical) ideas and methods – so long as they are technically sound.
>
> It is the late 80s, and my work is still very controversial among I/O psychologists, and I am feeling a little beleaguered with what seems like a lot of hostility toward the work. I arrive a little late at the SIOP conference and people are streaming down the steps from a large lecture hall. I learn that I had missed an invited talk by Marv, in which he said to about 300 people that I/Os have to stop beating up on Schmidt and

> Hunter, that our work was valuable. He said he'd tested our predictions about the generalizability of validity in his consortium study for the Edison Electric Institute and had confirmed our hypotheses in his data. He called this a paradigm shift. This talk of his had a very great impact. It was a major, major turning point in acceptance for our work.
>
> (Holt & Hough, 2005, p. 56)

- A legacy of lives and a profession changed.
  Notably, nine of the ten tips Marv ended his 1990 memoir entitled "Being There" reflect similar themes. For example:
- *Expect much from yourself and others* – let excellence be the primary value. Difficult goals result in high accomplishment.
- *Be there for both yourself and others* – grasp opportunity. Help others grasp it too.
- *Learn to write with clarity* – muddled writing is the mark of a muddled mind.
- *Expect change* – don't be satisfied with the status quo nor seek stability simply for the sake of stability.
- *Take yourself with a grain of salt* – have fun in what you do.
- *Live with ambiguity* – build new insights out of confusion.
- *Don't burn bridges* – this does not mean looking back. Build new bridges too. Extend and broaden your field of endeavor instead of constraining it.
- *Avoid pomposity* – pomposity is the precursor of much that is evil – the loss of self-knowledge, cessation of humor, the blunting of achievement, and the dulling of wisdom.
- *Prepare in the Fall and Winter for Growth in the Spring* – be prepared.

A measure of the success of a mentor is the success of the mentees – Marv's generated numerous innovative research streams, applications, interventions, and businesses. They are, indeed, a who's who in I-O Psychology. At present count, at least ten of his students, their students, and others who benefited directly from his mentorship became president of SIOP, an almost even number of academics and practitioners. He encouraged all of them in their pursuit of their own passions and interests.

Conclusion

During his life, Marv received many accolades, honors, and celebrations of his exceptionalism including SIOP's prestigious Distinguished Scientific Contributions award. The ones that he was most grateful for were the two instigated and funded by his mentees and colleagues. One, the Dunnette Chair in I-O Psychology at the University of Minnesota, is the only endowed chair at the University of Minnesota funded by former students and colleagues of the named person/chair. Its mission – Marv's passion – was Differential Psychology, the study of individual differences specifically as applied to the world of work. The second, the Dunnette Prize (a SIOP award with a $50,000 prize), also funded by former students and colleagues, honors living originators of fundamental scientific advances focused on research, development, or application that has expanded knowledge of the causal significance of individual differences.

References

Dunnette, M. D. (1966a). *Personnel selection and placement.* Wadsworth. (Published in English, French, Japanese, Italian, and Portuguese.) (Sections reprinted in two books of readings.)

Dunnette, M. D. (1966b). Fads, fashions, and folderol in psychology. *American Psychologist, 21,* 343–352. https://doi.org/10.1037/h0023535 (Reprinted in three books of readings.)

Dunnette, M. D. (Ed.). (1976a). *Handbook of industrial and organizational psychology.* Rand McNally.

Dunnette, M. D. (1976b). Mish-mash, mush, and milestones in organizational psychology. In H. Meltzer & F. R. Wickert (Eds.), *Humanizing organizational behavior* (pp. 86–102). Charles C. Thomas.

Dunnette, M. D. (1990) *Being there: A memoir.* Autobiography prepared for Society for Industrial and Organizational Psychology. Society for Industrial and Organizational Psychology.

Dunnette, M.D., & Hough, L.M. (Eds.) (1990). *Handbook of industrial and organizational psychology* (2nd ed.). Consulting Psychologists Press.

Holt, K., & Hough, L. (2005). *Celebration of Marv Dunnette: Scrapbook of letters to Marv.* Unpublished manuscript.

Latham, G. (2024, February 24). Personal communication. Summit Group meeting in Houston, TX.

McKenna, D. (1999, April). In M. Hakel & L. Hellervik (Eds.), *Marvin Dunnette, Master Creative Technician: Research Mentor, Monitor, and Motivator*. Special event at SIOP Annual Conference, Atlanta, GA. (Transcript, Tape No. 131, p. 23.)

Schmidt, F. (2005, November). Frank Schmidt's letter to Marv. In *Celebration of Marv Dunnette: Scrapbook of letters to Marv*. Unpublished manuscript (pp. 56–61).

Chapter 40

Edwin A. Fleishman (1927–2021)

Stephen J. Zaccaro and Steven Zhou

Edwin A. Fleishman celebrated a lifelong career with several notable contributions to the field of industrial-organizational (I-O) psychology, especially in the areas of leadership, human performance description and measurement, and by championing an international focus. His career rotated between academic and applied positions, making groundbreaking contributions in both domains. Fleishman's extraordinary career of over 60 years demonstrated the highest level of combined scientific rigor and application.

Biographical Overview

Edwin A. Fleishman was born on March 10, 1927, and died February 17, 2021. He received his Bachelor of Science degree from Loyola College in Baltimore. After stints in the United States Navy, University of Maryland for his Master of Arts, and the Army Personnel Research Office, Fleishman attended The Ohio State University (OSU) in 1949 at the invitation of Ralph Stogdill. This was a momentous time for leadership research in I-O psychology as the laboratory at OSU was in the process of fostering a paradigm shift, facilitated in no small way by Fleishman's work on the measurement of leadership behavior styles (Fleishman, 1953a, 1953b).

Fleishman's advisor at OSU was Harold E. Burtt, who in turn was mentored by Hugo Münsterberg (American Psychological Association [APA], 1999). This connection was influential because Münsterberg was one of the earliest industrial psychologists (Landy, 1992). Fleishman inherited from this lineage a strong, lifelong appreciation for applied psychology. His

DOI: 10.4324/9781003403258-40

career was marked by a series of transitions between academic and applied positions, including stints at Yale University (1956–1962), University of California, Irvine (1975–1976), and George Mason University (1986–1996) as well as at the Air Force (1951–1956), American Institutes for Research (1963–1975), Advanced Research Resources Organization (1976–1986), and Management Research Institute (1996–2021).

Fleishman's major contributions to the field of I-O psychology were in the areas of leadership, human performance description and measurement, and fostering the international spread of the field. The remainder of this chapter will elaborate on Fleishman's contributions in these three areas.

Leadership Behavior and Styles

The research at OSU in the 1940s–1950s focused on developing descriptions of leadership behavior. This focus was driven by disappointment in the leader trait approach that was dominant at the time and a desire to move away from the topic of "who leaders are" toward the question, "what do leaders do?" Accordingly, as a graduate student, Fleishman developed the Supervisory Behavior Description Questionnaire, which specified two major factors, *initiating structure* and *consideration* (Fleishman, 1953a). The first referred to the extent to which "the leader defined or facilitated group interactions toward *goal attainment*" including "planning, communicating, scheduling, criticizing, trying out new ideas, etc." (p. 2). The second referred to "the extent to which the leader was considerate of...workers' feelings" (p. 2). These two dimensions became ubiquitous in leadership research for the next several decades. Indeed, this influence resonates with current transformational leadership theories (Bass, 1985), in which individualized consideration is one of the dimensions of leadership.

Fleishman's research focused on how these behavioral styles influenced an array of work outcomes. His ideas were heavily influenced by the pioneering work of Lewin et al. (1939) (personal communication, April 14, 2003) who examined the effects on follower behavior of the social climates engendered by different leadership behaviors. Fleishman examined how combinations of initiating structure and consideration influenced employee grievances and turnover rates (Fleishman & Harris, 1962). He found that a leader's display of consideration moderated the effects of initiating structure on these outcomes, such that higher levels of consideration reduced the deleterious impact of structure. This classic work paved the way for later research on path goal theory (House, 1971) and functional team leadership perspectives (Zaccaro et al., 2001).

A major outcome of the OSU research was to shift the emphasis of leadership research away from trait perspectives (Day & Zaccaro, 2007). This shift is traceable to Stogdill's (1948) classic review that purportedly showed weak evidence for leader traits and argued for more situational perspectives of leadership. However, Fleishman noted that Stogdill did not intend to repudiate trait approaches (personal communication, June 14, 2005). Indeed, Fleishman interpreted leadership styles as fairly stable dispositional patterns (Harris & Fleishman, 1955; Fleishman & Peters, 1962). Research by Fleishman and colleagues over 25 years later offered frameworks of leadership problem solving behavior with attendant consequences for the specification of dispositional leader attributes (Fleishman et al., 1991; Mumford et al., 2000). Thus, throughout the arc of his career, Fleishman provided profound influences both on the demise of the leader individual differences perspective and on its renaissance.

Human Performance Description and Measurement

Fleishman also made major contributions throughout his career to the description and measurement of performance skills and abilities. His first position, with the Air Force Human Resources Research Center, involved the specification of psychometer skills linked to effective pilot performance. His methodological approach to this task (Fleishman, 1954) was one he used repeatedly throughout his career: he began by defining and classifying abilities that would contribute to performance differences in psychomotor performance. He developed a battery of 38 specific psychomotor tasks and administered them to 400 airmen.

He then factor-analyzed the results to come up with ten dimensions of psychomotor skill. Fleishman extended this approach to develop more fine-grained aspects of psychomotor skill (e.g., Fleishman & Hempel, 1956), culminating in selection tests for Air Force pilots (Fleishman, 1956). This work was important for I-O psychology because it established a foundation for the rigorous description and measurement of abilities linked to job performance.

Fleishman continued to build on this foundation throughout his career. In 1957, he expanded his focus on psychomotor abilities to examine a larger array of physical abilities linked to more complex tasks. In his research, he used a combination of experimental and factor analytical methods to uncover the dimensions of physical abilities that would apply across most tasks requiring such skills (e.g., Fleishman & Ornstein, 1960). Later, Fleishman continued to use this approach to examine human performance dimensions across multiple task categories. These dimensions were then used to examine individual differences in abilities related to skill learning and retention (Fleishman, 1972). The culmination of his research was the construction of multiple performance taxonomies including psychomotor, physical, perceptual, cognitive, and social/interpersonal abilities, as well as team performance functions (Fleishman & Quaintance, 1984; Fleishman & Reilly, 1992; Fleishman & Zaccaro, 1992).

The significance of these taxonomies is that they provided a systemic and conceptual foundation for the descriptions of abilities that underlie effective performance across a wide range of work tasks. Moreover, these taxonomic dimensions were constructed with corresponding behavioral anchored rating scales (Fleishman & Mumford, 1991) which contributed to important and widely used tools in job analysis, such as the Fleishman Job Analysis Survey (F-JAS) (Caughron et al., 2012). Moreover, Fleishman was part of the research team that developed O*NET (Peterson et al., 1999), the job classification system that replaced the Dictionary of Occupational Titles. O*NET, described at the time of its development as "the most important theoretical development in job analysis in recent times" (Campion et al., 1999, p. 287), adapted Fleishman's ability requirements scales for its classification system (Peterson et al., 1999).

Fostering International Outreach in I-O Psychology

Fleishman was particularly proud of his career-long efforts to foster international outreach and collaboration in I-O psychology. Such efforts began in 1956 when the Air Force sent him on a tour of psychology research laboratories in Europe (APA, 1999). Later, in 1960, Fleishman was one of eight psychologists to visit the Soviet Union and learn about the state of industrial psychology in that country. He described his observations of what was called "labor psychology" in the Soviet Union, noting their primary focus on training and engineering psychology but not on topics related to motivation, group dynamics, leadership, attitudes, test development, and personnel selection (Fleishman, 1963). On a later visit in 1976, Fleishman helped foster the first collaborative effort between American and Soviet psychologists (Fleishman, 1999).

In 1974, Fleishman was elected as president of the International Association of Applied Psychology (IAAP) and served for a period of eight years. In his role, he set out to broaden the international scope of this society, turning it from a primarily European-centered association to one that included 90 countries from all regions of the world in the 1998 IAAP Congress (Fleishman, 1999). He also revived and expanded the journal of the association, later renamed *Applied Psychology: An International Review*. He continued his international outreach by visiting psychologists in China in 1981. Fleishman contributed significantly to the globalization of I-O psychology, for which he was awarded the APA Award for Distinguished Contributions to the International Advancement of Psychology in 1999.

Conclusion

Fleishman's career lasted for over 60 years. In that time, he made groundbreaking contributions to multiple areas of I-O psychology. He also worked hard to extend the reach of applied psychology across the world. In his career, Fleishman demonstrated to the highest level the degree of scientific rigor and application prescribed by his "grand advisor," Hugo Münsterberg.

References

American Psychological Association (1999). Award for distinguished contributions to the international advancement of psychology: Edwin A. Fleishman (1999). *American Psychologist, 54*(11), 1004–1016.

Bass, B. M. (1985). *Leadership and performance beyond expectations.* Free Press.

Campion, M. A., Morgeson, F. P., & Mayfield, M. S. (1999). O*NET's theoretical contributions to job analysis research. In N. G. Peterson, M. D. Mumford, W. C. Borman, P. R. Jeanneret, & E. A. Fleishman (Eds.), *An occupational information system for the 21st century: The development of O*NET* (pp. 297–304). American Psychological Association.

Caughron, J. J., Mumford, M. D., & Fleishman, E. A. (2012). The Fleishman Job Analysis survey: Development, validation, and applications. In M. A. Wilson, W. Bennett, Jr., S. G. Gibson, & G. M. Alliger (Eds.), *The handbook of work analysis: Methods, systems, applications and science of work measurement in organizations* (pp. 231–246). Routledge/Taylor & Francis.

Day, D. V., & Zaccaro, S. J. (2007). Leadership: A critical historical analysis of the influence of trait theories. In L. L. Koppes (Ed.). *Historical perspectives in industrial and organizational psychology,* (pp. 383–405). Lawrence Erlbaum Associates.

Fleishman, E. A. (1953a). The description of supervisory behavior. *Journal of Applied Psychology, 37,* 181–210. https://doi.org/10.1037/h0056314

Fleishman, E. A. (1953b). Leadership climate, human relations training, and supervisory behavior. *Personnel Psychology, 6*(2), 205–222. https://doi.org/10.1111/j.1744-6570.1953.tb01040.x

Fleishman, E. A. (1954) Dimensional analysis of psychomotor abilities. *Journal of Experimental Psychology, 48,* 263–272. https://doi.org/10.1037/h0058244

Fleishman, E. A. (1956) Psychomotor selection tests: Research and application in the United States Air Force. *Personnel Psychology, 9,* 449–467. https://doi.org/10.1111/j.1744-6570.1956.tb01079.x

Fleishman, E. A. (1963). Some observations of industrial psychology in the U.S.S.R. *Personnel Psychology, 16*(2), 115–125. https://doi.org/10.1111/j.1744-6570.1963.tb01260.x

Fleishman, E. A. (1972). On the relation between abilities, learning, and human performance. *American Psychologist, 27*(11), 1017–1032. https://doi.org/10.1037/h0033881

Fleishman, E. A. (1999). Applied psychology: An international journey. *American Psychologist, 54*(11), 1008–1016. https://doi.org/10.1037/h0088214

Fleishman, E. A., & Harris, E. F. (1962). Patterns of leadership behavior related to employee grievances and turnover. *Personnel Psychology, 15*, 43–56

Fleishman, E. A., & Hempel. W. E. (1956). Factorial analysis of complex psychomotor performance and related skills. *Journal of Applied Psychology, 40*(2), 96–104. https://doi.org/10.1037/h0045587

Fleishman, E. A., & Mumford, M. D. (1991). Evaluating classifications of job behavior: A construct validation of the ability requirement scales. *Personnel Psychology, 44*(3), 523–575. https://doi.org/10.1111/j.1744-6570.1991.tb02403.x

Fleishman, E. A., Mumford, M. D., Zaccaro, S. J., Levin, K. Y., Korotkin, A. L., & Hein, M. B. (1991). Theoretical efforts in the description of leader behavior: A synthesis and functional integration. *Leadership Quarterly, 2*(4), 245–287. https://doi.org/10.1016/1048-9843(91)90016-U

Fleishman E. A., & Ornstein, G. N. (1960). An analysis of pilot flying performance in terms of component abilities. *Journal of Applied Psychology, 44*(3), 146–155. https://doi.org/10.1037/h0043480

Fleishman, E. A., & Peters, D. R. (1962). Interpersonal values, leadership attitudes, and managerial success. *Personnel Psychology, 15*(2), 127–143. https://doi.org/10.1111/j.1744-6570.1962.tb01855.x

Fleishman, E. A., & Quaintance, M. K. (1984). *Taxonomies of human performance: The description of human tasks*. Academic Press.

Fleishman, E. A., & Reilly, M. E. (1992). *Handbook of human abilities: Definitions, measurements, and task requirements*. Management Research Institute.

Fleishman, E. A., & Zaccaro, S. J. (1992). Toward a taxonomy of team performance functions. In R. W. Swezey & E. Salas (Eds.), *Teams: Their training and performance* (pp. 36 –56). Ablex.

Harris, E. F., & Fleishman, E. A. (1955). Human relations training and the stability of leadership patterns. *Journal of Applied Psychology, 39*(1), 20–35. https://doi.org/10.1037/h0046585

House, R. J. (1971). A path goal theory of leader effectiveness. *Administrative Science Quarterly, 16*(3), 321–338. https://doi.org/10.2307/2391905

Landy, F. J. (1992). Hugo Münsterberg: Victim or visionary? *Journal of Applied Psychology, 77*(6), 787–802. https://doi.org/10.1037/0021-9010.77.6.787

Lewin, K., Lippitt, R., & White, R. K. (1939). Patterns of aggressive behavior in experimentally created social climates. *Journal of Social Psychology, 10*(2), 271–299. https://doi.org/10.1080/00224545.1939.9713366

Mumford, M. D., Zaccaro, S. J., Harding, F. D., Jacobs, T. O., & Fleishman, E. A. (2000). Leadership skills for a changing world: Solving complex social problems. *Leadership Quarterly, 11*(1), 11–35. https://doi.org/10.1016/S1048-9843(99)00041-7

Peterson, N. G., Mumford, M. D., Borman, W. C., Jeanneret, P. R., & Fleishman, E. A. (Eds.). (1999). *An occupational information system for the 21st century: The development of O*NET.* American Psychological Association. https://doi.org/10.1037/10313-000

Stogdill, R. M. (1948). Personal factors associated with leadership: A survey of the literature. *Journal of Psychology, 25*(1), 35–71. https://doi.org/10.1080/00223980.1948.9917362

Zaccaro, S. J., Rittman, A., & Marks, M. A. (2001). Team leadership. *Leadership Quarterly, 12*(4), 451–484. https://doi.org/10.1016/S1048-9843(01)00093-5

Chapter 41

Frank L. Schmidt (1944–2021) and John E. Hunter (1939–2002)[1]

Jeffrey M. Cucina

With 69 joint publications, Frank L. Schmidt and John ("Jack") E. Hunter had one of the most prolific, successful, and impactful collaborations in industrial-organizational (I-O) psychology. These colleagues and friends made immense contributions to research methodology and the science of personnel selection and individual differences. Their work had significant impacts on the science and practice of I-O psychology.

Biographical Overview

Schmidt's Life[2]

Schmidt was born on April 29, 1944 and spent his early years in Jeffersontown, KY, a small town near Louisville. He grew up on a dairy farm with four younger brothers and one sister in a farmhouse with no running water. He enjoyed his time on the farm, where he cared for cows and chickens and had several outdoor hobbies including hunting and fishing. Schmidt's high school teachers required students in his track to fill out an application to Bellarmine College in Louisville. He was accepted with a full scholarship and later switched his major from biology to psychology after learning about I-O psychology in his introductory psychology course. He then attended Purdue University, obtaining a PhD in 1970. Schmidt became an assistant professor at Michigan State University (MSU). While interviewing for this position, Schmidt met his longtime collaborator, John E. Hunter.

Schmidt had a successful term at MSU, receiving early tenure after only three years. However, he craved more practical

DOI: 10.4324/9781003403258-41

"real-world" work and left for a new position at the United States (US) Civil Service Commission, which later became the US Office of Personnel Management (OPM). While there, he conducted research supporting the use of employment tests for US Federal Government positions and began a special appointment as a research professor at the George Washington University (GWU).

He was later recruited for a chaired professorship in the University of Iowa's business college. At first, Schmidt was not interested in leaving OPM and GWU; however, a professor in the college urged him travel to Iowa for three talks and pheasant hunting trips, which ultimately led him to accepting the position. Schmidt spent the rest of his career there but continued practical work as a scientific advisor for Gallup. At both GWU and the University of Iowa, he directed multiple students' dissertations, including those of the next generation of leading I-O psychology researchers and meta-analysts. He was known for his collaborative spirit and he often included multiple I-O psychologists in his projects, always mentoring junior scholars and giving credit for their contributions.

Hunter's Life[3]

Hunter was born on March 29, 1939, in what he described as "abject poverty." He lived in a tent during the first six months of his life and spent time living in an orphanage and a car. He later wrote that his family being on welfare saved his life. Hunter had a love for mathematics but developed a second passion for psychology given its emphasis on science and people. He double majored in both at the University of New Mexico and decided to pursue a doctorate in psychology because he felt it had a greater importance. He obtained his PhD from the University of Illinois in 1964, studying under Ledyard Tucker (co-creator of the Tucker-Lewis Index), Henry Kaiser (creator of the varimax rotation), and, his advisor, Lee Cronbach (who developed coefficient alpha). In 1964, Hunter obtained a position at MSU, where he spent the rest of his career. He developed a reputation for his brilliance (Kaiser and Cronbach attested that he was the smartest graduate student they encountered) and his selfless mentoring and development of students and colleagues.

Realizations Leading to the Development of Psychometric Meta-Analysis

Early in their careers, Hunter and Schmidt had similar but separate realizations that later inspired their subsequent collaboration. Hunter set out to apply mathematical methodology (whereby propositions or axioms would serve as a starting point for theories) to establish psychological theories. However, he had trouble finding psychological axioms. He had hoped to find axioms in literature reviews, but he found these to either be selectively one-sided or disappointing in their summaries of the existing research. He attributed much of his disappointment and frustration with literature reviews to sampling error.

Meanwhile, Schmidt was conducting his dissertation, which compared the prediction obtained from regression weighting to that from unit or equal weighting. He found that when typical sample sizes were used, unit weighting performed as well or better than regression when regression weights were applied to a new sample. He realized that many researchers did not understand the role of sampling error in the estimation of regression weights and the estimates of multiple correlations arising from the regression weights.

While in graduate school, Schmidt was enrolled in courses taught by Joseph Tiffin (his advisor) and Hubert Brogden. The courses covered the validity of personnel selection tests. Tiffin's validity findings were consistent with the theory of situational specificity – the validity of a particular personnel selection test could vary dramatically from one setting to another. A cognitive ability test might predict salesperson performance in one company but not in another. The notion was that situational aspects of the business setting impacted validity. In contrast, Brogden was involved with validity studies for the US Army, which had very consistent results from setting to setting. Schmidt asked Brogden to explain why the Army's validity studies were consistent and Tiffin's studies (which were often conducted in the private sector) were not. Brogden believed the differences were due to sampling error since the Army had samples sizes in the thousands whereas the private sector sample sizes were often 100 or less.

Schmidt was reminded of this realization one day in 1975 when he was sitting in his office at GWU and wondering why validity coefficients from OPM's validity studies varied across settings. He computed the percent of variance in distributions of validity coefficients obtained across multiple studies that could be attributed to sampling error and obtained a value of 70%–80%. After removing the effects of sampling error and other artifacts (e.g., unreliability in job performance measures and predictor range restriction) the validities generalized across different studies. He found his results so surprising that he was concerned he had made an error. He called Hunter to discuss his analysis. Hunter confirmed that the results were correct. Subsequently, the duo began refining the methodology, which they termed validity generalization.

Essentially, validity generalization is a quantitative methodology for combining correlation coefficients across multiple studies. It averages the correlations across studies giving greater weight to studies with larger sample sizes or smaller sampling error. By examining the variance in correlations after removing the artifactual variance (e.g., sampling error, unreliability) one can determine if there are meaningful moderators impacting the correlations. In the case of cognitive ability tests used for personnel selection, their analyses indicated that local settings were not serving as a moderator. Instead, they later found that job complexity was a moderator.

They drafted a paper but decided to submit it to the James McKeen Cattell Award for Research Design, which was an award for unpublished research sponsored by Division 14 of the American Psychological Association (APA). Although they won the award, the delay in the publication of their manuscript in 1977 resulted in Glass (1976) publishing the first article on this methodology, which he termed meta-analysis. Neither Gene Glass nor Schmidt and Hunter were aware of each other's independent efforts on the development of validity generalization/meta-analysis. Five years later, both teams of researchers independently published books on meta-analysis and again Gene Glass' work was published a year earlier. However, the latest edition of Schmidt and Hunter's (2015) book is considered the authoritative guide on meta-analysis in psychology.

The psychometric meta-analysis methodology developed by Schmidt and Hunter is a significant improvement over other meta-analytic approaches. Their approach corrects for biasing effects beyond just sampling error (e.g., unreliability, range restriction/enhancement, dichotomization). For example, variables are usually not measured with perfect reliability. Psychometric meta-analysis provides a method for correcting for unreliability allowing meta-analysts to estimate the true score correlation between variables. Range restriction occurs when the relationship between two variables is studied in a sample that has less variance in the variables than in the population. This artifact often leads to lower estimates of criterion-related validity for selection procedures. A useful feature of psychometric meta-analysis is that researchers can provide artifact distributions (e.g., an expected distribution of reliabilities) when the primary studies being analyzed do not provide this information.

Schmidt and Hunter's Work Applying Meta-Analysis

Schmidt and Hunter conducted numerous meta-analyses of personnel selection devices which shaped the field of I-O psychology. Hunter conducted a pivotal meta-analysis of the criterion-related validity studies for the General Aptitude Test Battery (GATB) conducted by the US Department of Labor. Applying psychometric meta-analysis to data from 515 jobs, he found that scores on the GATB predicted job performance for medium complexity jobs (which form the bulk of jobs in the US economy) with a validity coefficient of .51 after correcting for the distorting effects of sampling error, criterion unreliability, and range restriction. Working with his wife, Rhonda Hunter, he conducted additional meta-analyses for predictors such as biographical data, reference checks, interviews, and interests.

Collaborating with their students and colleagues, Hunter and Schmidt conducted meta-analyses of personnel selection procedures for clerical positions, computer programmers, petroleum industry positions, among others. This work culminated in Schmidt and Hunter's (1998) article summarizing meta-analytic validities of 19 predictors of job performance and 10 predictors of training performance. They later developed an improved indirect range restriction correction procedure which led to more accurate, and higher, validity coefficients for many predictors.

Other Contributions

The duo also made influential contributions in debates over null hypothesis significance testing and banding as well as utility analysis, individual differences, and measurement error. They developed a reputation for tackling misconceptions related to scientific practices and dispelling these misconceptions in a concise, logical, and persuasive manner.

Individually, Schmidt also worked on advancements of meta-analysis (e.g., second-order meta-analysis) and Hunter conducted impactful research in the communications field. Unfortunately, their collaboration came to an end in 2002 when Hunter passed away. Schmidt retired in 2012 but continued to be active in the field. He was the inaugural winner of the Society for Industrial and Organizational Psychology's most prestigious award, the Dunnette Prize, in 2015. Following his and Hunter's spirit of mentorship and development of the field, he donated the prize money back and created the Schmidt-Hunter meta-analysis award. In 2021, Schmidt suddenly passed away.

Conclusion

Schmidt and Hunter's contributions to the field of personnel selection and research methodology continue to have an impact today. Their writings are classic readings in personnel selection and meta-analysis courses, frequent citations in articles and technical reports, and a beacon of clear scientific thought and exposition. The validity generalization work conducted by the pair greatly improved the field's understanding of the relationship between individual differences and performance – many validities generalize across situations, organizations, and settings.

Notes

1 The views expressed in this chapter are those of the author and do not necessarily reflect the views of US Customs and Border Protection or

the US Federal Government. The author thanks Raymond Colangelo, Ilene Gast, Mark Hamilton, Huy Le, Michael McDaniel, In-Sue Oh, Deniz Ones, Kenneth Pearlman, and Chockalingam Viswesvaran for their feedback.

2 Much of this information is from Schmidt (2015).
3 Much of this information is from Hunter (2000).

References

Glass, G. V. (1976). Primary, secondary, and meta-analysis of research. *Educational Researcher*, *5*(10), 3–8. https://doi.org/10.2307/1174772

Hunter, J. E. (2000). John E. Hunter. [Autobiography]. *Research Methods Division Newsletter, 15*(2), 1–4. https://static1.squarespace.com/static/53143e7de4b0d2c24316913f/t/531d603de4b02c4ce261f90f/1394434109250/Hunter+Bio.pdf

Schmidt, F. L. (2015). *The importance of being frank: My life stories and anecdotes*. (4th ed.).Schmidt Consulting.

Schmidt, F. L., & Hunter, J. E. (1998). The validity and utility of selection methods in personnel psychology: Practical and theoretical implications of 85 years of research findings. *Psychological Bulletin, 124*, 262–274. https://doi.org/10.1037//0033-2909.124.2.262

Schmidt, F. L., & Hunter, J. E. (2015). *Methods of meta-analysis: Correcting error and bias in research findings*. (3rd ed.). SAGE.

Chapter 42

Five Additional Key Thinkers

Andrew J. Vinchur

As discussed in the *Preface*, not every key thinker in the history of industrial and organizational (I-O) psychology could be included in this volume; unavoidably, many deserving individuals were left out. In this concluding chapter, five key thinkers who were originally slated to have full chapters are briefly discussed.[1] *Max Weber* (1864–1920) is best known to I-O psychologists for his elucidation of the principles of bureaucracy. *Henry C. Link* (1889–1952) and *Harold E. Burtt* (1890–1991) wrote early influential textbooks and were pioneers in areas such as applying psychology to employee selection. *Douglas M. McGregor* (1904–1964) developed a very influential theory based on managerial belief systems: Theory X and Theory Y. And with his two-factor theory, *Frederick I. Herzberg* (1923–2000) was one of the first psychologists to study job content as a source of motivation and satisfaction.

Max Weber (1864–1920)

Within I-O psychology, the German scholar Max Weber is most associated with the study of bureaucracy. He attended the universities of Heidelberg, Berlin, and Göttengen, and while he did occasionally teach, he had the financial means to spend the bulk of his career as an independent scholar. Weber is now known primarily as a sociologist; however, it was not until late in his career that he identified as such, accepting chairs in sociology at the universities of Vienna and later Munich (Magnusson, 1990). Weber (1922/1946) characterized bureaucracies as organizations based on rules. In his view, bureaucracy represented an ideal

DOI: 10.4324/9781003403258-42

form of organization. Weber believed that managers should be appointed, not elected, and that authority should reside in the position and not be based on nepotism or personal characteristics. Organizational members should be hired based on their ability to do the work, and advancement should be based exclusively on work performance. Workers should be protected from arbitrary use of authority.

Other important characteristics of a bureaucracy include a clear hierarchy of authority; unity of command (each employee has one, and only one, direct supervisor); division of labor and function; clear communication channels; and rewards tied to performance. All these characteristics combined should result in a rational, efficient, and productive organization. While not without its critics, the bureaucratic structure has proven very durable as an organizing strategy for large organizations. With the 1947 English translation of Weber's book, *The Theory of Social and Economic Organizations* (Weber, 1947), his work become popular in the United States (Warr, 2007). Along with the American social activist Mary Parker Follett (1868–1933), and the French mining engineer and management theorist Henri Fayol (1841–1925), Max Weber is an example of an early organizational theorist who has had a substantial influence on I-O psychology.

Henry C. Link (1889–1952)

Henry Link received his doctorate from Yale University in 1916. He spent his career as an industrial psychologist working in industry, possibly the first PhD psychologist to do so full-time (Ferguson, 1962–1965). In 1916, Link conducted an early validity study that was quite sophisticated for its time. At the Winchester Repeating Arms Company, he used a series of tests on shell gaugers and inspectors to measure attributes such as accuracy of movement, steadiness of attention, reaction time, and visual acuity, to predict job performance. The job performance criterion was pounds of shells inspected in a day. Link (1918) was aware that measuring performance at a single point in time could be unreliable, therefore he averaged criterion performance across four weeks to increase reliability. He also engaged in one of the early instances of what today is called cross-validation, or replicating the study with a group other than the original one to assess whether the results are specific to the original group, or if they can be generalized.

In 1919, Link published *Employment Psychology*. The book has four major sections. Part I focuses on psychological tests and their administration and use in selecting various occupational groups, such as apprentice toolmakers, clerks, assemblers, machine operators, stenographers, and executives. Link included a discussion of general intelligence and intelligence tests, and of language and literacy tests. In Part II, he covered trade tests, training, and job analysis. Link emphasized the importance of job analysis and warns against conducting it by simply describing broad superficial human characteristics. He provided a systematic job analysis procedure for determining physical and psychological characteristics needed for successful job performance. The bulk of Part III concerns performance appraisal. In that section, Link described what came to be called the halo effect or error (he called it "prejudices"); raters who allow their assessment of one dimension to influence their ratings of other performance dimensions.

The concluding section, Part IV, is particularly interesting. Link included a discussion of the importance of a strong relationship between laboratory and applied psychology. He also discussed his concern that unqualified individuals were offering organizations quick fixes that have no empirical support. Relatively rare for his time, Link had a chapter on industrial psychology and organized labor, and he included a chapter of the employment process from the viewpoint of the job applicant. Link believed that job applicants should be treated fairly and with courtesy. He thought that administering unscored easy tests, or "shock absorbers," to build up applicant confidence is warranted. Link stated that it is too easy to view the applicant as a mere pawn in the selection process and that this should be avoided.

The book was viewed very favorably. Kornhauser and Kingsbury (1924) praised it for its sound scientific methodology in test construction and standardization. Viteles (1974) saw it as the first comprehensive American text in industrial psychology, and he referenced it heavily in his own groundbreaking 1932 text *Industrial Psychology* (Viteles, 1932).

Link could be critical when he thought it necessary. He saw scientific management as contributing to the belief by workers that outside consultants are cold-blooded and heartless, treating employees as machines to be exploited (Link, 1919). Link (1920) was highly critical of his own colleagues who expended little effort to understand the industries they were working in: there are many applications "of psychology *to* industry," he wrote, "but not so many *in* industry" (p. 336, emphasis in original). Link (1923) was very skeptical of the belief held by many psychologists at the time that intelligence is primarily innate. He believed intelligence tests measured examinees' attainment of knowledge, not their innate intelligence. Link saw the practice of using intelligence tests, such as the Army Alpha and Beta tests, to rank ethnic groups and races by intelligence as unwarranted, because the social, economic, and educational backgrounds of the examinees are not equivalent.

Harold E. Burtt (1890–1991)

Unlike Henry Link who spent his career in industry, Harold Burtt maintained an academic affiliation throughout a career that spanned much of the development of I-O psychology in the 20th century. Burtt received his BA from Dartmouth in 1911, where he graded papers for pioneering industrial psychologist Walter Van Dyke Bingham. Bingham encouraged Burtt to consider a career in psychology, and recommended Harvard University for graduate school and Harvard's Hugo Münsterberg for a mentor (Burtt, 1953). While at Harvard, Burtt worked with Münsterberg on assessing the effect of street illumination on reaction time and attention (Burtt, 1916).[2] After Burtt received his doctorate in 1915, he was an instructor at Harvard and at Simmons College from 1915 to 1917, and then a captain in Army Air Service in 1918, where he served as chair of the Committee on Psychological Problems in Aviation (Ferguson, 1962-65). He was hired by Ohio State University in 1919, serving as department head from 1938 until his retirement in 1960. Burtt, along with 1923 hire Herbert Toops (1895–1972), founded the industrial psychology program at Ohio State (Austin, 1992).

Burtt's major influences on I-O psychology were through his books (Burtt, 1926, 1929, 1948) and through his career accomplishments at Ohio State. In his 1926 text *Principles of Employment Psychology*, Burtt stated that his fundamental principle of employment psychology is testing the test, that is, demonstrating the relationship between test scores and job performance. Among the topics he discussed in the text are the threat of pseudoscience, various test types, rating scales, vocational interests, and job analysis. Notable was an entire chapter on criteria, which Burtt categorized as either subjective estimates of worker performance by supervisors, or as objective worker production figures. He defined the criterion as a job proficiency index that can be used to determine whether a test is predictive of performance; Burtt was possibly the first to define criteria in this way (Austin & Villanova, 1992).

Under Burtt's leadership, Ohio State became one of the preeminent I-O graduate programs in the country. In his 41 years there, he supervised 28 MA and 28 PhD students, including some who went on to great prominence in the field: Carroll L. Shartle, Edwin A. Fleishman, Donald L. Grant, and Paul W. Thayer all served as presidents of the American Psychological Association's I-O psychology division. On Burtt's 100th birthday, his PhD student former CBS president Frank Stanton and Stanton's wife endowed the Harold E. Burtt Chair in Industrial Psychology at the university (Thayer & Austin, 1992).

Douglas M. McGregor (1904–1964)

Early textbooks such as those by Link (1919) and Burtt (1926) paid little or no attention to motivation, leadership, or job satisfaction.[3] Two later theorists who focused on these topics are Douglas McGregor and Frederick Herzberg. Douglas McGregor earned his MA and PhD degrees in psychology from Harvard University. In addition to a career as a management consultant, he was a professor of management at the Massachusetts Institute of Technology (MIT) and President of Antioch College. While McGregor made contributions to the study of performance appraisal and other areas of I-O psychology, he is best remembered today for his work on motivation, leadership, and managerial belief systems: Theory X and Theory Y.

McGregor first presented Theory X and Theory Y in a 1957 speech at the Fifth Anniversary Convocation of MIT's Alfred

P. Sloan School of Management (Highhouse, 2021). He followed that with an article in *Management Review* (1957/1996) and a 1960 book *The Human Side of Enterprise* (McGregor, 1960). Heavily influenced by Abraham Maslow's need hierarchy theory of motivation and the idea that a satisfied need is not a motivator of behavior, McGregor (1957/1996) claimed that organizations do not give employees sufficient opportunities to satisfy upper-level ego and self-fulfillment needs. According to McGregor, the conventional view of management consists of the active intervention of managers to control employees, because of the belief that by nature employees are indolent, lacking in ambition, indifferent to organizational needs, gullible, and resistant to change. McGregor labeled this view Theory X. He saw this approach as inadequate, with managers confusing cause and effect: employees behave this way not because it is their nature, but because of the controlling, external rewards and punishment approach by managers. McGregor proposed a new theory of management, Theory Y, the view that employees have the potential for development, for assuming responsibility, and to work towards organizational goals. "The essential task of management is to arrange organizational conditions and methods of operation so that people can achieve their own goals *best* by directing *their own* efforts toward organizational objectives" (McGregor, 1957/1996, p. 180, italics in original).

Although sometimes interpreted as a blueprint for how managers should behave, McGregor's Theory X and Theory Y are best viewed as examples of how managerial beliefs can influence the motivation and general behavior of employees. His work has heavily influenced managerial thinking, and as Highhouse (2021) noted, McGregor also heavily influenced the work of prominent organizational theorists Chris Argyris, Mason Haire, Rensis Likert, and Edgar Schein, and among many others, Frederick Herzberg.

Frederick I. Herzberg (1923–2000)

Frederick Herzberg received his doctorate from the University of Pittsburgh under the supervision of John Flanagan. Herzberg used Flanagan's (1954) critical incident technique to collect data from a sample of engineers and accountants to determine the factors that made them feel very good or very bad about their jobs. When Herzberg and Bernard Mausner and Barbara Snyderman analyzed the results, they found factors associated with the job itself (job content factors) were the primary sources of satisfaction and motivation, while contextual factors were the source of dissatisfaction (Latham & Budworth, 2021).

Termed two-factor theory or motivator/hygiene theory, Herzberg's theory stressed the importance of the job itself (Herzberg et al., 1959). To avoid a dissatisfied worker, contextual or hygiene factors such as pay, fringe benefits, working conditions, supervision, and coworker relations need to be at a satisfactory level. Satisfying these hygiene factors, however, will not result in a satisfied, motivated worker, the result will be an employee in a neutral state. For a satisfied, motivated worker, job content or motivator factors, such as the job providing challenge, interest, and autonomy, are paramount. These motivators are intrinsic to the work itself. Sole emphasis on external factors such as pay is inadequate. For a motivated, satisfied worker the job must be enriched, that is, the job content itself must be challenging, interesting, and provide for autonomy and responsibility.

While two-factor theory has had its share of criticism (see Locke, 1976), Herzberg's ideas have been influential in I-O psychology. He was one of the first psychologists to focus on characteristics of the job as a source of worker motivation and satisfaction and to propose a method, job enrichment, to achieve it. Herzberg's distinction between intrinsic and extrinsic factors in motivation has also had an influence (Jex & Britt, 2008). The notion of job enrichment has been particularly useful, notably in the job enrichment theory of Richard Hackman and Gregory Oldham (1975).

Closing Remarks

The five individuals covered in this chapter are not the only key thinkers that the selection process, described in the *Preface*, identified as worthy of inclusion but who do not have an individual chapter in this volume. Others include *Agostino Gemelli* (1878–1959), who as early as 1915 was using aptitude tests for pilots in Italy; *Isaak Shpil'rein* (1891–circa 1930s), who was instrumental in establishing industrial psychology in Russia before disappearing in one of Stalin's purges; and Fritz Roethlisberger (1898–1974), who was integral to the iconic Hawthorne Studies. There is also *Edward Webster* (1909–1989), a guiding force for I-O psychology in Canada; and *Joan Woodward* (1916–1971) of Great Britain, for her work on the effect of type of technology on organizational structure. A convincing argument could be made for many others who contributed to our understanding of behavior in organizations. Researchers today continue to test and refine the ideas of these key thinkers in I-O psychology. Some of these current researchers will develop groundbreaking theories and conduct innovative research, and perhaps, one day, they will be honored with a chapter in a future volume of *Key Thinkers in Industrial and Organizational Psychology.*

Notes

1 Reasons for exclusion were either the editors' inability to find an interested, qualified author, or due to unforeseen circumstances, authors unable to complete their chapters.
2 While Münsterberg was a mentor to Burtt at Harvard, his PhD research was on imagery under H. S. Langfeld, who "saw me first." Burtt noted while not particularly interested in the topic, he completed the study for "diplomatic reasons" (Burtt, 1953, p. 2). Burtt was an assistant to Münsterberg and in the classroom when Münsterberg passed away during a lecture at Radcliffe College in 1916.
3 One exception is Walter Dill Scott's (1911) *Increasing Human Efficiency in Business* with its focus on motivation.

References

Austin, J. T. (1992). History of industrial-organizational psychology at Ohio State. *Industrial-Organizational Psychologist, 29,* 51–59.

Austin, J. T., & Villanova, P. (1992). The criterion problem: 1917-1992. *Journal of Applied Psychology, 77,* 836–874. https://doi.org/10.1037//0021-9010.77.6.836

Burtt, H. (1916). The effect of uniform and non-uniform illumination upon attention and reaction-times, with special reference to street illumination. *Journal of Experimental Psychology, 1,* 155–182. https://doi.org/10.1037/h0071640

Burtt, H. (1926). *Principles of employment psychology.* Harper.

Burtt, H. (1929). *Psychology and industrial efficiency.* Appleton.

Burtt, H. (1948). *Applied psychology*. Prentice-Hall.
Burtt, H. (1953, January 14). [Letter to Leonard Ferguson]. Carnegie-Mellon University (Ferguson Collection, Box 2), Pittsburgh, PA.
Ferguson, L. W. (1962-65). *The heritage of industrial psychology* [14 pamphlets]. Finlay Press.
Flanagan, J. C. (1954). The critical incident technique. *Psychological Bulletin, 51,* 327–358. https://doi.org/10.1037/h0061470
Hackman, J. R., & Oldham, G. R. (1975). Development of the job diagnostic survey. *Journal of Applied Psychology, 60,* 159–170. https://doi.org/10.1037/h0076546
Herzberg, F., Mausner, B., & Snyderman, B. S. (1959). *The motivation to work*. Wiley.
Highhouse, S. (2021). The dubious legacy of early "O"-side interventions. In L. Koppes Bryan (Ed.), *Historical perspectives in industrial and organizational psychology* (pp. 184–202). Routledge. https://doi.org/10.4324/9780429052644
Jex, S. M, & Britt, T. W. (2008). *Organizational psychology: A practitioner approach* (2nd Ed.). Wiley.
Kornhauser, A. W., & Kingsbury, F. A. (1924). *Psychological tests in business*. University of Chicago Press.
Latham, G. P., & Budworth, M-H. (2021). The study of work motivation in the 20th and 21st centuries. In L. Koppes Bryan (Ed.), *Historical perspectives in industrial and organizational psychology* (pp. 203–226). Routledge. https://doi.org/10.4324/9780429052644
Link, H. C. (1918). An experiment in employment psychology. *Psychological Review, 25,* 116–127. https://doi.org/10.1037/h0072742
Link, H. C. (1919). *Employment psychology: The application of scientific methods to the selection, training, and grading of employees.* Macmillan.
Link, H. C. (1920). The applications of psychology to industry. *Psychological Bulletin, 17,* 335–346. https://doi.org/10.1037/h0075868
Link, H. C. (1923). What is intelligence? *The Atlantic Monthly, 132,* 374–385.
Locke, E. A. (1976). The nature and causes of job satisfaction. In M. D. Dunnette (Ed.), *Handbook of industrial and organizational psychology* (pp. 1297–1349). Rand-McNally.
Magnusson, M. (Ed.). (1990). *Chambers biographical dictionary.* Chambers.
McGregor, D. M. (1957/1996). The human side of enterprise. *Management Review, 46,* 22–28. Reprinted in J. M. Shafritz & J. S.

Ott (Eds.), *Classics of organization theory* (4th ed.) (pp. 176–182). Wadsworth.

McGregor, D. M. (1960). *The human side of enterprise*. McGraw-Hill.

Scott, W. D. (1911). *Increasing human efficiency in business*. Macmillan.

Thayer, P. W., & Austin, J. T. (1992). Harold E. Burtt (1890-1991). *American Psychologist, 47*, 1677. https://doi.org/10.1037//0003-066x.47.12.1677

Viteles, M. S. (1932). *Industrial psychology*. Norton.

Viteles, M. S. (1974). Industrial psychology: Reminiscences of an academic moonlighter. In T. S. Krawiec (Ed.), *The psychologists* (Vol. 2, pp. 440–500). Oxford University Press.

Warr, P. (2007). Some historical developments in I-O psychology outside the United States. In L. L. Koppes (Ed.), *Historical perspectives in industrial and organizational psychology* (pp. 81–107). Lawrence Erlbaum Associates.

Weber, M. (1922/1946). *From Max Weber: Essays in sociology*. Oxford University Press.

Weber, M. (1947). *The theory of social and economic organizations*. Free Press.

Index

Note: End of chapter notes are denoted by a letter n between page number and note number.

FSC
www.fsc.org
MIX
Papier | Fördert gute Waldnutzung
FSC® C083411

Kolibri 360 GmbH
Ferdinand-Jühlke-Straße 7
99095 Erfurt, Deutschland
produktsicherheit@kolibri360.de